D1520998

Studying the Image

Studying the Image

Critical Issues in Anthropology for Christians

by
ELOISE MENESES

Foreword by
SERAH SHANI

CASCADE *Books* · Eugene, Oregon

Cascade Books
An Imprint of Wipf and Stock Publishers
199 W. 8th Ave., Suite 3
Eugene, OR 97401

www.wipfandstock.com

PAPERBACK ISBN: 978-1-5326-3667-7
HARDCOVER ISBN: 978-1-5326-3669-1
EBOOK ISBN: 978-1-5326-3668-4

Cataloguing-in-Publication data:

Meneses, Eloise

Title: Studying the image : Critical issues in anthropology for Christians / Eloise Meneses.

Description: Eugene, OR: Cascade Books, 2019 | Includes bibliographical references and index.

Identifiers: ISBN 978-1-5326-3667-7 (paperback) | ISBN 978-1-5326-3669-1 (hardcover) | ISBN 978-1-5326-3668-4 (ebook)

Subjects: LCSH: Anthropology—social and cultural. | Theological anthropology Christianity. | Christianity and Science.

Classification: BT701 .2 M43 2019 (paperback) | BT701 .2 (ebook)

Manufactured in the U.S.A.   03/25/19

To Rev. Dr. Lesslie Newbigin
"Well done, thou good and faithful servant."

and

To my students,
who have made my work rewarding.

Contents

Figures

Foreword

By Serah Shani

Eloise Meneses is a seasoned cultural anthropologist with extensive knowledge of cultures around the world. Her research interests span diverse areas in anthropology that include faith and science, global economic systems, India, women's experience, race and ethnicity, comparative religions, international development, and Christian missions. In addition to her fieldwork in India, she is conversant with the experiences of other people and cultures. Reading this book exposes one to these cultures as she comparatively discusses them to present key ideas. This knowledge provides a wide and holistic view and will appeal to a variety of readers. Readers will make connections, comparisons, and sometimes identify with various aspects of the book as real-life cultural situations are used. Meneses is currently a professor of anthropology at Eastern University in the Department of Global Studies and Service where she has worked for more than twenty-five years as a professor and scholar. She is also a Christian anthropologist, and a second-generation anthropologist in her family. Meneses is devoted to blending theological and scientific anthropologies to form a holistic entity. Funded by the John Templeton Foundation, she founded and became director of the Master of Arts in Theological and Cultural Anthropology at Eastern University. She embraces the significance of engaging theological understandings with anthropological knowledge in order to holistically address multiple aspects of the human condition.

This book, *Studying the Image: Critical Issues in Anthropology for Christians,* is an illustration of how theological and anthropological perspectives can be engaged to illuminate and further deepen understandings of cultures. It is about engaging the missing links between the two perspectives, and in the process repairing misconceptions caused by overreliance on naturalistic explanations and the neglect of theological insights. Since the period of the Enlightenment, scientific explanations based on empirical findings have taken a front seat, while theological explanations that sometimes did not have, or were perceived not to have, tangible and evidential proofs were relegated to secondary and even marginalized peripheral positions. Yet, religious belief systems continue to shape people's worldviews and greatly influence their behaviors. In addition, these behaviors can have consequences that are either beneficial or detrimental to humanity. While not dismissive of science, but delving into Christianity, Meneses takes a proactive approach to make sense of the scientific explanations of cultural customs and habits, and to understand them through a Christian biblical and theological lens.

The book attracts a broad audience in its content and readability. It is written in a style that is easy for readers to understand. Also, the content is applicable to many kinds of readers as it addresses topics that are relevant to everyone's social realities; topics like art and religion are subjects that exist in all cultures around the world. Covering ten topics, the book can be used together with any introduction to anthropology course book, allowing space for further investigation into these topics than a textbook is able to provide.

I have used the book *Studying the Image* as a supplemental text in all of my introduction to anthropology classes for over four years. Approximately 200 or more of my students have read this book. My students, in both schools at which I have taught, Eastern University and Westmont College, have described how the book has helped them learn, understand, and appreciate anthropology from a Christian perspective. This has made it easier for me to integrate faith in the classroom, a crucial requirement in most Christian colleges and universities. I find that my students understand and use this book as a resource especially when discussing the connections between my teaching and contemporary and global Christian processes. I think most anthropology, mission studies, international development, and cross-cultural communication classes could benefit from this book. I have received positive comments regarding the book's usefulness in explaining, critically analyzing, comparing, and drawing conclusions on critical issues in anthropology for Christians.

Christian liberal arts colleges are faith-centered institutions. The coursework is expected to enable students to integrate learning with faith in most studies and to understand learning from a Christian perspective. Learning involves integrating secular scientific disciplines with Christian intellectual thought. It involves integrating biblical principles into the teaching such that students become well rounded, addressing every aspect of our lives as human beings so as to live a more productive life with ourselves and others, to be effective and informed members of society, and to be ready to meet Christ. While all liberal arts colleges aim to impart a broad general knowledge and to develop general intellectual capacities, Christian liberal arts colleges make knowledge more impactful by working for God's kingdom and a heavenly future, without compromising quality and rigor, and by providing space for students to excel both as learners and as Christians. *Studying the Image* provides such space in the teaching of various topics in anthropology that are important to Christians.

Eloise Meneses addresses some of the most difficult questions Christian anthropologists encounter in trying to make sense of pertinent issues in the understanding of humanity. Throughout the book, she tackles challenging topics. As an example, in a scientifically charged world where a high value on empirical evidence coupled with plural truths is prevalent, how do we know what is true? And how can we engage biblical knowing in a world where religious beliefs are questioned and at the same time respect those with different opinions? In a high-tech and highly globalized world, most people are likely to meet and interact with people from other cultures through travel and virtual interactions. In addition, with the increased levels of migration and transnationalism, these cultures can now be found in our own backyards. Sometimes these cross-cultural interactions will give us good experiences, but sometimes there will be experiences that are disturbing, and even outright unpleasant. In this book, Meneses challenges readers to explore answers to the following questions: How should Christians respond to beliefs and practices from other cultures which they find disturbing or repulsive? How do we distinguish ethnocentrism from legitimate commitment to beliefs and practices? How does the Christian theological conception of the "cultural mandate" differ from the Western secular conception of the theory of progress? How can we as Christians best give service to our cultures as part of our membership in the kingdom of God? The book is very engaging as she explores controversial topics like evolutionary theory, deconstructing race and ethnicity, social order and social change, politics and the kingdom of God, the role and purpose of aesthetics in culture, Christianity and the other religions, and finally "studying and living the image." By reading this book, you can allow the author to take you into cultural spaces where she discusses, questions, elaborates, and answers questions both from scientific and from theological perspectives.

Preface

The chapters of this book are a series of essays on issues in anthropology that are important to Christians. Over the past few decades, interest in anthropology has been growing in Christian circles for its ability to provide information useful to church growth, missions, development, and ministry in general—as well as to help Christians understand and adapt to living in plural societies. Christian colleges and universities, along with many seminaries, are teaching introductory anthropology classes as a regular part of their curriculum. There, anthropology must be "integrated" with biblical and theological insights to create a holistic understanding of the study of people and cultures. Secular textbooks provide the latest findings from the field of anthropology, but frame the discussion in naturalistic terms and make assumptions that Christians contest. This book provides the opportunity to dig deeper into selected topics using tools and insights from biblical and theological scholarship.

As it is a book about special topics, I have made no attempt to "cover" the material of an introductory anthropology class. Rather, I have assumed that the reader is familiar with basic terms and concepts and ready for an in-depth conversation about relativism, evolution, ethnicity and race, governments and war, the global economy, religions, and other such topics. It is, however, self contained enough that it might also be used by discussion groups such as adult Sunday school classes or church small groups, or by Christian student groups on university campuses. And, of course, it will be of interest to general readers wanting a holistic Christian understanding of cultures. At the core is an ongoing discussion about epistemology, how we can know things to be true and in what manner we can know them as Christians. So the book will also be relevant to those seeking to find solid ground for their faith in a multicultural world.

Each chapter has been examined by reviewers from the subfields addressed. These reviewers are acknowledged in footnotes at the chapter beginnings. I especially thank Dr. Andrea Pampaloni for preparing the manuscript and the team at Wipf and Stock for assisting me through the process. All Bible quotations are from the New Revised Standard Version unless otherwise indicated.

Eloise Meneses
Eastern University, Philadelphia, PA
February 27, 2018

Chapter 1

How Do We Know What is True?
A Christian View of Knowledge

> Two preteens, siblings, were sparring with one another in disagreement about a fact. "Yes, it is!," said the sister. "No it isn't!," said the brother. "Yah-hahn!," said the sister, louder. "No way!," said the brother, louder still. There was a pause. "Well, in *my* world it is!" said the one. "Well, in *my* world it isn't!" said the other, as they both burst into giggles at the solution.

These two children had learned well from their American culture.[1] Disagreements over the truth of a situation can be resolved by retreating into separate worlds. But not really. The children also realized that there is a ludicrous character to the solution they have been taught to apply in situations of conflict. If reality only exists in our minds, not between us, then nothing is true at all. As is commonly the case, the children could see through the mythology of their culture to a reality beyond it.

Perhaps no issue is more critical at this time in the plural West, and in the globalizing world, than the matter of how we know things to be true. In times when people were less mobile, and cultures less influenced by each other, a psychologically innocent absorption of the beliefs and values of one's own culture created a sense of confidence about the truth that probably made life a good deal simpler (though not necessarily better). Of course, there were disagreements among culture members. People

---

1. This chapter was read and reviewed by Rev. Michael Meneses and Holly Meneses Smith. I thank them both for their theological and philosophical insights on epistemological matters.

1

never fully conform to their cultures' norms, and cultures change over time. Furthermore, disagreements can be produced by the very structure of the society, as for instance with the natural tensions arising between rival political leaders. But fundamental beliefs and values about the nature of the world, the purpose of life, and the definition of good and bad behavior were generally held in common, giving a relative stability to everyone's sense of what is true.

This is not to say that these beliefs were in fact true! Many cultures have explained unfortunate things by blaming socially ostracized members of the community as witches. Some have justified oppressing the lower strata of their social structure by insisting on a natural hierarchy of inferiority and superiority based on birth. Such beliefs provide a sense of security to the mainstream of the culture at the expense of a portion of its members. But, by presenting the world as coherent, they inculcate a sense of confidence that the world can be understood, and therefore acted upon, in a reasonably predictable way. It is this sense of confidence that is missing in the contemporary world, where colliding views of the truth, both of what it is and of how it is obtained, are creating a mockery of the notion that we can know anything at all.

A CRISIS IN KNOWING

Our first impression of how we know things is that we "see" them. They are immediately apparent to us because we perceive them through our senses. Babies know things in this way; in fact, they are limited to this level of knowledge. The psychologist Jean Piaget has demonstrated that babies under the age of eight or nine months become distressed when their mother is hidden from their view (Piaget 1969). It is as if she no longer exists. But as they grow older, babies develop the cognitive ability to realize that their mother is not really gone when she has stepped behind another object. Instead of distress, they show signs of anticipating her return. So, while the requirement to see in order to believe is a fundamental first way of knowing things, it is quickly and necessarily followed in normal human development by another requirement, the requirement to think.

Thinking, too, is rooted in human biology and development. At base level, people around the world have the same capacity to reason (Lee and Johnson-Laird 2006). What they think about is different, of course, and the conclusions they draw vary widely because the culture-based assumptions they think *with* are different. Even the manner in which they reason may be influenced by cultural values (Luria 1976). But, the pure ability to reason does not differ by ethnic background, regional location, or cultural upbringing. This should not be surprising if we remember that our brains are fundamentally the same. Since it is vital to our survival to be able to use our mental capacities effectively in our interactions with one another and with nature, we are actually physically constructed to believe, in the initial instance, that the combination of our senses and our reason will produce for us clear and uncontestable truth.

The difficulty with this simple, or innocent, view of knowledge comes when we discover that others do not agree with us. How can it be that others, who also have senses and can reason, do not "see" things the same way that we do? The problem is a serious one because, again, the viability of our lives depends upon our ability to comprehend the world around us correctly. Someone must be wrong. Perhaps the easiest solution, and certainly the most commonly selected one, is to decide that others are wrong. Looking at it this way protects our sense of confidence in our own ability to function well. It has the benefit of providing a sense of security and stability to our lives.

There are, however, two detriments to this solution. The first is that deciding we are right at the outset closes us off from further information that might alter our viewpoint in valuable ways, or even completely change our minds about the subject. If we are no longer listening for truth, we become increasingly detached from it by the "hardening of our categories." The second is that refusing to consider what others have said leads to conflict with them. Since they too must be concerned about their ability to determine the truth, others will argue with us and be unhappy if we do not grant them a real hearing. Moreover, coming to some agreement on the matter may be absolutely necessary. For instance, the members of a society can hardly agree to disagree on the definition of murder, nor can the members of a church agree to disagree on their most central notions of God or of morality. So, as the discussion heats up, with important matters at stake, differences can lead to conflict, sometimes even to violence, and finally to separation or alienation from one another.

It is this fear, of conflict and alienation, that has caused many in Western cultures to espouse a doctrine of pluralism. Pluralism attempts to solve the problem of disagreement by privatizing some kinds of truth while coercively insisting upon others. As a result, some of our most deeply held and highly valued beliefs about the nature of reality, which are usually religious beliefs, are relegated to the private sphere of cultural life, considered subjective in nature, and therefore treated as matters on which it is best to agree to disagree. Religious matters are considered to be located in people's minds, not in the external world; to be matters of personal choice, rather than of group consensus; and ultimately, to be about the construction of an image of reality that is personally beneficial, rather than a set propositions about truth or a model of reality.

At the same time, scientific propositions about reality are considered to be above the distortions of subjectivity. Science's objective character is thought to derive from two sources, the scientific method, which stresses the removal of the bias of the researcher, and scientific consensus, which requires that the truth be verified by the replication of studies by other scientists. The removal of subjective bias by the scientific method in favor of a purported objectivity is believed to produce certainty and universal agreement. So, while our religious beliefs must be kept to ourselves, or expressed only tentatively as private opinions, our scientific beliefs can be stated boldly, and debated openly, since they are matters of public truth. As the missiologist and theologian Lesslie Newbigin has pointed out, "If two scientists, using the same materials, the same instruments, the same methods, under the same circumstances, conduct the same experiment and produce contradictory results, they do not embrace each other and say, 'what a joy it is to live in a pluralist society!'"[2] That is, they do *not* agree to disagree! Instead, they debate the matter until one or another of them is proved wrong, or until some third way of understanding emerges.

Since the 1970s, however, under the influence of the "postmodern" movement, even science has come under the criticism that it is subjective. Science is a product of Western culture, and more narrowly of the Enlightenment. Its seventeenth-century founding philosophers declared as their purpose to establish completely incontestable truth, and to develop a massive and coherent body of knowledge that would provide a universal understanding of all people and the natural world. That knowledge could be used to enhance human life through expanding technology under the paradigm of "progress." This seems a benign and benevolent purpose. But, historically, science and technology have been used to promote the West's power over the rest of the world, especially under colonialism. So, according to some now, science is tainted, even fundamentally flawed, by its association with people in positions of dominance. Others from other places, times, and circumstances, have had other perspectives on the truth that are equally valuable. No one is in a position to determine which "truths" are really true, and which are not, not even scientists.

The challenge to publicly agreed upon truth in the Western world has, at one and the same time, freed and empowered people from non-dominant

2. "The Gospel as Public Truth." Lecture presented to the Beeson Divinity School of Samford University in 1997. See videotape, "Lesslie Newbigin," produced by Gateway Films.

positions or places and created a deep uncertainty for everyone. Having the confidence of holding innocent or homogeneous views is no longer possible, not even in science, and the danger of retreating into private worlds of subjectively held opinions to avoid incoherence and conflict is perhaps more real to us now, and on a more massive scale, than ever before in human history. Yet, as the children in the story above understood, pluralism is not a real answer. It can in fact be a dangerous position for a society to take. Newbigin notes that high levels of agnosticism with regard to the truth make a culture ripe to be coercively taken over by those who claim they can provide the certainty that people need to live meaningful lives.[3]

THE KNOWING SUBJECT

Actually, the claim to our having completely objective, transcendent knowledge was false to begin with, in science and in culture generally. Only God can know us and the world he has created with perfect certainty. We, as situated human beings, are always limited in our ability to comprehend reality. Moreover, we all cast a slant on what we know that is a direct result of our cultural backgrounds, historical circumstances, and personal experiences. This has been established repeatedly by the findings of scholars in the fields of the sociology of knowledge, symbolic interactionism, and cognitive anthropology. In science, it was established in a now-classic work by Thomas Kuhn (1996), who demonstrated that scientific understanding proceeds not by an accumulation of incontestable facts, but by a series of "paradigm shifts." Paradigms are mental models of reality constructed to incorporate a body of knowledge into an understandable whole. But as such they are products of history, of the particular configuration of knowledge of the time. During the period in which they hold sway, anomalous facts, or low-level truths that do not fit the paradigm, are simply rejected. This is actually a good thing, because in many instances such anomalies can eventually be explained without destroying the paradigm. But over time, increasing numbers of anomalies arise and the paradigm loses its explanatory power. Eventually all paradigms fail in favor of new ones that can incorporate more of the facts by presenting the field of knowledge in a different way.

Kuhn established the *inevitability* of subjectivity in science. But it was another philosopher of science, Michael Polanyi, who made the case for the *value* of subjectivity in the act of knowing. Polanyi was a world-class chemist before he began to write as a philosopher, so he was very familiar with the practice of science and able to challenge popular stereotypes about how

3. Ibid.

it is actually done. In his primary work, *Personal Knowledge*, he compared the way in which a scientist considers a problem to the manner in which a craftsman molds or shapes a product, or an artist creates a work of art. In all three of these cases, the *passion* with which a person works is vital to the success of the project. All knowing begins with caring to know. It is caring to know that drives us forward toward "making a new, more extensive contact with reality" (1974: 137). Initially, it prevents us from wasting huge amounts of time studying unimportant things. Were we to study everything equally and dispassionately, says Polanyi, we would spend most of our time examining interstellar dust! (3). Our passion assists us to choose matters of importance, and then to pursue them with the discipline and through the tedium needed to discover new information. Polanyi notes that "obsession with one's problem is in fact the mainspring of all inventive power" (127). Thus our subjectivity is a critical element in the success of our endeavor to pursue truth.

The next step after developing a passion to know the object, says Polanyi, is to "indwell" the circumstances of its existence. Mentally, we enter into the situation, both pondering and "feeling," that is, vicariously experiencing, its reality. For instance, Einstein first intuited the theory of relativity by imagining himself traveling alongside a wave of light (Polanyi 1974: 10). In the process of indwelling the object, the instruments of our research, such as telescopes or microscopes, become extensions of our own body as we sense our way toward understanding. Indwelling also focuses our mental efforts. Our concentration on the object of study blocks out our immediate surroundings and all irrelevant data similarly to the way in which concentrating on a good book causes us to not hear the telephone or realize the passing of time. In fact, when reading, the book itself may "disappear" as the world that it opens up comes into mental focus. In this way, our ability to indwell the circumstances of the object of study provides us with a fuller, richer, and deeper understanding than would be possible from a purely objective distance, and we develop what Polanyi calls a "personal knowledge" of it.

However, concentrated study such as this produces a sort of understanding that is difficult to communicate to others. In fact, says Polanyi, the more deeply we know a thing, the less we can articulate what we know. This is in part because of a difference between the focal point of our concentration and a subsidiary awareness of the particulars that Polanyi calls "tacit knowing." For instance, when we recognize a friend's face, we do it not by adding up the particulars—specific eyes, a certain nose, a distinctive mouth—but by an instant recognition that incorporates all of these things without really knowing how it does so. Furthermore, higher levels of understanding subsume lower ones. So fluent knowledge of a language, for instance, allows a person to concentrate on what they are saying rather than on the grammar. In fact, fluent speakers may lose their ability to describe the rules of grammar, though they know well when a mistake has been made. Or, in another example, the specifics of how to drive a car are "forgotten" by skilled drivers who learn to react automatically so that they can concentrate on where they are going.

The significance of the point about tacit knowing is in what it says about how we know anything at all. As the above examples demonstrate, in order to consciously focus on one thing, we must at least temporarily accept other things uncritically, including the basic skills and assumptions with which we are operating. The same is true in science. Polanyi notes:

> The actual foundations of our scientific beliefs cannot be as-
> serted at all. When we accept a certain set of pre-suppositions
> and use them as our interpretive framework, we may be said to
> dwell in them as we do in our own body. Their uncritical ac-
> ceptance for the time being consists in a process of assimilation
> by which we identify ourselves with them. They are not asserted
> and cannot be asserted, for assertion can be made only *within* a
> framework with which we have identified ourselves for the time
> being; as they are themselves our ultimate framework, they are
> essentially inarticulate. (1974: 60) [Emphasis in the original.]

The reason tacit knowledge is inarticulate, then, is that it is a framework of understanding that is the *means* by which we are able to focus on the object of study.

Still, tacit knowing is the result of a history of previous investigations, and that history is fraught with choices along the way, including not only choices about what to study, but choices about what to believe in a certain instance. The "facts" are never 100 percent clear (as Kuhn established). The interpretation of them is even less certain, always allowing for multiple ex-planatory theories. So, at critical points in the process of coming to under-stand an object of study, says Polanyi, scientists must *choose to believe* one way or another about it. At the moment of decision, such a choice is actually a faith commitment to one viewpoint over others, and the scientist makes the choice intuitively:

> Every deliberate mental act has to decide its own timing. The
> risks of further hesitation must be weighted against the risks
> of acting hastily. The balance of the two must be left to be de-
> rived from the circumstances, as known to the person making
> up his mind . . . To postpone mental decisions on account of

> their conceivable fallibility would necessarily block all decisions
> forever, and pile up the hazards of hesitation to infinity. It would
> amount to voluntary mental stupor. Stupor alone can eliminate
> both belief and error. (1974: 314)

The choice of what to believe is a risky one! To the degree that we have
chosen well, our later investigations will be productive (that is, yield comprehensible results); to the degree that we have chosen badly, they will be
unproductive. But choose we must. And the choices we make now will contribute to the construction of the framework of tacit knowing that will guide
our further investigations.

According to Polanyi, then, *all knowing is rooted in prior believing*, and
all believing is a personal commitment. Polanyi makes powerful statements
on the subject: "We must now recognize belief once more as the source of
all knowledge . . . no intelligence, however critical or original, can operate
outside such a fiduciary framework" (1974: 266). In fact, ". . . to avoid believing one must stop thinking" (314).

Still, personal knowledge is not an abandonment of the pursuit of
objective truth. Anyone who cares about the truth, says Polanyi, holds personal beliefs with "universal intent" (1974: 150). That is, they believe what
they believe to be true for everyone. To suggest otherwise is to be disingenu-
ous at the least, and dangerous at worst. If you believed an avalanche was
coming, would you be wise to keep it to yourself and not warn others who
are in the way? Actually, holding personal beliefs with universal intent is an
act of responsibility (309). Polanyi chides science heavily for its failure to
take moral responsibility for its findings. For example, it was investigations
into the nature of the atom that led to the development of the atomic bomb.
More recently, investigations into the functioning of DNA have made technologies possible that threaten the sanctity of life. Thus, knowing is always
a public activity, in science as elsewhere, and *asserting what we believe to be
universally true is a morally responsible act*.

This sense of responsibility, together with a sense of our own vulnerability, is the reason we care deeply whether others acknowledge our understanding of the truth or not:

> Heuristic passion . . . raises a claim that makes a tremendous
> demand on other [people]; for it asks that its gift to humanity
> be accepted by all. In order to be satisfied, our intellectual pas-
> sions must find response. This universal intent creates a tension:
> we suffer when a vision of reality to which we have committed
> ourselves is contemptuously ignored by others. For a general

unbelief imperils our own convictions by evoking an echo in us.
Our vision must conquer or die. (Polanyi 1974: 150)

To some extent, the value of our belief depends on its acceptance by others, and the value of their beliefs depend on our acceptance as well. What is needed is a community of discussion and debate, investigation and inquiry, speaking and listening. So we must continue to talk, and to try to persuade one another of our viewpoints, not only in science but also in culture, and in matters of religious faith as well.

THE KNOWING COMMUNITY

All knowledge is contextualized within a knowing community. A knowing community exists in a specific place and time, with a particular culture composed of social structure, language, religion, and worldview. In fact, knowledge only *makes sense* within the context of a community, just as a spoken sentence only makes sense within the framework of the language in which it is spoken. The belief system of a community is inculcated in its members by years of education. This does not mean that it is explicitly taught. The most powerful way to inculcate beliefs is to simply assume them in actions (Bateson 1978). For instance, the organization of children into large classrooms by grades in Western education is predicated upon two beliefs: that biological development is the same in all people, and that, by effort, individuals can achieve success in competition with one another. Viewing education like a ladder, teachers carefully stair-step assignments to help students take small steps that lead to bigger accomplishments as they grow. By assuming and acting upon these beliefs (and sometimes by demonstrating a sense of outrage if they are explicitly challenged), the worldview of egalitarianism, individualism, and achievement is transmitted to American students, and to others around the world who receive a Western education. Within a culture, the same implicit messages are transmitted to people in multiple contexts, reinforcing the notion that the views of the community are not just arbitrarily chosen, but are normal, natural, and good.

Scientific knowledge is no exception to this rule about the influence of community life upon belief. Polanyi notes that science is also rooted in a tradition:

> Science . . . [is] a vast system of beliefs, deeply rooted in our history and cultivated today by a specially organized part of our society . . . [it] is part of our mental life, shared out for cultivation among many thousands of specialized scientists throughout the

world, and shared receptively, at second hand, by many millions.
(1974: 171)

Of course, science operates by debate, claims, and counter-claims about the
nature of reality. Yet, as Polanyi points out, entrance into the community of
scientists has an exceedingly long period of apprenticeship, requiring the
learning of a very technical and complex language (53). "When I speak of
science," he says, "I acknowledge both its tradition and its organized authority, and I deny that anyone who wholly rejects these can be said to be a
scientist, or have any proper understanding of science" (164). So, the community of scientists, along with its traditions, values, and beliefs, is necessary to the production of scientific knowledge.

Put in another way, the sociologist Peter Berger suggests that all beliefs
exist within certain "plausibility structures." Plausibility structures are social
and cultural institutions that confirm the validity of beliefs by making them
seem believable:

> With the possible exception of a few areas of direct personal
> experience, human beings require social confirmation for their
> beliefs about reality . . . It follows from this that there is a direct
> relation between the cohesion of institutions and the subjective
> cohesiveness of beliefs, values, and worldviews. (Berger and
> Luckmann 1967: 17)

Berger is suggesting that when the customs and practices of a community
are well coordinated they create experiences in the lives of their members
that confirm the community's beliefs. In Hinduism, for instance, there is a
belief that women who commit suicide at the death of their husbands (*sati*)
will be reborn as goddesses. That belief is confirmed in the Hindu community by institutions such as the general worship of goddesses, a daily ritual
in which wives subordinate themselves to their husbands, folktales about
specific women and their reincarnations, the stigmatization of widows for
not committing *sati*, and the praise given to women who have committed
sati in the past. Without these institutions, the belief in the apotheosis of
self-sacrificing women would be much harder to accept. With these institutions, ideas to the contrary, such as the notion that we have just one life on
earth, or that all people have the same intrinsic worth, seem less likely to be
true. As a relatively cohesive set of practices, the plausibility structures of a
community operate in people's daily lives to make their beliefs seem more
realistic.

In small scale societies, it is possible for social and cultural institutions
to consistently affirm the belief system without a great deal of contradiction.

In large and complex societies, this sense of a fully coherent understanding of the world can only be had in subcultures, such as religious or ethnic communities. The dominant public arena, which is the realm of politics, must construct a base level agreement between different subcultures on how to live together. The public arena cannot offer the complete set of beliefs and practices needed for a meaningful life because it must accommodate groups with different religious and cultural commitments. Still, it must claim to offer truth that is relevant to all in order to successfully coordinate the groups. In the West, science has played the role of provider of truth for the public arena, and so it has become "the supreme interpreter of human affairs," says Polanyi (1974: 141). That is why, since the Enlightenment, science has replaced religion at the center of public life:

> When the supernatural authority of laws, churches and sacred texts had waned or collapsed, man tried to avoid the emptiness of mere self-assertion by establishing over himself the authority of experience and reason. But it has now turned out that modern scientism fetters thought as cruelly as ever the churches had done. It offers no scope for our most vital beliefs and it forces us to disguise them in farcically inadequate terms. (1974: 265)

Science is a very poor substitute for religion at the center of public life. It offers little in the way of meaning and hope to our existence, and is even more coercive in its claims to truth than the church once was.

Because of science's power and prestige in Western culture, it is important to identify the faith-based claims science is making. Roughly, these are the beliefs of philosophical naturalism: the universe is self-contained (that is, needs no explanation from outside of itself), operates according to discernable laws, and is fundamentally material in nature. Human beings are part of the universe, though they transcend it in the sense that they can understand it through observation and reason. Only science can provide complete and universal certainty through its method of skepticism, controlled testing, and proven results. Through science, people can come to agreement on essential matters, and progress toward a common future with a good life.

Years of indoctrination, in the educational system as well as through the media and in the culture at large, make assumptions such as these seem realistic to most people in the West. But Polanyi challenges this worldview at perhaps its most critical point, the notion that doubt or skepticism can produce truth:

> Doubt has been acclaimed not only as the touchstone of truth, but also as the safeguard of tolerance . . . It remains deeply

ingrained in the modern mind . . . that though doubt may become nihilistic and imperil thereby all freedom of thought, to
refrain from belief is always an act of intellectual probity as
compared with the resolve to hold a belief . . . [which] is felt to
be a surrender of reason. (1974: 271)

The idea that doubt is a safer path to truth than belief, is not only wrong,
says Polanyi, it is foolish. First, the normal form of doubting, which is used
in science to test hypotheses, can only be done from a vantage point that
rests firmly on belief, as we saw in the above discussion on tacit knowing.
For instance, it is possible to doubt the effectiveness of herbal medicines, but
only from the vantage point of a belief in the natural processes of the body
and of their susceptibility or insusceptibility to certain kinds of biochemical
influences. Or, it is possible to doubt the existence of spirits in nature, but
only from the vantage point of a belief in regular laws of nature that function independently of outside forces. Even our ability to perceive the world
around us rests on an uncritical acceptance of the input of our senses (which
we *know* can fool us!), and on an interpretation of the data in terms of the
beliefs we have already accepted about what could reasonably be true. It is
simply not possible to doubt one belief without simultaneously accepting
others.

Actually, this sort of critical doubt that rests on other uncritically accepted beliefs has been valuable, according to Polanyi, because it has assisted us to detect error. But there is a second form of doubt which has had
a very pernicious effect on Western culture. It is the belief that skepticism
is the best guide to truth, and that the more skeptical you are, the more
"reasonable" are your beliefs. This idea is truly foolish, since the attempt to
doubt everything at once would result in "imbecility," says Polanyi (1974:
295). Science cannot function at all apart from its commitment to certain
beliefs about the nature of reality and about how we as humans can know
that reality. Ironically, when science's skepticism is turned on itself, its entire
project is threatened. Polanyi remarks:

The critical [doubt-based] movement, which seems to be near-
ing the end of its course today, was perhaps the most fruitful
effort ever sustained by the human mind. The past four or five
centuries, which have gradually destroyed or overshadowed the
whole medieval cosmos, have enriched us mentally and morally
to an extent unrivalled by any period of similar duration. But
its incandescence had fed on the combustion of the Christian
heritage in the oxygen of Greek rationalism, and when this fuel

was exhausted the critical framework itself burnt away. (1974: 265–6)

The final result of relying solely upon doubt to establish truth is nihilism; without faith, we cannot know anything at all.

It is important to know that Polanyi is not disputing the value of scientific practice. Science has provided us with a vast knowledge of the world that we did not previously have due to its careful method of investigation. But some of the claims that science makes for itself are inaccurate, even dangerous. Science claims to have complete objectivity, to be able to establish incontestable truth, and to do so by blindly rejecting all tradition and authority. Yet within the scientific community, authority actually does play an important role. Polanyi notes the following when describing how people become scientists:

> To learn by example is to submit to authority. You follow your master because you trust his manner of doing things even when you cannot analyse and account in detail for its effectiveness. By watching the master and emulating his efforts in the presence of his example, the apprentice unconsciously picks up the rules of the art, including those which are not explicitly known to the master himself. These hidden rules can be assimilated only by a person who surrenders himself to that extent uncritically to the imitation of another. A society which wants to preserve a fund of personal knowledge must submit to tradition. (1974: 53)

It is neither possible nor valuable to attempt to gain certain knowledge by relying solely on our own observation and reason. We must trust the community of which we are a part, submitting to its authority, learning its traditions, and accepting its premises by faith. Of course, communities can be wrong. As Christians, we do not believe that women who commit *sati* will become goddesses. But as human beings we have no other choice; we must join a believing community of one sort or another. Truth, especially in the form of meaning, is not found in the minds of isolated rational individuals; it is embedded in living communities of faith and practice.

BIBLICAL KNOWING

For Christians, it should be neither surprising nor alarming that we cannot independently know the world with complete certainty. We have always believed that human understanding is limited. The Bible warns of the dangers of relying too heavily on our own judgment. In Proverbs (3:5), we are instructed to "Trust in the Lord with all your heart, and do not rely on your own insight." In Isaiah (55:8–9) God says, "For my thoughts are not your thoughts, nor are your ways my ways, says the Lord. For as the heavens are higher than the earth, so are my ways higher than your ways and my thoughts than your thoughts." It is possible that in Genesis (3:6), Adam and Eve's desire to know good and evil was a sinful attempt to be like God in knowing *everything* (Gordon and Rendsburg 1998: 36). If so, the first human beings fell from grace because they could not accept the limitations of their own knowledge and power.

But human understanding is not just limited, it is also *distorted* by the effects of sin, especially the sin of self-centeredness. Theologians down through the centuries of the church, from the Apostle Paul to St. Augustine to the Reformers, have acknowledged the flawed character of human reason. Reason can lead us away from God and truth as easily as toward them, and it can be used to defend illegitimate purposes. Lesslie Newbigin suggests that we have an overly innocent view of our own motives in the reasoning process:

> We are not honest inquirers seeking the truth. We are alienated from truth and are enemies of it. We are by nature idolaters, constructing images of truth shaped by our own desires. This was demonstrated once and for all when Truth became incarnate, present to us in the actual being and life of the man Jesus, and when our response to this Truth incarnate, a response including all the representatives of the best in human culture at that time and place, was to seek to destroy it. (1995a: 69)

A typical human response to truth, then, is to reject it . . . and to threaten the life of the messenger! (cf. Matt 21:33–44).

The distortion in our thinking that is caused by sin makes God's ways seem mysterious to us, even foolish. The Apostle Paul wrote:

> Where is the wise person? Where is the teacher of the law? Where is the philosopher of this age? Has not God made foolish the wisdom of the world? For since in the wisdom of God the world through its wisdom did not know him, God was pleased through the foolishness of what was preached to save those who believe. Jews demand signs and Greeks look for wisdom, but we preach Christ crucified: a stumbling block to Jews and foolishness to Gentiles, but to those whom God has called, both Jews and Greeks, Christ [is] the power of God and the wisdom of God. For the foolishness of God is wiser than human wisdom,

and the weakness of God is stronger than human strength. (1
Cor 1:20–25, NIV)

Paul was giving an account for people's rejection of the Christian message
of salvation through Christ's death. He was aware of how foolish such a
message must appear to the Greek philosophers (the intellectual ancestors
of our modern-day rationalists). Paul argued that God, in his wisdom, had
not chosen human reason as the means of revealing his plan for salvation.
Rather, he had chosen to act in history in a way that appeared foolish to
those who trust only their own judgment, but wise and powerful to those
who believe.

None of the above passages suggest that we should not use our God-
given abilities to perceive and to reason. There are many other passages in
the Bible that encourage us to develop wisdom. The Bible praises people
such as Joshua (Deut 34:9), Solomon (1 Kgs 4:39), Daniel (Dan 1:20), the
woman of Proverbs (31:26), and Jesus himself (Isa 11:2; Matt 13:54; Luke
2:40,52) for their wisdom; and it declares wisdom to be a gift from God,
urging that we pursue it (Ps 51:6; Prov 1–9; Eph 1:17; Jas 1:5). Perhaps one
of the strongest such passages is Proverbs 2:1–10:

> My child, if you accept my words and treasure up my command-
> ments within you,
>
> Making your ear attentive to wisdom and inclining your heart
> to understanding,
>
> If you indeed cry out for insight and raise your voice for
> understanding,
>
> If you seek it like silver and search for it as for hidden treasures,
>
> Then you will understand the fear of the Lord and find the
> knowledge of God.
>
> For the Lord gives wisdom; from his mouth come knowledge
> and understanding,
>
> He stores up sound wisdom for the upright; he is a shield to
> those who walk blamelessly,
>
> Guarding the paths of justice and preserving the way of his
> faithful ones.
>
> Then you will understand righteousness and justice and equity,
> every good path,
>
> For wisdom will come into your heart and knowledge will be
> pleasant to your soul.

The passage states that if we seek wisdom, God will give it to us, including a knowledge of himself. The wisdom we gain will add to our moral character, making us both righteous and just.

Still, the Bible repeatedly states that wisdom begins not with our own abilities, but with the fear of (or reverence for) the Lord (Ps 111:10; Prov 1:7; Job 28:28). Jesus said that in order to know truth we must become his disciples (John 8:31–2), that is, trust him first. On one occasion, he claimed, "I am the light of the world. Whoever follows me will never walk in darkness, but will have the light of life" (verse 12). The Pharisees challenged him to show by what authority he was saying such a bold thing! Jesus answered that it was by his own authority and by God the Father's. Later he commented to his followers, "If you hold to my teaching, you are really my disciples. Then you will know the truth and the truth will set you free" (verse 31). His followers insisted that they were already free because they were descendants of Abraham, the chosen people. But Jesus declared that they were in fact slaves to sin, and that only he could free them. The followers then tried to claim that God was their father. Jesus rebuked them:

> "If God were your Father, you would love me, for I came from God and now I am here. I did not come on my own, but he sent me. Why do you not understand what I say? It is because you cannot accept my word. You are from your father the devil, and you choose to do your father's desires. He was a murderer from the beginning and does not stand in the truth, because there is no truth in him. When he lies, he speaks according to his own nature, for he is a liar and the father of lies. But because I tell the truth, you do not believe me. Which of you convicts me of sin? If I tell the truth, why do you not believe me? Whoever is from God hears the words of God. The reason you do not hear them is that you are not from God." (John 8:42–47)

Jesus made it clear that our inability to recognize him as having come from God, and to understand and accept the truth that he offers, is due to our allegiance to the devil! And that allegiance causes us to prefer lies.

In the last section, we saw that human knowing must take place within a community if it is to have meaning. Yet we also saw that human communities can be wrong. Now we can see why. Human beings are inclined to sin not only as individuals but also as groups arrayed in rebellion against God. Jesus' followers thought that their Jewish heritage would save them. But Jesus rejected membership in a traditional or religious community as being enough to open our eyes to truth. If this was the case for the Jewish people, who were chosen by God to bear truth as a "light to the nations" (Isa

49:6), then it is certainly true of all other human communities. As we will see in chapter five, traditional communities can be very powerful opponents of the Christian message.

What then is the solution? Jesus repeatedly referred to the limits and distortions of human understanding as a kind of blindness (Matt 13:10–17; Matt 15:14; Matt 23:16; Luke 6:39; John 9:39–41). Ultimately, that blindness can only be healed by God; we cannot heal ourselves. As Christians, we believe that God has revealed redeeming and healing truth to humanity throughout history. God began by speaking through the prophets to the people of Israel, then sent his son, Jesus, followed by the Holy Spirit who inspired the apostles to bring life-giving truth to the world. The record of God's messages and acts in history is in the Bible, along with an interpretation of what these things mean in the context of the whole story of time. As Christians, we enter into that story through faith, in a process that Lesslie Newbigin likens to Polanyi's process of indwelling the object of study:

> The Christian life [is] one in which we live *in* the biblical story as part of the community whose story it is, find in the story the clues to knowing God as his character becomes manifest in the story, and from within that indwelling try to understand and cope with the events of our time and the world about us and so carry the story forward. At the heart of the story, as the key to the whole, is the incarnation of the Word, the life, ministry, death and resurrection of Jesus. In the Fourth Gospel Jesus defines for his disciples what is to be their relation to him. They are to "dwell in" him. He is not to be the object of their observation, but the body of which they are a part. As they "indwell" him in his body, they will both be led into fuller and fuller apprehension of the truth and also become the means through which God's will is done in the life of the world. (1989: 99)

Newbigin makes an important point regarding the stance we must take on knowing truth, especially the Truth who is Jesus. We do not study Jesus, or the Bible, as an object over which we have superior judgment. Rather we submit ourselves to him, and to the biblical text, in such a way as to have our blindness removed by faith. Jesus said that our knowledge of him comes from abiding, or remaining, in him (John 15:5–7), that is, by committing ourselves to trust in him. Likewise, says Newbigin, we indwell the Bible as the uncritically accepted framework with which we observe everything else. Remember that according to Polanyi *all* knowing must be done from such a framework! It is simply a matter of which framework we choose to accept as our ultimate guide to truth.

Of course, we can learn many good things about Jesus and the Bible, as we can about the rest of the world, through collecting information and thinking it through, that is, through study. There is no need for Christians to reject the findings of science or of good scholarship outright. But we cannot learn the most important things, such as about the nature of God or of life's purposes, by our intellectual efforts alone. Nor can we interpret what we know correctly apart from the deep connection with God that we get from indwelling his Word. We need God's healing touch and his revelation of truth in order to understand.

For instance, by faith, we Christians believe that Jesus, who is now at the right hand of God, is sovereign over all the universe (John 1:1–5; Col 1:15–20). But that truth is not evident, or seemingly even rational, to most people. Why should Jesus' reign not be evident to all? Theologically, the answer is that God has chosen to partially hide the truth of his presence in order to give us the freedom to choose whether or not to relate to him. Newbigin reminds us that we live in a period of time, between the first and second comings of Jesus, during which "signs are granted of that hidden reign [of Christ] but in which the full revelation of its power and glory is held back in order that all the nations—all the human communities—may have the opportunity to repent and believe in freedom" (1989: 128). In fact, a full revelation of the truth of Jesus' reign would make it impossible for us to resist him, and therefore *be* the Day of Judgment, says Newbigin.

So God's truth is in part secret, hidden especially from those who do not know him. The Apostle Paul says, "Among the mature we do speak wisdom, though it is not a wisdom of this age or of the rulers of this age, who are doomed to perish. But we speak God's wisdom, *secret and hidden*, which God decreed before the ages for our glory" (1 Cor 2:6–7) [emphasis added]. It is only through faith that our eyes can be opened to secrets such as these. St. Augustine began his intellectual life as a fourth-century professor of rhetoric. He was well versed in Greek philosophy and the use of reason to determine truth. But after his conversion to Christianity, Augustine recognized the necessity of faith for such knowledge and wrote words that have been remembered throughout the history of the church: *nisi credideritis non intelligetis*, "without belief there is no understanding." Through belief we are put into relationship with God in such a way as to be able to accept his revelation of hidden truth.

Thus God's revelation comes to us in two forms: first generally, in ways that are relatively accessible to observation and reason (such as through nature), and then specifically, through messengers. Most immediately, this second way of revealing truth can seem to us to be unfair. Theologians call it "the scandal of particularity." In the Bible, God called certain people in specific places and times to be the recipients of his revelation; he did not communicate directly with everyone. Adam and Eve were called to bear God's image in creation, Abraham and Sara were called to leave their families and found a new nation, Moses was called to liberate the Israelites and give them the law, the Israelites were called out from the pagan nations around them to be a "chosen people" for God, and the prophets were called, one by one, to deliver messages to Israel from God. Each of these messengers lived in a certain time and place and reached only a limited number of people. Even Jesus, who was himself *the* revelation of God, was not given to everyone, but to the people of Palestine in the first century. Then, the apostles were called one by one to be Jesus' first disciples and to found the church, and now the church is called to represent Jesus as God's revelation to the world in one local community after another. God gives specific revelation through earthly messengers, who are then responsible to share the good news with others.

Specifically revealed truth is not shared primarily through rational argument, debate, study, or contemplation, but through witness. Witnesses claim to have "seen," or had direct contact with, an event. They report on what they know by observation. In the Old Testament, witnesses were the cornerstone of the legal system. Important decisions, such as guilt or innocence in crimes, were made by the testimony of witnesses. Two were needed to establish the truth by agreeing with one another, and each witness had to make a personal commitment to the truth of the report (similar to the oath given to witnesses in our own legal system). Sometimes they were even expected to help punish the offender.[4] They were required to speak up if they had information (Lev 5:1), and were punished if they were discovered to have given a false report (Exod 20:16). Hearers too had a responsible role. First, they had to judge the validity of the reports based on the integrity of the witnesses. The judgment was made with a knowledge of the person—his or her access to information, general reliability, and evidence of conviction about the point being made. Then, they had to make decisions about how to act based upon the testimony they had received. They could not simply listen and walk away. All parties were personally invested in the process in such a way as to promote the moral responsibility of the whole community to the truth.

In the New Testament, God chose to inform the world of his plan of salvation, *not* by having Jesus write a book or found a school of philosophical thought, but by sending out witnesses to Jesus' life, death, and resurrection.

---

4. See William Vermillion, "Witness, martyr" in the *Holman Bible Dictionary*, ed. by Trent C. Butler (Nashville, TN: Broadman and Holman, 1991).

These witnesses told others of what they had seen and heard, and later wrote books and letters about the events they had witnessed. Most people did not believe them. Remember, we human beings do not really want to hear the truth, in part because it requires a response from us. Hearers must choose to listen and obey ("believe") the truth, or refuse it with possible consequences. But the conviction of those witnesses, and of the many others after them in the history of the church, was so strong that they staked their very lives on their reports, becoming martyrs (the word means "witness") for the gospel ("good news") of Jesus Christ.

Of course, in the world of beliefs, people are witnessing to different things, some of them mutually contradictory. This situation is parallel to Polanyi's description of scientists debating the merits of different theories. Polanyi said that risk and personal commitment are necessary for a scientist to advance a theory. Scientists must declare their theories to be universally true (not just true for themselves), and then stake their reputations on being right. The validity of the theory can only be established in the long run by its fruitfulness. In the meanwhile, scientists must witness to the truth as they see it, and do so with conviction despite the disagreements. Likewise, as Christians, we must witness to our faith with conviction by staking our own lives and reputations on what we believe to be true—that is, by risking other people's condemnation, and by *living* according to the truth that we proclaim. Newbigin states, "I can only affirm the objectivity of a truth claim which I make by committing myself to live and act in accordance with this claim" (1995a: 75). In the long run, God will reveal all truth to humanity on the day of judgment. But, in the meanwhile, it will be our *personal* commitment to Christian truth that will convince other people of it (Matt 7:15–20).

Newbigin reminds us that the humility with which we must represent our understanding of truth should not cause us to shy away from stating it with confidence (1995a). In the New Testament, the early Christian believers prayed for the ability to speak out with boldness under persecution (Acts 4:29), and their hearers noticed the confidence with which they spoke (Acts 4:13). The Apostle Paul wrote to the Philippians, "It is my eager expectation and hope that I will not be put to shame in any way, but that by my speaking with all boldness, Christ will be exalted now as always in my body, whether by life or by death" (Phil 1:20), and he asked the Ephesians to pray for him for boldness: "Pray also for me, so that when I speak, a message may be given to me to make known with boldness the mystery of the gospel, for which I am an ambassador in chains. Pray that I may declare it boldly, as I must speak" (Eph 6:19–20). In the last verse of the last chapter of Acts, Luke records that Paul did indeed receive this gift from the Lord; to the end of his life, he was "proclaiming the kingdom of God and teaching about the Lord Jesus Christ with all boldness" (Acts 28:31).

As Christians, we can sometimes be confused about what it means to be humble. We can imagine that speaking up is proud, while keeping quiet is humble. But, it is perfectly possible to speak humbly, or for that matter, to maintain a proud silence! Remembering the original meaning of the word *confidence* can be helpful: con-fidence means, "with faith." We can be humble yet bold so long as our faith is in God, not ourselves. Newbigin writes, "The confidence proper to a Christian is not the confidence of one who claims possession of demonstrable and indubitable knowledge. It is the confidence of one who has heard and answered the call that comes from the God through whom and for whom all things were made: 'Follow me'" (1995a: 105).

So our confidence comes very simply from the strength of our personal commitment to believe in and to follow Jesus. With this epistemological stance—recognizing the limitations of our own understanding; yet holding to truth in a faith lived out in practice; indwelling Jesus, the Bible, and the church in order to be recipients of God's revelation; and declaring that revelation humbly yet boldly to others as witnesses—we *can* have a "proper confidence," says Newbigin (1995a). The desire for complete certainty as human beings has always been an attempt to do without God. But our confidence does not rest on a certainty derived from our own abilities. Rather it rests on the faith we have placed in God as our Creator, in Jesus as our Savior, and in the Holy Spirit as our Guide.

KNOWING PEOPLE

Finally, it is possible to view knowledge as existing not just in individual minds, but relationally between people. Anthropology is the study of people. Since scientists are also people, anthropologists (and other social scientists) are in the unique circumstance of being both subject and object of study. They can be both observer and observed, knower and known. This circumstance is both a benefit and a detriment to the work. On the one hand, unlike natural scientists, anthropologists can intuitively understand those they study because they share a common humanity. They can also communicate directly with the "objects" of study, listening to their reports. But, on the other hand, anthropologists can skew their depictions by over-identifying in culturally specific ways, or by imposing theories or assumptions on the data. A difference can emerge between the perspectives of observer and observed.

It might seem easiest to simply take either the anthropologists' perspective, or the informants' (anthropologists' term for the people they are interviewing), to be the more truthful one. But anthropologists have long had a more complex approach to the matter. Due to the work of a Christian linguistic anthropologist and missionary, Kenneth Pike, a distinction has been made in the field between *etic* and *emic* perspectives. The former is that of the observer, and describes the situation as viewed from outside the culture. The latter is that of the informant, and describes the situation as experienced from inside the culture. Rather than insist on the complete objectivity of the outsider, which we know is impossible anyway, or the superior knowledge of the insider, which is often tainted with interests of various sorts, anthropologists have affirmed the value of *both* perspectives working interactively with one another. There are differences in emphasis between anthropologists, with some giving preference to the richness of people's own explanations, and others giving preference to laws and principles of human behavior determined by the scholarly community. But, on the whole, most anthropologists have accepted the value of both perspectives, *emic* and *etic*, for arriving at a fuller understanding.

All this fits well with the notion that knowing is essentially relational. Parker Palmer is a Christian educator who describes this notion well. "Knowing is a process in which subjective and objective *interact*," says Palmer (1993: 36) [emphasis added]. The word *truth,* he says, comes from "troth," which means loyalty or faithfulness—as in "betrothal." "To know something or someone in truth is to enter troth with the known, . . . to enter into the life of that which we know and to allow it to enter into ours. Truthful knowing weds the knower and the known" (31). Thus, an anthropologist who comes to know a people does so by developing a trusting relationship with them. Even in the study of the physical world, knower and known must relate to one another in order for information to be passed between them. If you try to walk through a wall, for instance, the wall will "talk back" in the sense that it will forbid you to enter. How much more so, then, is this true of our attempts to know people! We must *relate* to others in order to learn about them, and that relationship must be a two-way street.

Palmer traces the history of the Enlightenment, or "modernist," project to know the world with complete certainty through objectivity. That project was a one-way street, with the knower completely in control of the process. By artificially stressing the value of a detached curiosity, science ironically produced in Western culture a deep desire to control the world and everything in it (1993: 7). Scientists saw themselves as merely investigating the world, and took no responsibility for how the knowledge they produced would be used. That left technology to develop on its own trajectory without the supervision of the knowledge producers. The research on the nature of the atom was done by scientists who did not consider themselves responsible for the atomic bomb that was constructed using their findings. "Curiosity sometimes kills," says Palmer, "and our desire to control has put deadly power in some very unsteady hands" (1993: 7).

But curiosity and control are not the only possible motivations to investigate the world. A third motivation, says Palmer, is compassion. This motivation differs qualitatively from the others because it has a different goal:

> The goal of a knowledge arising from love is the reunification and reconstruction of broken selves and worlds. A knowledge born of compassion aims not at exploiting and manipulating creation but at reconciling the world to itself. The mind motivated by compassion reaches out to know as the heart reaches out to love. Here, the act of knowing *is* an act of love. (1993: 8) [emphasis in the original.]

In our relationships with one another, we mean something different by *knowing* than science does by that term, something richer and more penetrating. Relational knowledge includes a concern for the well-being of the other person, with a willingness to *act* on their behalf. The Bible uses the term *know* in this sense. To know, biblically, is to relate to another, to participate in their life, and ultimately to defend them. Thus, we are to know God, but not know evil. And God knows us, not as objects of a detached curiosity or a desire to control, but as recipients of his compassion.

When we know someone with compassion, we want to listen to them. Palmer says that true listening involves *obedience* to the truth (1993: 65). That is, rather than controlling the conversation with the other person, we listen to them in order to submit ourselves to the truth that emerges. Newbigin agrees: "Personal knowledge only becomes a possibility when I abandon the sovereign claim of autonomous reason, the claim to know the other person without that person's self-communication in speech and art and gesture; when I am ready to stop my investigations and listen, to be addressed, to be called in question, to be summoned to an adventure of trust" (1989: 61). Truth emerges from loving relationships partly because we hold one another accountable to it. That is why the community is so important. We must "create a space in which obedience to the truth is practiced" through deep listening (Palmer 1993: 69).

Within the space created for listening and learning, if we are willing to make ourselves open and vulnerable, we can expect a "conversion" to truth, says Palmer (1993: 48). Jesus claimed to *be* the truth himself, that is to embody the truth we need to know about God (John 14:6). Before Pilate, he said, "For this I was born, and for this I came into the world, to testify to the truth. Everyone who belongs to the truth listens to my voice" (John 18:37). Listening to truth, especially the Truth who is Jesus, converts us; it changes *us*, rather than our circumstances. Ultimately, our willingness to be changed by truth is what enables us to contribute positively to a better world.

Most anthropologists are functioning atheists. But their encounter with people of other cultures has made them relatively aware of the shortcomings of objective knowledge and the value of relational knowing. Knowing people, listening to them, and learning about them is the whole purpose of the discipline, and anthropologists have learned much about people and cultures. As Christians, we root our own knowing ultimately in God's revelation, not in any human understanding. But we can benefit from what anthropology has learned through relational knowing and apply that knowledge to a better understanding of ourselves and others as part of our participation in God's kingdom work.

(CHAPTER 1) DISCUSSION QUESTIONS

1. On what basis can we claim to know truth as human beings and as Christians?

2. In disagreements, how can we show respect for others' views while not abandoning the quest for truth?

3. In a world in which faith-based beliefs are trivialized, how can we communicate what we believe with confidence?

4. At what points must we admit our own ignorance and trust God for matters we cannot understand?

RECOMMENDED READINGS

Kuhn, Thomas. 1996. *The Structure of Scientific Revolution*. Chicago: University of Chicago Press.

Newbigin, Lesslie. 1995a. *Proper Confidence: Faith, Doubt, and Certainty in Christian Discipleship*. Grand Rapids, MI: Eerdmans.

Palmer, Parker. 1993. *To Know as We are Known*. New York: HarperOne.

Polanyi, Michael. 1974. *Personal Knowledge: Towards a Post-Critical Philosophy*. Chicago: University of Chicago Press.

Chapter 2

Isn't Our Way Just Natural?
Understanding Culture

It was just too much. The college student in "Heritage of India" class had read about bloody wars, pagan rituals, and a social system that deemed some people divine and others dirt. And now there was a ritual symbolizing the mating of the queen with a horse! The student was trying to be as tolerant as she could. But when writing her weekly paper on the readings, she felt forced to express her real feelings. "I *struggle* with some of these ideas," she wrote. "But," she quickly added, "I know that if I disagree, it means I'm ignorant."

Is this true? Is it the case that disagreement always reflects ignorance?[1] If so, all disagreements should be easily resolvable by the provision of further information. It is a tempting idea, because it suggests that all we need to do to avoid cultural conflict is to better educate ourselves about one another. But history and ordinary experience hardly reveal this to be the case. It is people who know one another who disagree the most bitterly, and it is groups with a history of previous contact that fight wars. Sometimes, coming to understand one another more fully can be the basis for even deeper disagreement. "It ain't those parts of the Bible that I can't understand that bother me, it is the parts that I do understand," quipped Mark Twain.

The student in this case did not really mean she lacked information. It was the information in front of her that was disturbing her. She meant that

---

1. This chapter was read and reviewed by Eric Flett. I am grateful for his rich theological insights and clarifications.

her own inability to agree with the things she was reading about reflected a lack of the liberal perspective that is commonly associated with a general education. Incorporated into her thinking was the model of a plural society currently being promoted in American culture through the school system. That model suggests that all cultures are equal (in some undefined manner), and that no one should criticize, or "judge," any other culture's beliefs, values, customs, or habits. In this way of thinking, tolerance is the supreme virtue, and intolerance the most serious sin. The student did not question the model. She had learned it in childhood, had it constantly reinforced in classes, conversations, and the media since, and had never been given a serious alternative to it. Everyone in her world seemed to agree on this point about the equality of cultures, so it must be true. Yet she "struggled" when she found that the real world of cultures was a far more diverse place than she had anticipated, and more disturbing than the model had seemed to promise.

THE CONCEPT OF CULTURE

Culture is the special province of anthropologists because it is the main object of their study. As a result, no group has done more than anthropologists have to encourage the acceptance of all cultures on their own terms and to discourage any outside critique of them. Anthropologists have successfully campaigned for a view of cultures as: inherently good and necessary to human life, adaptive to local social and natural environments, internally consistent and comprehensible, and, in the end, morally inviolable. The ethic is that differences between cultures should be tolerated, even celebrated, and that outside influences should not be allowed to damage cultures, which are viewed as a fragile balance of pristine systems. This view of cultures is so pervasive in Western societies now that some are calling it "cultural fundamentalism" (Sanneh 1996: 9).

It is important to remember that the term *culture* is a highly constructed one. A review of the history of the term will help us to understand its current meaning. In the early days of the discipline, anthropologists used the term *civilization* rather than culture. Civilization was not considered to be universally distributed; rather societies were believed to have more or less of it. Of course, nineteenth-century anthropologists considered their own societies to be the most civilized, and the ones they were studying they considered "primitive." It seemed self-evident to them that the technological inferiority of other societies reflected a total inferiority of ways of life. The social systems, political orders, religions, and arts associated with cities (the root meaning of civilization) were presumed to be an advance over simpler forms of organization. Furthermore, the specific forms of these things in European societies were considered to be the pinnacles of human achievement. Thus, all societies, anthropologists thought, could be arranged along a single line of cultural evolution, from "savagery" to "barbarianism" to "civilization" (Morgan 1985), and all could be expected to progress in the same way toward the same future through human "progress."

This evolutionary model of culture had two problems with it. First, since anthropologists were not yet doing serious fieldwork, it was short on the facts about human beliefs and practices in remote places. Second, due to the influence of the natural prejudice we all have in favor of our own beliefs and practices, it took as a starting assumption the superiority of Western societies over all others. Thus, as anthropology developed into a serious science, this model turned out to be fatally flawed. Careful collection of ethnographic data made it clear that so-called "primitive" societies had previously unsuspected complexities of their own, especially in the areas of language and kinship. And, by learning local languages and spending time in local communities, ethnographers such as Franz Boas and his students were able to report that seemingly strange customs were reasonable in their own contexts, practically useful, and even morally right for the circumstances.

A new concept was needed to replace "civilization" as the object of study. So the term *culture* was invented, or rather reinvented, to suit the purpose. Originally the term had been a derivative of the words "agriculture" and "horticulture," referring to the careful tending of plants to increase their yield. Then it had been adapted to refer to a similar tending of human beings to improve their refinement and appreciation of literature and the arts. Upper class people were more "cultured" than lower class people, just as horticultural plants were more cultivated than wild ones. But anthropologists such as Edward Tylor, with increasing insight into the complexities of human ways of life, repackaged the term to include *all* learned and shared human behavior, regardless of class, education, or technological development (Tylor 2016). They distinguished culture from human nature, or instinct, and solidified the concept by identifying the structures and internal consistencies that cause customs to make sense when understood in the context of the whole.

As the project grew and developed, anthropologists envisioned a world of multiple cultures, each equal to the others for its ability to produce a viable way of life in a particular environment, each associated with a territory of its own with distinct boundaries separating it from its neighbors, each internally complete and self-sufficient, each intrinsically valuable and worth preserving for both scientific and humanitarian purposes, and each providing a morality for its members that must not be altered by any outside influence. The only need was to appreciate cultures as they are, to guard them from unnecessary interference, and to expect that they would thrive best in isolation. For some time, anthropologists were the marginalized front runners of this perspective. But with the breakup of the colonial empires into nation states in the middle of the twentieth century, each nation with a supposed unique people, the concept of culture gained currency in the general public. Now, it serves the purpose of providing a moral value for the pluralist model that is considered essential to resolving conflict in a time of globalization. So long as we do not interfere with one another's cultures, the moral suggests, we will have a peaceful coexistence in a multicultural world.

THE PROBLEM OF ETHNOCENTRISM

There was, and is, real reason to adopt the pluralist stance, at least initially, with regard to the customs and habits of unfamiliar people. Things that strike us as strange, even abhorrent, can turn out to have important purposes that are not immediately apparent. Sometimes they can challenge our own culture-bound expectations in ways that make us realize the strangeness of our own behavior. For instance, there are societies in which people do not wear clothing. For those of us from societies that do, and where modesty is associated with dress, it is a natural assumption that people who are naked must be promiscuous. But nakedness has no necessary connection to promiscuity. In fact, people from societies without clothing sometimes imagine *us* to be the promiscuous ones, given that we ornament our bodies so elaborately. Of course, the "lack" of clothing is actually associated with warm weather, and the need to put time, resources, and energy into the production of things more useful than clothing in such an environment. In any case, the initial judgment about promiscuity is wrong on the facts due to prior assumptions about what cultural customs mean.

Or, in another example, in many societies large amounts of wealth are spent on weddings, funerals, and other sorts of feasts. Sometimes, people too poor to send their children to school will spend extravagantly on the burial of their parents, or the ushering in of the new year. Such expenditures seem foolish and wasteful to those of us from societies where the careful management of wealth for purposes of individual success is valued. But feasting societies do not value the accumulation of wealth for its own sake. For them, wealth is for the purpose of "investment" in relationships and in community life. It is social success, not financial success, that is the measure of a person. And it is relationships, not bank accounts, that make one truly "wealthy." In this case, our interpretation of other peoples' behavior is being guided by our own materialist values, leading to a misjudgment of their conduct. A more careful look at the situation can actually produce a critical evaluation of our own conduct. Perhaps we are the ones in the wrong!

In a final example, the illustration above about the symbolic mating of the queen with a horse can be understood, if not approved, by the simple remembrance that rituals depict deeper truths than surface conversation can express. In this case, the horse represented the king's authority, and was subsequently let loose to roam the land and establish the power of the monarchy. It was the king himself who was being symbolized by the horse, and the ritual symbolic mating with the queen, just prior to letting the horse loose, was a means of establishing that authority. Our own Christian faith uses symbolism in the same way (but with a different message). In communion, we "eat" and "drink" the body and blood of Jesus to symbolize the ingestion of Christ into our lives. Outsiders encountering this idea for the first time must surely find it strange, if not repulsive! But to those of us who engage in the ritual, it is a deeply meaningful way of "speaking" about things too deep to articulate in ordinary conversation. The power of ritual is its ability to penetrate the heart with deeper understanding than is possible with everyday words. If we remember this simple truth, a lot of very strange behavior associated with ritual becomes much more understandable, and we are able to avoid the temptation to imagine that other people are "primitive" or "barbaric."

As we can see in these examples, the further we penetrate the strange ways of other peoples, the more we find them to be not unlike ourselves. And, in general, the more we remember our common humanity, the less likely we are to treat others with cruelty or to ignore their suffering. *Ethnocentrism* is the term anthropologists use to describe the combination of ignorance and prejudice that causes people to misinterpret one another's customs, or to lack sympathy for them. It is a mindless judgment based on an unexamined use of one's own cultural values to evaluate other people's ways. Not only is it detrimental to our relationships, it is harmfully restrictive of our understanding of the larger world in which we live.

Ethnocentrism is in all of us, without exception. It is there because it is a by-product of the normal process of enculturation (children's learning of their own culture). Children are naturally experimental, and will try out various means of accomplishing their goals: shoving food in their mouths with their fingers, poking around and pulling apart things that grown-ups want undisturbed, or asking inappropriate questions at awkward moments. When they don't like the restrictions they have been given, they will try to circumvent them. Parents and other caretakers handle these situations with a variety of responses ranging from mild disapproval to severe criticism and physical punishment. It is the caretakers' job to make sure that children properly adopt the customs, habits, values, and perspectives of the cultures in which they live.

The process of enculturation is most intense when children are between three and six years old, a time when they are biologically and psychologically vulnerable and receptive. At an earlier age, children care little for adults' approval and much more for getting what they want. But once they become ready for social life, the shame they feel for having transgressed a norm can be acute. That shame becomes the basis for their increasing conformity to their cultures as they grow up . . . and the real reason for their disapproval of other cultures as adults. Having paid a painful price in childhood to learn the "proper" way to function, adults then become incensed, even horrified, when "improper" ways are discovered to be customary for other people.

Yet the fact that ethnocentrism is inevitable in all of us does not make it good! After all, sin is inevitable in us too. Ethnocentrism causes us to view others as children, as animals, and even as devils, and it gives us a false sense of superiority. Furthermore, because we imagine that our own ways are exclusively the right ones, we are likely to engage in the sins of our own culture without questioning them. We may even try to defend our cultural ways in religious terms. This possibility is especially dangerous in a country such as the United States, where the culture is believed to be Christian. Here, the over-conformity to our own culture that ethnocentrism encourages may be the greatest evil of its effects (as we will see in some of the following chapters).

It was to remedy the ill effects of ethnocentrism, both in scientific and in moral terms, that anthropologists turned from the notion of degrees of civilization to the concept of many cultures. Early anthropologists had misconstrued the lives and mentalities of "primitive" peoples in ways that distorted the data upon which they were building their scientific theories. After Boas, anthropologists adopted the position that the researcher must suspend all judgment and attempt to understand customs strictly in their own contexts. Even theorizing about cross-cultural differences was suspect. Each culture was viewed as a self-contained whole, and all customs were understood exclusively in relation to that whole. Anthropologists such as Ruth Benedict demonstrated that cultures had core themes or patterns that provided them with internal coherence (2006). It was these patterns that made it possible not only to comprehend strange customs, but also to appreciate them. Tampering with a culture's customs in any way was believed to be detrimental to the system as a whole. Study after study demonstrated this point, and, with the wholesale destruction of indigenous cultures taking place at the time (Bodley 2008b), such instances were not hard to find. The result was that anthropologists embraced the "prime directive" of not interfering with cultures under any circumstance.[2]

Still, it is important to realize that this model of the human situation, that we are all members of distinct and equal cultures, is as much a social construct as the earlier model of human societies ranged along a continuum from relatively less to more civilization. Furthermore, the model has a strong normative agenda. All cultures *must* be considered equal, as a precondition to the discussion. No one *may* judge anyone else's ways, no matter how problematic they are. As we will see below, this solution to the problem of ethnocentrism has many shortcomings. But, before critiquing it, we will turn to the Bible for a deeper understanding of the purpose of culture from God's point of view.

THE CULTURAL MANDATE AND HUMAN SIN

Culture can be defined simply as the ways of life of a people that assist them to live in creation and to relate to one another and to God. With this definition, there is much in the Bible to assist us in understanding culture's value. First, theologians refer to the following passage in Genesis as the "cultural mandate:"

> Then God said, "let us make humankind in our image, according to our likeness; and let them have dominion over the fish of the sea, and over the birds of the air, and over the cattle, and over all the wild animals of the earth, and over every creeping thing that creeps upon the earth." So God created humankind in his image, in the image of God he created them; male and female he created them. God blessed them, and God said to them, "Be fruitful and multiply, and fill the earth and subdue it; and have dominion over the fish of the sea and over the birds of the air and over every living thing that moves upon the earth." (Gen 1:26–28)

There are two important points here and they are linked to one another. The first is that we are made in God's image, and the second is that we are

---

2. The television series *Star Trek* makes good use of classic anthropological insights and values. The crew of the starship Enterprise are to explore and make contact with other worlds, but not to interfere in any way with their cultures or the course of their histories.

to have dominion over the rest of creation. The link is that our dominion is part of what it *means* to be made in God's image. We have been given some of God's sovereignty over creation, and thus over our own lives. And we are to use that sovereignty to construct families, communities, economies, governments, and global systems that promote *shalom,* or "peace," for ourselves and for the rest of creation.

Richard Middleton summarizes the history of Christian scholarship on the nature of the *imago Dei,* the "image of God," in which we are made (2005). For centuries, Christian scholars from Augustine to Aquinas, who were under the influence of Greek philosophical thought, identified the image with various human abilities, especially with rational thought and social relationships. But recent biblical scholarship has suggested that the true meaning of the phrase may refer not to any special ability, but to our *role* in creation. Middleton notes that it was common practice in the ancient Near East for kings to set up statues, or "images," of themselves in the remote areas of their kingdoms. These statues represented the king's authority over the territory. They were physical reminders of the king's power in places where the king himself could not be seen. Thus, says Middleton, "The *imago Dei* refers to humanity's office and role as God's earthly delegates . . . Imaging God thus involves representing and perhaps extending in some way God's rule on earth through the ordinary communal practices of human sociocultural life" (Middleton 2005: 60). In this understanding, we are "corporeal representation of the divine" (25), God's vice-regents on earth!

Moreover, we are also "priests of creation." Middleton points out that the creation account in Genesis parallels the construction of the tabernacle in Exodus 31 (Middleton 2005: 77–84). This parallel implies that creation is God's house, palace, or temple, and that God's Spirit inhabits the earth as a tabernacle. Kings in the ancient Near East were not only political rulers, but priests as well. Thus, the Bible is implying that, as God's representatives on earth, we are priests in the temple of his creation. This point is affirmed by the theologian T. F. Torrance, who calls us "midwives" of creation, and "mediators of order" (Flett 2011: 116, 137).

In our role as vice-regents and priests of creation, we are to care for the created order through the construction of peaceful communities. The Hebrew word *shalom* refers to a community in which a holistic and healthy reconciliation is evident in our social relationships, in which peace and prosperity are evident in our relationship to nature, and in which God is acknowledged as the source of all wellbeing. Christopher J. H. Wright depicts the order that God has set up as a triangle of relationships (2004: 19). Initially, God created the earth, placed humanity in it, and entered into relationship with them both:

Figure 2.1: Triangle of Creation

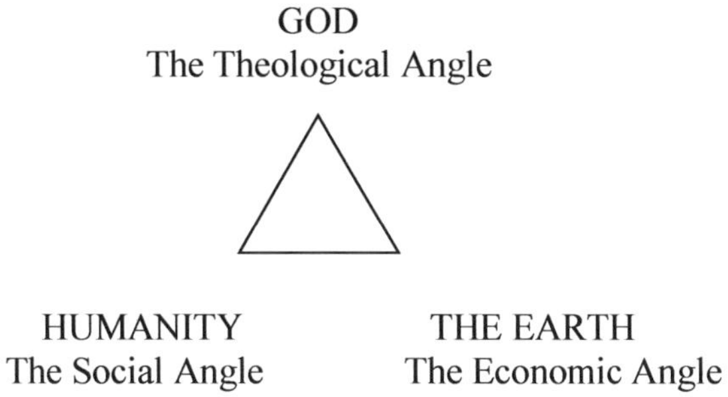

GOD
The Theological Angle

HUMANITY   THE EARTH
The Social Angle   The Economic Angle

Source: Wright (2004: 103)

This created three "angles" of relationship. The theological angle is God's own character, will, action, and purpose, which we are to imitate (23). He has purposes for our lives that we are to discover and to live out. Above all, we are to respond to his loving call and enter into relationship with him. The social angle is our relationship to one another as human beings. We are called to live in communities of *shalom* in accordance with God's original purposes for us. The economic angle is our relationship to the earth, that is, to the rest of creation. Creation exists first and foremost to glorify God. But we as human beings have a unique relationship to it. The earth sustains and nourishes us, and we are expected to exercise responsible dominion over it as "servant-kings" (122–23).

After humanity's fall into sin, God's original plan for our health and happiness was destroyed and we became alienated from him, from one another, and from the earth. So God, in order to redeem humanity, chose Israel to be "a priestly kingdom and a holy nation" for the rest of the world (Exod 19:4–6):

Figure 2.2: Triangle of Redemption: Old Testament

GOD
The Theological Angle

ISRAEL   THE LAND
The Social Angle   The Economic Angle

Source: Wright (2004: 19)

Israel's role was to be "a light to the nations" (Isa 42:6; 49:6; 60:3). In order to live out that calling, God gave to the Israelites the promised land of Canaan, where they were to demonstrate the relationships of *shalom*—with God, with one another, and with the land—which God had originally intended for all of humanity. This does not mean that the Israelites were sin-free! The Bible repeatedly refers to them as "a stubborn and rebellious" people (eg: Deut 31:27; Isa 63:10; Neh 9:16–31). Yet, God's intent was that they should become a people set apart to show his plan of redemption to the world.

With the life, death, and resurrection of the Messiah, Jesus, God's plan of redemption reached beyond Israel to the Gentiles, and was spread "to the ends of the earth" (Acts 1:8; 13:47). How was this accomplished? As Christians, we believe that Jesus offered himself as the sacrificial lamb for our sins (John 1:29). Furthermore, he made it possible for us to take up our true role as bearers of God's image. Peter Enns writes:

> Jesus is the *true* image-bearer. You might say that Jesus is the only truly and fully human figure who has ever lived. By looking at the crucified and risen Son, we see what "human" really means, not the corrupted dysfunctional version that stares back [at] us from the mirror, or that we see in others . . . By his resurrection, Jesus is the first to embody fully the image-bearing role conferred on all humanity in Genesis.[3]

Jesus was fully God, and thus able to save us from our sinful nature, and fully human, and thus able to restore the image of God within us.

Since Jesus' resurrection, says Christopher Wright, it is the church, the body of Christ, that has become a light to the nations, demonstrating God's goodness and holiness along with his love and forgiveness.

Figure 2.3: Triangle of Redemption: New Testament

GOD
The Theological Angle

THE CHURCH   KOINONIA
The Social Angle   The Economic Angle

Source: Wright (2004: 196)

3. Biologos.org. http://biologos.org/blog/series/what-does-image-of-god-mean. Written July/August 2010. Accessed 7/21/15.

It is through Christian fellowship, or *koinōnia*, that God provides for our needs. And it is through the church's relationship to the world that we live out our role as God's vice regents and priests of creation. Finally, at the end of time, yet another triangle will "break through," establishing fully restored relationships between God, a redeemed humanity, and a new creation (Wright 2004: 137, 184).

In the meanwhile, however, while awaiting God's final redemption we still experience the alienating effects of our own sin. Kent Smith suggests that in Genesis 3 we can see four different types of alienation that have resulted from human sin (Van Rheenen 1997: 35). First, we have become alienated from ourselves, as evidenced by Adam and Eve's need to cover themselves, and by our own continuing sense of shame. Second, we have become alienated from one another, as evidenced by Adam's blaming of Eve, and by our own ongoing brokenness in relationships. Third, we have become alienated from creation, as evidenced by God's cursing of the ground as punishment for Adam and Eve's disobedience, and by our own continuing destructive treatment of the earth. Fourth, and most disastrously, we have become alienated from God, as evidenced by Adam and Eve's expulsion from the garden of Eden, and by our own chronic fear of God and further rebellion against him.

Alienation, then, is a pervasive factor in our lives, causing us to behave in detrimental ways toward ourselves, others, the environment, and God. In the words of theologian Eric Flett, humanity has become "disoriented and turned in upon itself through a primordial act of fear, pride, and denial, resulting in the gifts and powers of humanity being used for the destruction of creation, others and self" (Meneses et al. 2014: 86). Sin reorients the image of God within us toward the pursuit of self-centered ends, causing us to try to rule by and for ourselves. The result is a continuing destruction that we wreak upon one another and the earth, and a deafness to God's loving attempts to guide us toward his plan for redemption.

Behind human evil is the hand of Satan, luring us into further disobedience and alienation. It is "the ruler of this world" (John 14:30, KJV) who destroys our happiness and robs us of the loving relationships that God intended. Because we have rejected God's sovereignty over our lives and shirked our responsibility to maintain appropriate dominion over the earth, we have placed ourselves under the dominion of the devil and are subject to his torments. We, who were to have been servant-kings of creation, have become slaves to the would-be usurper of God's power.

For culture, this means that our families, communities, economies, governments, and global systems, not to mention our beliefs, attitudes, and values about these things, are inevitably distorted from their original purposes. Families and communities, which are supposed to promote our best welfare through loving relationships, in fact commonly injure us both physically and emotionally. Economies and governments, which are supposed to provide for and protect us, commonly rob us of what we need and oppress us. Global systems, which might bring us into fruitful and productive relationships, instead become the means of exploiting one another and abusing creation. The alienation that we experience as sinful human beings is woven into the very fabric of all that we think, make, and do—that is, of our cultures.

A MORE COMPLEX VIEW OF CULTURE

None of this means that cultures have completely lost their value. At their best, they still provide us with the relationships and understandings that are essential to healthy and fruitful lives. But it does mean that all cultures are a mixture of good and evil, of health and sickness, of constructiveness and destructiveness. These days, even secular anthropologists are beginning to acknowledge this complex reality. Clifford Geertz, for instance, has described the institution of cockfighting in Bali, and demonstrates its relevance for status rivalry in a hierarchical society (1973: 412–53). The cockfight is a bloody fight to the death for the chickens themselves, and a symbolic fight between the cock owners and other bystanders who are betting on the fight. Men who cannot challenge higher ranking men in ordinary life, can "enjoy and savor" for the moment a win against them in the cockfight (443). Thus for the Balinese, said Geertz, the cockfight is a depiction of the raw struggle for rank that lies beneath the surface of polite social interaction, "a story they tell themselves about themselves" (448). The seemingly spontaneous eruption of violence in 1965, when thousands of Balinese people suddenly massacred one another, makes more sense when one realizes that the Balinese believe their politeness to be a necessary cover for an animal nature that comes out in competition and rivalry.[4]

Until now, most anthropologists have been reluctant to admit what they know about internal forms of violence such as abuse, exploitation, and murder. (We will investigate external violence, or war, in chapter seven.) Internal violence contradicts the notion that cultures are integrated seamless wholes, based on the full consensus of the culture members. Anthropologists have been quick to criticize the violence being committed against indigenous peoples by outsiders, but have explained away internal conflict

4. For other comments by Geertz on conflict and violence, see *Available Light* (2000:167–86; 218–63).

as functional to the maintenance of the social structure, implying that it is not truly destructive.

Recently, however, some anthropologists have begun to study internal violence directly. One describes the case of a village chief who systematically starved his own people over a period of years in order to force them to submit to his wishes (Hatch 1983: 86). Another describes the beatings that women commonly endure at the hands of their husbands in a Belizian community (McClusky 2001). The traditional practice of female circumcision has come under scrutiny, as it is generally more severe than male circumcision and serves a more oppressive purpose. Robert Edgerton, a long-time critic of the idealized depiction of cultures in anthropology, writes:

> Humans in various societies, whether urban or folk, are capable of empathy, kindness, even love, and they can sometimes achieve astounding mastery of the challenges posed by their environments. But they are also capable of maintaining beliefs, values, and social institutions that result in senseless cruelty, needless suffering, and monumental folly in their relations among themselves as well as with other societies and the physical environment in which they live. People are not always wise, and the societies and cultures they create are not ideal adaptive mechanisms, perfectly designed to provide for human needs . . . Traditional beliefs and practices may be useful, may even serve as important adaptive mechanisms, but they may also be inefficient, harmful, and even deadly. (Harrison and Huntington 2000: 131)[5]

All of this is to say that we need a more complex view of culture. Geertz has suggested that at the heart of any culture is a bifurcation between the way that people think life ought to be and the way that it is actually experienced (1973: 87–125).[6] That is, people everywhere interpret their lives in terms of an interplay between their culture's prescriptions for a good life and its analysis of the ways in which people are falling short of that life. Pain, disease, and death, not to mention conflict and harm, are universally recognized to be at variance from the way that life should be. It is the job

5. This point by Edgerton is well taken. However, Edgerton's stance on the evaluation of cultures is one that a Christian cannot accept. All religious beliefs and practices are "folly" to Edgerton, and his understanding of the definition and role of rationality in science is one that I have worked hard to refute in chapter one of this volume (cf. Harrison and Huntington 2000: 134).

6. In context, Geertz is referring to religion, and we will examine this definition of religion further in chapter nine. But his comments are relevant to our examination of culture here since religion, as Geertz defines it, is at the heart of the culture.

of culture (especially through religion) to create the orderliness, the sense of meaning, that we need to guide our behavior and to have hope for the future.

Geertz has proposed that cultural behavior can best be understood as a form of conversation (1973: 3–30). The language of that conversation is a system of symbols that include things, words, actions, and events that are sometimes communicated directly, sometimes in ritual, and sometimes in nonverbal behavior, or actions. These symbols, taken together, form "an imaginative universe within which [people's] acts are signs" (13), that is, have meaning. Through ethnographic fieldwork, the complex layers of meaning coded in messages being circulated between culture members can be interpreted by and for outsiders, people who come from other "imaginative universes." Because we all have humanity in common, the best ethnography "exposes [others'] normalness without reducing their particularity" (14). That is, it elucidates the imaginative universe of a people so well that it is comprehensible to outsiders, while at the same time bringing differences into focus. "The whole point," says Geertz, "is . . . to aid us in gaining access to the conceptual world in which our subjects live so that we can, in some extended sense of the term, converse with them" (24).

The value of Geertz's definition of culture, is that it a) depicts the human condition as problematic, b) explains the difficult relationship between the ideal and the real, c) describes the nature of meaning and how it is constructed in a culture, d) acknowledges the freedom of individuals and institutions to "say" things that may be constructive or destructive of the relationships between them, and e) addresses the matter of cross-cultural understanding. As Christians, we are reminded that our culturally constructed interactions with one another and with the earth can be mutually beneficial, or exploitative and harmful. And, we can place this understanding of culture as communicated meaning in the larger context of God's communication with us for the purpose of our redemption.

RELATIVISM RECONSIDERED

With this more complex view of culture, let us reexamine the ethic of cultural relativism that anthropologists have advocated and continue to promote. As described above, relativism was adopted to solve the problem of ethnocentrism and to promote the understanding and appreciation of all cultures. In its extreme form, the basic tenets of the ethic are that a) morality is no more than a cultural construct, which varies from place to place (moral relativism), b) truth is a matter of perspective and ultimately unknowable, if it exists at all (epistemological relativism), and therefore c) no one may claim to know truth or to be morally superior to anyone else (a normative statement about how we should relate to one another). Geertz has suggested that such an extreme set of beliefs has not really been held by anyone, and that it is actually the fear of these ideas that is most damaging to the discussion (Geertz 2000: 42–67). But for nearly a century now, most anthropologists have strongly defended cultural relativism.

Anthropologists have been most adamant about the value of moral relativism, the belief that no culture may be criticized for any behavior that it legitimizes. This belief is defended with the argument that all the customs of a culture are vitally necessary to the functioning of the whole. Tampering with or removing any part will have a domino effect on the entire system of beliefs and practices. As a result, anthropologists have expended much time and energy in demonstrating the functional necessity of unusual practices. Customs as dubious as child marriage, witch hunting, raiding for women and cattle, ax fights, and headhunting have all been defended.

Remember, it is not individual misbehavior that we are considering here, but culturally legitimized practices. But a simple survey of recent news reports will illustrate that there are many culturally legitimized practices that are problematic. In 1987, Roop Kanwar, an educated young woman of north India who had just been widowed, committed suicide according to the ancient Hindu custom of *sati* by being cremated alive with her husband. In 2006, also according to ancient Hindu religious beliefs, a child was sacrificed to the goddess Kali. There were reports of 200 more such child sacrifices in the area. In 2008, twenty-five albino people in Tanzania were killed for their body parts, which are used by witch doctors in sorcery to make other people rich.[7] Today in the United States, abortion, capital punishment, neglecting the elderly, and making one's self fabulously rich at other peoples' expense are all part of the culture. Extreme moral relativism would make it impossible to contest or even criticize any of these behaviors.

Historically, anthropology's defense of moral relativism reached a critical point in 1947 when the American Anthropological Association (AAA) refused to support the United Nations' Universal Declaration of Human Rights (UDHR). In a formal statement, the AAA declared that there were no human rights upon which all cultures could agree, that as a science

7. News reports for these events can be found at the following websites respectively:
    Kanwar's suicide: http://news.bbc.co.uk/2/hi/south_asia/5278898.stm. Accessed 10/18/16.
    Child sacrifice: http://news.bbc.co.uk/2/hi/south_asia/4903390.stm. Accessed 10/18/16.
    Albino killings: http://news.bbc.co.uk/2/hi/africa/7518049.stm. Accessed 10/18/16.

it was not anthropology's place to affirm one morality over another, and that any set of values chosen would be an imposition of one people's views on another (Goodale 2006). It is important to note the inconsistency between the last two points. On the one hand, the AAA was washing its hands of any responsibility for determining human morality, and on the other it was declaring the imposition of any one culture's values on another to be immoral! This is, in fact, a classic problem with moral relativism. It claims to stand above the fray, but then becomes adamant in the defense of a presumed value on "tolerance." In the end, it declines all responsibility for the consequences of tolerating any and every moral system.

It has been more than a half century since 1947, and yet most anthropologists continue to vigorously defend moral relativism. Even applied anthropologists (who work to solve human problems) are criticized for their involvement in changing cultures through governments, businesses, and other social institutions. Still, the AAA has moderated its position on human rights to some degree. In 1992, it established a Commission for Human Rights, and in 1999 it sponsored its own "Declaration on Anthropology and Human Rights." The document is very general, and largely defends the right to "the capacity for culture" (thereby evading the real issue). But it does support the UDHR, along with other declarations on international law, and it supports in principle an expansion of human rights to include "collective as well as individual rights, cultural, social, and economic development, and a clean and safe environment."[8]

Anthropologists have been far more ambivalent, however, about epistemological relativism. Coming from Western societies which emphasize personal liberty, they have found it relatively easy to accept other peoples' moral behaviors. But as members of the academy, committed to anthropology as a science, they have found it much more difficult to accept the fact that sensible, rational people have differing perspectives on the truth. Right from the beginning, in their ethnographic encounters, anthropologists have been confronted with a wide variety of beliefs, often partly religious in nature, that seem obviously false. For instance, there are Native American groups that believe their various clans are physically descended from different animals. There are African groups that believe illness is the result of witches eating peoples' souls in the middle of the night. There are Melanesian groups that do not believe men have anything to do with pregnancy (they believe spirits invade women's wombs to impregnate them). These beliefs are not just symbolic for the people who hold them; they are believed

8. http://humanrights.americananthro.org/1999-statement-on-human-rights/. Accessed 10/18/16.

to be true in the most literal and concrete terms. Yet to cultural outsiders they seem to be, very simply, wrong on the facts.

Initially, anthropologists assumed that "false" beliefs were the result of a lack of scientific information. Given the "real" reasons for descent lines, illness, or pregnancy, these "superstitions" would be given up. But ethnographers quickly discovered that attempts to talk people out of such "irrational" beliefs were almost wholly ineffective. So, still confident that their own views on reality were the truth, anthropologists proceeded to account for the beliefs in terms of various functions: cognitive (explaining the unexplainable), social (binding the group together), political (supporting traditional leaders), psychological (assisting with fears and/or uncertainties), or religious (providing a coherent worldview). The belief in descent from animals, for instance, supported the solidarity of the clans and structured their relationships to one another; the belief in witches was a psychological expression of jealousy and a means of conflict resolution; the denial of men's role in pregnancy established and maintained inheritance laws through the mother's line. Describing beliefs in terms of their functions seemed to explain their necessity.

Moreover, the functional view of other peoples' beliefs permitted anthropologists to avoid questioning the validity of their own beliefs, at least for a time. But, in a classic study of the Azande of the Sudan, E. E. Evans-Pritchard (who was a Christian) described a whole *system* of these types of beliefs in such detail that the possibility for a different sort of rationality became evident (Evans-Pritchard 1976). The Azande believe that all significant misfortune is the result of witchcraft. Accidents, natural disasters, and even intentional acts by human beings such as murder, are only the most immediate causes of events. Behind them lie the envies, jealousies, and evil intentions of witches (who are either male or female). Unless the *real* reason for the trouble is addressed, all efforts to plant crops, build homes, cure sicknesses, or heal relationships will be futile. So, the Azande conduct oracles to determine who the witches are, and to warn or punish them for their evil acts. Oracle procedures are constructed such that any ambiguities in their results, or any mismatch with the facts, can be resolved through further procedures. Furthermore, they are designed so that relatively antisocial members of the community will be identified as witches. Accused witches are given the opportunity to apologize for their behavior, but not to deny it. Hence, the system is self-contained and complete, impervious to external challenges to its validity.

Evans-Pritchard's study was significant because it demonstrated that peoples' beliefs are parts of systems of belief that resist alternative interpretations of reality. This ability to resist other explanations is actually vital to the maintenance of any belief system, as otherwise day-to-day life would chaotically destroy all understanding by its pure variability.[9] For instance, agriculturalists cannot afford to abandon all their beliefs about raising plants based on a single, or even several, crop failures. They assume they are correct about general principles, and look for a specific cause that explains the failures instead. Communities cannot afford to abandon their belief in the value of social institutions, or in the basic good intentions of their friends and family, based on the conflict they experience. Rather they look for reasons, either internal or external, why behavioral norms are being violated. Most importantly, people cannot afford to abandon their most cherished religious beliefs based on experiences that seem to contradict them. In fact, it is in the very nature of religious beliefs to suggest that the most central truths of life cannot be directly observed or established through experience and rationality alone. As we have seen in chapter one, our most important beliefs, including those that support the scientific project, are accepted by faith in the context of a community that legitimizes them.

Before Evans-Pritchard's work, anthropologists had been quick to judge other peoples' beliefs to be false whenever those beliefs contradicted their own Western, science-based, and functionally atheist common sense. They had also been reluctant to recognize that science itself is a system of beliefs. Instead, they had viewed science as having a privileged position of epistemological transcendence over cultural constructions of the truth. By demonstrating the rationality of another people's understanding of reality, Evans-Pritchard brought anthropologists' own assumptions out into the open where they could be questioned.

Since the 1970s, anthropology has been caught up in a broader philosophical movement that is rocking the very foundations of the Western academy. "Postmodernism" is a radical form of epistemological relativism making the case that there is no transcendent position on truth at all.[10] All truths are mere assertions, made in order to gain power over others. Postmoderns point out that, historically, science emerged in Europe along with the developing colonial enterprise. Its knowledge and technology were used to dominate the non-Western world. In fact, early anthropologists were often funded by colonial governments wanting ethnographic information

---

9. It was the philosopher David Hume who first challenged scientific thinking with this point. Hume suggested that we cannot know for sure that the sun will rise on the following day based on its having done so in previous days. We must simply believe that it will and act on that expectation (Hume 1993).

10. Actually, there are relatively stronger and weaker forms of postmodernism, with the milder ones very much resembling the stance on truth that I have recommended here in chapter one.

to "keep the peace" (i.e. exercise control) in the colonies. Thus science is a Western project rooted in the grand narrative (a socially constructed story) of the European Enlightenment, stressing human achievement and progress at the expense of other people's ways of life and used to legitimize their oppression through the silencing of their voices, or points of view.[11]

In anthropology, epistemological relativism (or postmodernism) has challenged the complacency with which ethnographers can claim to know better than their informants what is happening in a certain situation. If the informant suggests a death was due to witchcraft, but the ethnographer believes it was an accident, then who is right? The answer to this question matters to the ethnographer because beliefs that are deemed "irrational" must be given an alternate explanation in the ethnography. It also matters to informants because beliefs about what is true lead to moral and practical courses of action that have real consequences. If it is witchcraft, the witch must be found and punished.[12] It might be tempting to side with the unbelieving ethnographer in this case, but remember that anthropologists have given similar functional explanations for all religious beliefs, including our own Christian ones. So there is actually value for us as Christians in the postmodern challenge to science. Postmodern ethnographers may or may not believe what they hear, but they are more likely to record informants' own views directly, allowing them to speak for themselves. And, they are willing to acknowledge the limitations of their own perspective and experience.

Actually, anthropology has always been ambivalent about its designation as a "science." It has straddled the border between the social sciences and the humanities because of the nature of its subject, human beings. Its primary product, the ethnography, has been part scientific record and part informational novel. So, the effect of postmodernism in anthropology has been a shift away from a scientific orientation, and toward a more literary approach to the work. But this shift has caused a heated debate in the

---

11. It was the philosopher Friedrich Nietzsche who first expressed this very counter-cultural view in the nineteenth century. Postmoderns identify with Nietzsche's critique of knowledge as power in disguise, and advocate for an epistemological democracy in which all truth claims, which are the expressions of different life experiences and backgrounds, are seen as equally valuable.

12. In this sense, epistemological relativism cannot be separated from moral relativism, as many anthropologists would like to have it. Geertz suggests that our beliefs about reality and our beliefs about morality are intertwined in a mutually reinforcing way. Beliefs about reality indicate the moral action to be taken, and beliefs about morality help to formulate our experience and to legitimize the epistemology we use to establish our sense of reality (Geertz 1973: 87–125).

field over anthropology's true purpose and the nature of its value to society. Some have felt the loss of the certainty of truth keenly.

There are ways of deriving benefit from a moderate postmodernism without being caught in extreme relativism's internal contradictions. For instance, many anthropologists now distinguish between moral relativism, epistemological relativism, and *methodological relativism*, "the practice of suspending judgment until a belief or practice can be understood within its total context" (Brown 2008: 367). It is not necessary to embrace either moral or epistemological relativism in order to adopt methodological relativism. In fact, being willing to lay aside one's own beliefs temporarily can be necessary to perceiving the truth at all, especially in social situations. It is also necessary for good communication with other people, even if the goal is to eventually propose one's own viewpoint. The Apostle Paul's statement, "I have become all things to all people that I might by all means save some," was made in this spirit (1 Cor 9:22b). Methodological relativism requires us to listen to and understand other people's explanations before we critique their beliefs and practices. This does not mean that we cannot do critical thinking on the matters that come up. It just means that we must do so based on real understandings, not misconceptions or prejudices. With a judicious use of methodological relativism, we can build good relationships with people who are different from us, and learn from their thoughts and experiences *before* we voice our own views.

THE COURSE OF HISTORY

So where does this leave us on the matter of culture? We have traced the history of the concept in anthropology, considered a theology of culture's original purpose, noted its fallen state, identified its essential nature as communicated meaning, and found a means of understanding it fairly through methodological relativism. What is left is the question of culture's destiny in human history. Will culture be a source of our salvation through divinely inspired human progress? Or will it be the means by which we destroy ourselves and our environment through human foolishness and rebellion against God? Are cultures getting better or worse in time? What is the big picture for the future of culture?

To review, God's original purpose for culture was to enable people to create communities of *shalom* in which relationships with him, each other, and the rest of creation are established to promote human flourishing. Humanity was given a limited dominion under God's authority to accomplish this purpose. But we have rebelled against God and have abused that dominion, alienating ourselves from God, nature, and each other, and turning our cultures into sources of evil, as well as good. Yet God, by coming in person as Jesus, has ushered in a new era of redemption, one in which the legacy of our past and present sinfulness overlaps with the advent of the kingdom of God, our present and future hope.

What really is the kingdom of God?[13] It is the arena in which God's will, including his will for us for *shalom*, is perfectly done. And its advent on earth is the cornerstone of God's plan of redemption. Repeatedly Jesus declared that announcing the kingdom was his primary task. In the beginning of his ministry, "Jesus came to Galilee, proclaiming the good news of God, and saying, 'The time is fulfilled, and the kingdom of God has come near; repent, and believe in the good news'" (Mark 1:14–15). Later, when crowds tried to keep him with them, Jesus said, "I must proclaim the good news of the kingdom of God to other cities also, for I was sent for this purpose" (Luke 4:42–44). Twice during his ministry, Jesus sent his disciples out to proclaim the kingdom throughout Judea (Luke 9:2; 10:1), and after his death and resurrection the apostles announced the kingdom beyond Judea's borders (Acts 8:12).

Much of Jesus' teaching was about the character of the kingdom. In some parables he used images from nature, comparing it to the harvesting of a crop (Mark 4:26–29), the sowing of seed on various kinds of ground (Matt 13:1–23), the growth of a mustard seed (Mark 4:30–32), and the rising action of yeast in dough (Luke 13:20–21). All of these images imply growth from something small and seemingly insignificant to something large and powerful, good and nourishing. But in other parables Jesus used images of conflict and exclusion. He compared the kingdom of God to a dinner in which outcast people are welcomed, but the original invitees rejected (Luke 14:15–24), and to a wedding for which some are prepared, and some are not (Matt 25:1–13). He warned that wealth could be a hindrance (Luke 18:24–25), and that much would be expected of the kingdom's members (Luke 19:11–27; Matt 5:19–20; Matt 7:21–27). Only those with a knowledge of their own poverty (Luke 6:20), the humility of a child (Mark 10:14–16), and believing obedience (Matt 21:28–44) would be able to enter the kingdom at all. In fact, the requirements are so stringent, said Jesus, that entry is impossible without the help of God (Luke 18:26–27) and the willingness to be reborn (John 3:3–6).

Jesus also made it clear that he was himself the only way into the kingdom (John 14:6). This declaration was very unwelcome to his hearers, partly

---

13. The following theology of the kingdom of God is drawn from the work of Lesslie Newbigin in *The Gospel in a Pluralist Society* (1989: 105–11).

because it seemed to diminish God's power, and partly because it threatened their own. In fact, the crowds were eventually so offended at Jesus' "blasphemy" that first they stopped following him (John 6:60–69), and then they turned him over to be tortured and killed by the Roman authorities. But there were signs from God accompanying Jesus' works and legitimizing his claim, including the events of his baptism (Luke 3:21–22), his healings and exorcisms (Luke 11:19–20), his transfiguration (Matt 17:1–13), and above all else, his resurrection (Matt 12:38–42; Acts 1:3). The signs affirmed that Jesus was in fact the king of this new kingdom (John 5:31–37).

Where is the kingdom of God located? It is not immediately apparent to us, especially given the evil we see at work in and around us. First, theologically, we believe that God has chosen to keep his presence hidden from full view in order to create a space in which people may choose whether or not to be reconciled to him. Were he to reveal his presence to us fully, we would be forced to acknowledge him. Out of love, God does not want to put us in that position; he wants us to choose him freely. Lesslie Newbigin explains:

> This hiddenness is what makes possible the conversion of the nations. The unveiling of the glory of God's kingdom in all its terrible majesty could leave no further room for the free acceptance in faith which Jesus called for. Only when that glory was veiled in the lowliness of the incarnation could it call out freely given repentance and faith. (Newbigin 1989: 108)

Then, we believe that the kingdom is of a spiritual nature. On one occasion, the Pharisees, who expected an earthly political kingdom, asked Jesus when the kingdom would come. Jesus answered, "The kingdom of God is not coming with things that can be observed; nor will they say, 'Look, here it is!' or 'There it is!' For, in fact, the kingdom of God is [within/among] you" (Luke 17:21). The Greek word, *entos*, means both "within" and "among." So the kingdom of God is *within* us, in our hearts and minds, and it is *among* us, in the relationships that we create with one another and with God. Once again, it exists wherever God's will is being accomplished.

Does this mean that the kingdom is without an external presence? Not at all! First, the church, despite its many failings, is a visible sign of the presence of the kingdom. The church is the assembly of Christians worshipping their king and witnessing to the kingdom's existence by living out God's will on earth. Yet the kingdom is not confined within the walls of the church. It reaches out into the world bringing healing and hope to people who do not yet know the king. So second, the kingdom is observable in the activities of Christian people and in the work of the Holy Spirit in cultures. Newbigin points out that the Holy Spirit goes before Christian mission to convict people of sin and to reorient them to God.

> The active agent of mission is a power that rules, guides, and goes before the church: The free, sovereign, living power of the Spirit of God. Mission is not just something that the church does; it is something that is done by the Spirit, who is himself the witness, who changes both the world and the church, who always goes before the church in its missionary journey. (Newbigin 1995b: 56)

Finally, when people's lives are transformed by Christian faith, they begin to change not only themselves, but things in the world around them.

The observable changes being promoted in cultures by members of the kingdom may initially be welcomed if they are not too disruptive. But, at some point, kingdom workers will find that they must challenge cultural institutions that are unwholesome or unjust. When they do, they must not be surprised to encounter a backlash from the culture. After all, Jesus warned that his followers would encounter conflict and persecution:

> If the world hates you, be aware that it hated me before it hated you. If you belonged to the world, the world would love you as its own . . . If they persecuted me, they will persecute you; if they kept my word, they will keep yours also. But they will do all these things to you on account of my name, because they do not know him who sent me. (John 15:18–21)

Much of the church even now is under persecution. In many non-Western countries it is direct persecution in the form of intimidation and violence. In the West, it is indirect persecution in the relatively mild but insidious form of mockery and criticism that discourages belief. Jesus tells us to remember that the persecution we endure is no worse than what he himself endured before us.

When persecuted, it is important for us as Christians to stand firm for the kingdom of God, that is, for the kingdom of which Jesus is the true king. But it is equally important that we do so in the *manner* used by Jesus himself, that is, by being willing to suffer rather than inflict harm, and by forgiving our enemies. According to the Apostle Paul, Jesus "disarmed" the rulers and authorities of this world by his death on the cross (Col 2:15). That is a very confusing idea for the world—and sometimes for us! How does martyrdom produce victory? It seems most immediately to be a defeat. And yet, down through the centuries, Christians under persecution have willingly faced death to stand firm for Christ in a way that expresses their love for their enemies. The secret is in remembering the spiritual world. What looks like a defeat in earthly terms can be a tremendous victory for the kingdom. Kingdom victories are characterized by God's transformative purpose. God is in the process of bringing all of creation back into relationship with himself, and love in the face of persecution powerfully accomplishes that purpose by inviting people to repentance. So Christians who "turn the other cheek" (Matt 5:38–41), repaying hate with love, demonstrate another way to conquer evil, the transformative way of the kingdom.

Summing these things up, Newbigin suggests the following are the essential characteristics of the kingdom of God: First, the purpose of the kingdom is to bring all of creation back into relationship with God, doing his will and giving glory to him (1989: 179).[14] Second, the king of the kingdom is Jesus, who has full authority over it (134). Third, for the present, it is in the nature of the kingdom to be partially hidden from view. Its full reality will only be made manifest at the end of time (105). Fourth, in the meanwhile, we are to proclaim its existence, bringing change to the world around us, and expect to be persecuted for doing so (221). Fifth, we are to suffer this persecution in the same way that Jesus did, by standing firm while paying the price of the conflict ourselves (134). Then, finally, if we do these things, says Newbigin, we will "indwell" the story of the Bible, embody it in our own lives, and thereby give witness to the world of the kingdom's existence and of God's offer of salvation (99).

How does this Christian narrative of the kingdom dovetail with the world's narrative of human history? We have yet to answer our question, are cultures getting better or worse in time? The Western theory of progress assumes that they are getting better: that technology will solve our physical and natural problems, that better government will solve our political problems, that therapy and social institutions will solve our emotional and relational problems. The theory of progress rests heavily on science to provide the information and principles needed to build a better future. Yet the influence of science-based policies on our lives has been mixed at best! Natural science–based technologies have produced not only increased agricultural yields, greater travel capabilities, and a wide variety of creature comforts, but also nuclear war and environmental disasters. The public policies of governments have not only promoted ordinary people's welfare,

14. To American ears, the idea that God requires glory may seem self-serving. The American value on egalitarianism precludes the notion that hierarchical relationships can be close and mutually beneficial. But traditional cultures celebrate the notion of glorifying those above you and receiving glory from those below. They know that such a relationship can fill our deepest need for dependency and care, as well as provide us with an object of admiration and trust.

but sent them to war and restricted their free expression of religious and political ideas. Social science–based techniques have given us insights into our social and emotional lives, but have also made us individualistic and self-centered.[15] It would be very difficult to argue that human character is improving, or that human relationships are getting better, due to the work of the social sciences.

In general, anthropologists have become as disillusioned with the theory of progress as they have with the concept of civilization. Initially, they had been optimistic that the developments in Western thought and practice known as modernity would be beneficial to cultures around the world, bringing them out of dark ignorance and into the light of rational scientific knowledge and enlightened social institutions. But the events of World Wars I and II sobered anthropologists tremendously about the possibilities for human advancement. Science, it seemed, had not eradicated the irrationality of mutual destruction, not even in the most "civilized" of nations. Thus, after the world wars, anthropologists swung heavily to a pessimistic view of modernity, and to an idealization of the past and of cultures previously considered "primitive." This pessimism is still in the discipline today. Rather than a theory of progress, anthropologists seem to be embracing a theory of modernity's increasing destructiveness.

As Christians we believe that we know the end of the story: God's period of waiting for people's repentance will come to a close, Christ will return, and the kingdom now hidden will be made manifest. Yet the Bible is clear that history will *not* be a straight-line ascent from the sinfulness and suffering of "Babylon" to the glory of the New Jerusalem. In passages about the end times, the Bible consistently refers to wars and destruction on a global scale (Dan 12; Matt 24; 2 Pet 3: Rev 8ff). In this sense, we share anthropologists' pessimism for humanity's ability to solve its own problems through "progress."

But does this mean that all efforts to improve human life are wasted because of the evil that may eventually overtake them? Not at all. Jesus explained the circumstances of the end of time with a parable:

> "The kingdom of heaven may be compared to someone who sowed good seed in his field; but while everybody was asleep, an enemy came and sowed weeds among the wheat, and then went away. So when the plants came up and bore grain, then the weeds appeared as well. And the slaves of the householder

15. Psychological counseling, for instance, has been critiqued for encouraging radical individualism at the expense of community (Vitz 1994), and for maintaining a political conservatism that disempowers people by convincing them that their problems are psychological rather than social (cf. Bellah et al., 2007).

came and said to him, 'Master, did you not sow good seed in
your field? Where, then, did these weeds come from?' He answered, 'An enemy has done this.' The slaves said to him, 'Then
do you want us to go and gather them?' But he replied, 'No; for
in gathering the weeds you would uproot the wheat along with
them. Let both of them grow together until the harvest; and at
harvest time I will tell the reapers, Collect the weeds first and
bind them in bundles to be burned, but gather the wheat into
my barn.'" (Matt 13:24–30)

The disciples were unsure of Jesus' meaning, and asked him about it. So he
explained:

"The one who sows the good seed is the Son of Man; the field is
the world, and the good seed are the children of the kingdom;
the weeds are the children of the evil one, and the enemy who
sowed them is the devil; the harvest is the end of the age, and
the reapers are angels. Just as the weeds are collected and burned
up with fire, so will it be at the end of the age. The Son of Man
will send his angels, and they will collect out of his kingdom all
causes of sin and all evildoers, and they will throw them into
the furnace of fire, where there will be weeping and gnashing of
teeth. Then the righteous will shine like the sun in the kingdom
of their Father. Let anyone with ears listen! (Matt 13:36–43)

According to Jesus, *both* good and evil are growing, and they are growing
together. In fact, they are so deeply intertwined that it is not possible to
uproot one without damaging the other. In the story, the master specifically
forbid his servants from attempting to uproot the weeds before the harvest
because of the negative effect it would have on the wheat. So, we must expect
that our good works for the kingdom, which involve the transformation of
cultures, will be side by side with the evil works of the enemy in this world.

Two practical problems emerge when we think about our work to
improve cultures. First, what is the real value of human projects, given that
there will be an end to time—projects such as helping the poor, fighting
injustice, or simply contributing to local communities through art, education, or civic participation? What difference do these efforts make if God
is going to bring history to a close? And second, why should we ourselves
participate, given that much of what we work for we will not live to see?
Newbigin points out that it is death that creates these difficulties for us by
dividing our personal futures from the future of humanity.

[Death] cuts across the attractive picture of an unbroken ascent
from the origins of the world to the final consummation of

history. A chasm cuts across the landscape between the place
where I stand and the glorious vision of the holy city that I see
on the horizon of my world. The path goes down into the chasm,
and I do not see the bottom. (1995a: 105)

Death makes it tempting for us to think that our salvation is just an escape
from this world to the next, and that the work done here has no connection
with our lives in heaven. But Newbigin reminds us that it is precisely this
chasm, the chasm of death, that Jesus dealt with on the cross:

The gospel is good news because in Jesus Christ God has dealt
with sin and death, has opened a way that goes down into that
chasm and leads out into the uplands beyond it, and has thereby
released me from the dilemma in which I was trapped. The life,
death, and resurrection of Jesus have opened up a way on which
I can travel toward the city [the New Jerusalem], knowing that
the end of the journey will be a real consummation *both of my
personal history and of the public history in which I have shared.*
(1995a: 105) [Emphasis added.]

Newbigin goes on to explain that because Jesus has conquered the effects
of death we can pour ourselves fully into projects that benefit humanity,
knowing that their completion is ultimately in the hands of God:

Trusting [Jesus], therefore, I can follow that way and lose myself
in the service of God's cause, knowing that though I cannot create the city, God can raise up both me and my works, purged in
the fire of judgment, to take a place in the life of the city. I am
no longer in the dilemma between meaning for the personal life
and meaning for the public life. I can live fully the life of a real
person, part of the real world of society, history, and nature, and
know that, because Christ has risen, my labor in the Lord is not
futile (1 Cor 15:58). (1995a: 106)

As Christians, then, we must see our work in this world as being part of
God's own project to redeem humanity, work that will be "raised up" on the
final day and offered to Jesus as a gift in the service of his kingdom.

Cultures are necessary to our lives as human beings. They provide us
with a livelihood, relationships with one another, and a sense of meaning
and purpose. This is all as God intended it to be. But our natural sinfulness
distorts our culture-making work, and causes us to create cultures that are
a mix of good and evil things. Still, as members of the kingdom of God, we
Christians *must* participate in cultural life, promoting its ultimate benefit as

a form of service to our King. If we do so, we will be helping to extend God's kingdom to all the world for its redemption.

(CHAPTER 2) DISCUSSION QUESTIONS

1. How should Christians respond to beliefs and practices from other cultures which they find disturbing or repulsive?

2. How can we distinguish ethnocentrism from legitimate commitment to our own beliefs and practices?

3. Describe a type of relativism that would be appropriate for a Christian to entertain in order to understand cultural differences.

4. How does the Christian conception of the "cultural mandate" differ from the Western secular conception of the theory of progress?

5. How can we as Christians best give service to our cultures as part of our membership in the kingdom of God?

RECOMMENDED READINGS

Geertz, Clifford. 1973. *The Interpretation of Cultures*. New York: Basic.
————. 2000. *Available Light: Anthropological Reflections on Philosophical Topics*. Princeton, NJ: Princeton University Press.
Flett, Eric. 2011. *Persons, Powers, and Pluralities: Toward a Trinitarian Theology of Culture*. Eugene, OR: Pickwick.
Newbigin, Lesslie. 1989. *The Gospel in a Pluralist Society*. Grand Rapids: Eerdmans.

Chapter 3

Are Monkeys Our Cousins?
Engaging Evolutionary Theory

The adult Sunday school class was in heavy discussion. The subject was Christian witness, and one of the class members was describing a friend she thought might be encouraged to come to church. "Is your friend a Christian?" someone asked. "Oh no!" said the class member, "She's an evolutionist."

A re *Christian* and *evolutionist* mutually exclusive terms?[1] Are they even comparable terms? Why did the Sunday school class member think that her friend could not be a Christian if she accepted evolutionary theory? As the discussion proceeded, it turned out that the friend had been attending church, but had quit when the college class she was taking in evolutionary theory started to make sense to her. She too thought that it was impossible to accept both Christianity and evolution.

Although the Catholic Church has had little difficulty in accepting evolutionary theory (in modern times), Protestant churches, especially in America, have put up a challenge for a number of reasons. First, there is an apparent conflict between the stories told by the first few chapters of Genesis and by evolutionary theory. How can evolution be true if God created the world and everything in it in just six days? If people have descended from other animals, why does the Bible say that Adam and Eve were made from the dust of the earth? Why is there no indication in Genesis of animals

1. This chapter was read and reviewed by David Wilcox. Dr. Wilcox's own work in this area has been helpful in providing me with the relevant facts to make an informed judgment.

and plants, or people, changing their forms over time? It would appear that science and the Bible are at odds in regard to the origin of the universe, of life, and of human beings.

Second, evolutionary theory seems to reduce human beings to mere animals, without souls, without uniqueness before God, and therefore without responsibility. If humans are just another species, and nature a blind force, then there is little purpose to our lives other than the struggle to survive. Scientists seem to be saying that all of life is an accident of the forces of nature. The various species are engaged in a competitive battle with one another, and we are simply another accident, attempting to win the battle. There is neither meaning nor purpose nor protection for us in such a world. If an asteroid of sufficient size strays off course and hits the earth, we will all be destroyed and our deaths will be as pointless as our lives. According to evolutionary theory, life in the state of nature is just "nasty, brutish, and short."[2]

Yet, American Protestants have not found it so easy to dismiss the practical and concrete findings of science. This country is built upon a kind of fascination with new ideas, new discoveries, and a strong theory of human progress. In other areas, such as psychology or economics, American Christians grab eagerly at the latest scientific findings and apply them relatively uncritically to problems they are facing. Thus, it is not surprising that some have tried to solve the problem of evolution by developing an alternative science of human origins. "Creationism" claims to prove that a literal reading of Genesis can be established with scientifically produced facts, including evidence that humans were alive at the same time as dinosaurs, that Noah's flood was a worldwide event (not a regional one), and that the earth is no more than about 6,000 years old. Ironically, by taking this approach, Creationists uncritically *accept* the claim of science to be able to establish incontestable truth. Yet they do not accept the overwhelming evidence from science in favor of evolution. They selectively choose, and sometimes claim to find, facts that suit their purpose, straining to find a gnat, while ignoring the elephant in the room.

Some Christians have suggested that God has designed the world to *look* as if evolution has occurred, when in fact he created it as described in a literal reading of the Genesis account. So, the fossils in the earth that show a progression of species, or the strata of the soil that indicate the earth's 4 ½ billion year age, are there because God made them that way in an instant. It is worthwhile to note that this explanation is actually more reasonable than the one made by the Creationists. To say that you are following the methods of science, but then ignore most of the evidence, is not honest. But to say

2. This well-known phrase is from Thomas Hobbes, a seventeenth-century English philosopher, who suggested in his book, *Leviathan,* that life in the state of nature (i.e. without government) is "the war of all against all."

that the world is illusory is possible so long as you give an adequate reason as to why it should be that way. The challenge for those who take this position is to explain why God would want to fool us by making it appear that evolution has occurred, when in fact it has not.

In this chapter, you will have an opportunity to examine the evidence and the arguments for yourself (though I will also try to persuade you of certain parameters of the debate). We will begin by reviewing the data from biology, anthropology, geology, and a number of other sciences to see what appears to have occurred in the earth's history. Then we will turn to theology to remind ourselves of the essential beliefs that we as Christians must hold about God, people, and the natural world when interpreting the data. In order to reconcile the findings of science with Genesis, we will bring in hermeneutics, the study of how to read the Bible. Finally, we will conclude with a discussion of the creative understanding that is possible when Christians study both of the "books" that God has given us, the Bible and the book of nature.[3]

THE EVIDENCE

Most people, when considering the evidence for evolution, think first of fossils. This is because fossils are direct and tangible evidence that evolution has occurred. But it was not fossil evidence that first suggested the idea of evolution to the scientific community. Rather it was the emerging field of comparative anatomy in biology. Scientists in the nineteenth century were enthusiastically collecting, describing, cataloging, and classifying the various plant and animal species of the world as they knew it. Carl Linnaeus constructed a master classification of all known living things, coining the Latin terms that we still use today. His interest, and the interest of other naturalists at the time, was in piecing together the grand puzzle of the design in nature. It was fascinating work! As European explorers went out to previously unknown parts of the world and returned with written descriptions, sketches, and sample specimens, the full beauty and complexity of creation was being revealed to the scientific community. Furthermore, careful inspection of known species was producing some surprises. Species that occupied the same environments had internal structures that were remarkably different from one another, and species from different environments

3. The early church fathers suggested that nature is a second "book" that should be read along with the first book, the Bible (or faith). In the thirteenth century, Thomas Aquinas developed the idea of a convergence between Scripture, which is revealed by God, and nature, which can be studied with observation and reason.

showed inexplicable similarities. Why were plants and animals not more directly designed to fit their environments?

For instance, in the oceans we find animals with a basically similar shape, something like a torpedo, obviously because that shape works well for swimming through water. These animals also have fins and tails that are similar to one another to propel them. But if we take a look at the internal structure of species such as sharks, penguins, and dolphins, we will see that they are not the same at all. In fact, they seem to be based on very different structural designs (see figure 3.1). The internal organs of sharks include a swim bladder, while the internal organs of a dolphin include lungs. This difference affects how the two animals function in the water. Sharks can remain submerged, while dolphins must emerge from time to time to breathe. Both are adapted to obtaining oxygen while living in the water, but they do it differently. Furthermore, sharks lay eggs to reproduce, while dolphins birth live young and suckle them. Both strategies work in the water, but they are fundamentally different ways of reproducing. If the environment is the same, why should these two animals have such different structures and use such different strategies for living in it?

Figure 3.1: Water Animal Fins Compared

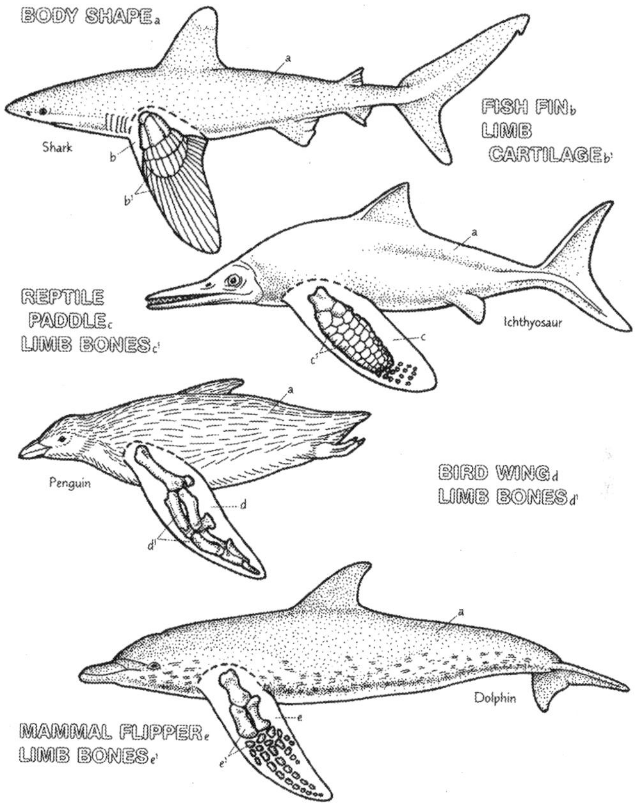

Source: Zihlman (2000: 1–8)
Artwork by Coloring Concepts, Inc.

When we compare species across environments an even more striking thing emerges. Animals in very different environments have the same or similar structures and strategies. Dolphins not only have lungs and wombs like many land animals, from "tip to tail" they share all the characteristics of what we call "mammals" (and that is why they are classified as mammals). Along with whales, porpoises, and some others, they are water-dwelling mammals that are structurally the same as land-dwelling mammals such as elephants, cats, zebras, and people. In a word, they are not fish.

If we compare the animals that look alike internally, rather than the ones that occupy the same environments, we notice further that there seem to be basic designs that are altered between the species depending on functional needs. So, for instance, all mammals have skeletal structures with four limbs. The front two of these limbs have the following pattern of bones: a long heavy bone extending from the shoulder, followed by two parallel bones, a set of articulating bones (the wrist), and five jointed digits. In human beings, this structure allows us to use our arms to carry things, and to manipulate our fingers for a wide variety of purposes. But this same structure is found in mammals that do not use their front limbs in anything like the same way. Elephants use their front limbs for walking on hard surfaces, bats use them as wings for flying, and moles use them for digging. The dolphin uses them as fins to swim with. Yet, the internal bone structure of each of these species is based on the same pattern: a single heavy bone, two parallel bones, articulating bones, and digit bones . . . whether they actually form digits or not!

Figure 3.2: Mammalian Forelimbs Compared

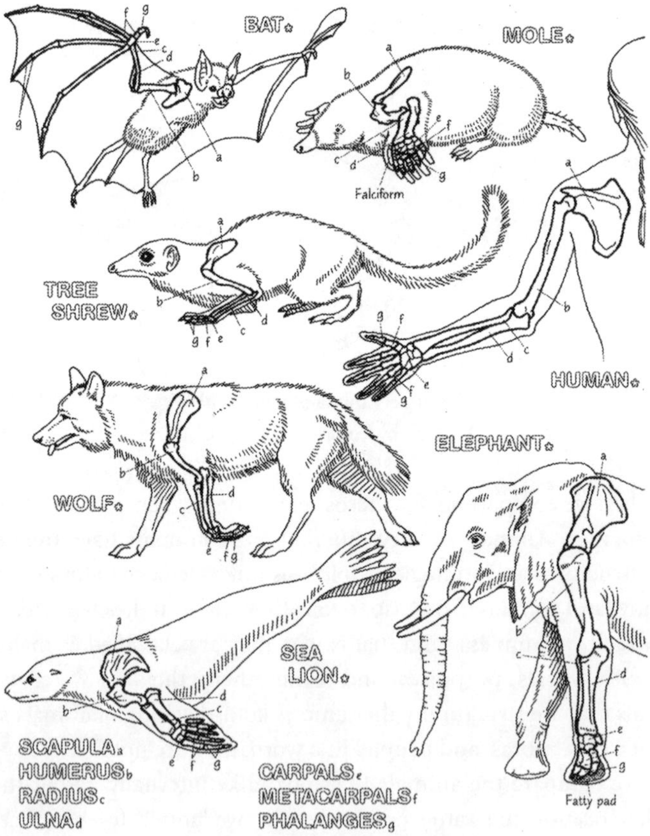

Source: Zihlman (2000: 1–6)
Artwork by Coloring Concepts, Inc.

What are we to make of all this? The simple explanation[4] is that dolphins, porpoises, and whales are "related" to land mammals more closely than they are to fish, despite their surface appearance and watery environment. Normally, we all recognize that similarity in appearance indicates common ancestry. Siblings who look alike do so because they have common parents. So, it would seem reasonable to think that the approximately 170,000 varieties of moths and butterflies have probably descended from a common ancestor. In fact, there may have been an ancestral species of insect that gave rise to the basic pattern found in all insects now. Reasoning in this fashion, similarity can be explained by ancestry. Is it possible that similarity may be an accident? Sure it is, especially when single traits are compared to one another, such as coloration or blood types. But an overall pattern of structural similarity is very unlikely to be accidental. So, when a thorough analysis of species is made, and they are classified by anatomical structure, the members of these classifications are assumed to be related to one another through common ancestry. Comparative anatomy, even now, provides some of the strongest evidence in favor of evolution.

Since the advent of genetics, scientists have been able to be much more specific in their comparisons between species. Rather than observing the outward forms, the phenotypes, geneticists can look directly at the mechanisms that produce those forms, the genotypes. Genes are patterns of chemicals (bases) in chromosomes that give instructions for how to grow anatomical parts and maintain physiological functions. The total sequence of DNA bases on chromosomes, or genomes, identify the species. So comparing genetic similarities between species is a good way to compare their presumed relatedness. Human beings, for instance, are most closely related to chimpanzees (with more than 98 percent genetic similarity), then to gorillas, then to other apes, then to other mammals, and so on.

This evidence for relatedness is true not only of genes, which are the blueprints for constructing our bodies, but also of the inter-genetic material on chromosomes that turns genes on and off at appropriate times. And it is true of certain viruses, known as retroviruses, that insert themselves into the nuclear DNA. If successful, retroviruses are replicated to all succeeding generations of the host. Thus, when they find the same retroviruses in two different species, scientists assume that the invasion occurred in an ancestor to both of them. The chances of finding the exact same set of retroviruses in two different species by accident is "vanishingly impossible," says David

---

4. One of the most fundamental principles of science is that the simplest explanation must be accepted unless there is clear evidence or reason not to do it. This is known as Occam's Razor, after the sixteenth-century Franciscan monk who promoted it. So, if we are to hypothesize complex explanations, we must demonstrate the need for them.

Wilcox, a Christian geneticist (2004: 101). Retroviruses, then, are a kind of genetic fossil evidence of common ancestry.

Keeping in mind these signs of relatedness from comparative anatomy, let us turn to the matter of the fossil evidence. If evolution has occurred, then we should expect that the fossil evidence will yield ancestral forms that are in some sense intermediate between the currently living forms of plants and animals (or more basic). Fossils are the remains of species found in the earth. They may be direct remains, as in the case of bones, or indirect, as in the case of impressions on rock. The existence of fossils, in any particular case, is actually a minor miracle. A variety of natural processes such as decay, the food chain, and climactic forces, combine to eliminate almost all remains of animals and plants quickly after they have died. The earth recycles biological material to the next generation of living beings. Optimal conditions, such as isolation, dryness, or freezing temperatures, are needed for fossils to form. Still, fossils are not hard to find, and scientists have collected far too many of them to count, or even estimate.

The fossil evidence indicates a remarkable thing about the history of the earth. It is not just that there are a few extinct species, such as the dinosaurs, that must be added to the current catalog of living species. It is that, in the past, there has been a succession of *whole worlds* that are almost entirely unfamiliar to us. These worlds consisted of hundreds of thousands of species that are no longer around today. More significantly, they do not contain the currently living species at all! During the time of the dinosaurs, for instance, the world was composed of a wide variety of reptiles and conifer trees. Until late in the period, there were no flowering or fruit-bearing trees, no mammals other than small rat-like creatures, and of course, no human beings. Prior to this time there were only smaller reptiles and giant ferns; prior to that only fish and trilobites, prior to that only tiny multi-celled "animals," and prior to that only single-celled beings. The history of the earth has been a series of epochs in which all of the plants and animals were different than they are now.

How do we know this? First, fossils are found in layers of the earth. The layers, if they are undisturbed, show which species lived at the same time as one another, and which preceded or succeeded the others. Then, there are a variety of dating methods that can establish the approximate ages of fossils. None of these dating methods will work in every instance, and all of them have known margins of error. But a careful investigation of how they are used will reveal most dating methods to be reasonable when properly conducted. Potassium argon dating, for instance, measures the amount of potassium that has broken down into argon in volcanic rock. Since potassium breaks down at a known rate, the amount of argon accumulated in the rock will tell how old it is (since the rock was lava), and thereby date the fossils found between the layers. Carbon dating measures the amount of carbon-14 remaining in organic fossils after the plant or animal has died. Carbon-14 breaks down with a half-life of 5,730 years, allowing scientists to date the fossil directly. Potassium argon dating cannot be used for time periods less than 100,000 years ago because too little argon will have built up in the rock, and carbon dating cannot be used for time periods greater than 50,000 years ago because too little carbon will be left in the fossil. But there are other dating methods that scientists can use to help fill in the gaps when identifying the ages of fossils.

Establishing the facts of the existence of previous species from the fossil evidence is fairly straightforward. But the next step in constructing an account of earth's history requires a good deal more guesswork. Assuming that all living beings are related, lines of descent must be drawn between currently living species that appear related to one another and fossil species that might, or might not, have been their common ancestors. In some cases, there are fossil species that are well established (with plenty of fossil evidence) and have the right characteristics to be established as ancestors. In other cases, there is a lack of fossils, or the right kinds of fossils, creating "missing links." Most often, there are a number of possible ancestors to any particular group of later species, causing scientists to battle it out over which species is the most likely ancestor to the others. In general, it is easier to establish evolutionary links between species, past and present, that are related to one another at the lowest taxonomical levels, such as families, where there are strong similarities to be observed. It is more difficult to do so at the highest levels, such as phyla, where there are much bigger differences involved. Still, scientists are working to link all species together into a single evolutionary tree that describes the history of life on earth.

THE MECHANISM

It is important to distinguish the general idea of the evolution of species and common ancestry from the matter of *how* evolutionary changes occur. This is because, while the former is very well established by the evidence from a wide variety of scientific fields, the latter is more narrowly a theory, and one that is contested even within the scientific community. Scientists in the nineteenth century who were trying to piece together the puzzle of earth's history were able to establish that plants and animals were changing in response to changing environments, but they had no means of explaining the mechanism that brought about this change. Charles Darwin provided a mechanism. He did so by drawing a simple parallel between "artificial selection," which is animal breeding such as is done on farms, and "natural selection," which he postulated happens by itself in nature (Darwin 1968: 67). Animal breeders alter the morphologies of domesticated animals and plants by selecting out individuals that have the characteristics they want and mating these individuals to one another. The result is future generations that have more of the characteristics that are desired, and less of the ones that are unwanted. In nature, Darwin suggested, animals or plants that are not well adapted to their environments will not survive to reproduce at the same rate as those that are well adapted. The result over time will be a shift in the morphology of the species as adaptive traits are retained and maladaptive ones are lost.

The full significance of this theory is twofold. First, an explanation of how change can occur (by differential reproduction rates), and why it should occur (for purposes of adaptation) is provided. Second, the explanation fits in with the notion of a mechanical universe with natural processes, rather than a created world miraculously formed by God. The nineteenth century was the heyday of the modern period of European history, characterized by the split between science and religion, a tremendous optimism over human progress, and the birth of atheism as a significant force in Western history. Essentially everyone in the sciences was looking for ways to explain things without reference to God.[5] In truth, they were so successful at this that today it is essentially impossible to publish scientific works that integrate God's powerful and creative activity into the general understanding of what happens in the natural world. We will consider this matter more below.

First, let us take a closer look at Darwin's theory. He suggested that: variations in individual characteristics occur naturally (Darwin did not know why), some variations increase the individual's ability to survive and reproduce in a certain environment and others reduce that same ability, variations that are adaptive are passed on to the next generation in greater frequencies than those that are not, thus over time the entire population will shift in the direction of the beneficial changes. Also, adaptation is not just to the environment in general, but to a specific niche (food source) within that environment, and species are in competition with one another for these niches. This produces a situation of the "survival of the fittest," not only between individuals, but also between species. The competitive pressure for

5. There have always been Christian scientists, however, working to integrate what they see in nature with theology. An example from this time period is Asa Gray, a nineteenth-century American botanist who defended Darwin's theory of natural selection while yet holding to an orthodox Protestant belief in God. Likewise, Teilhard de Chardin, who did paleoanthropological work himself, wrote books about the glory of God in creation.

niches accelerates the tendency for adaptive characteristics to be selected, and maladaptive ones to be lost.

Darwin's theory has proved very fruitful in explaining microevolution, the relatively small changes that occur in species over an observable period of time. Furthermore, the field of genetics, which developed after Darwin, has added tremendously to our understanding of how natural selection occurs. Mutations, or accidental changes in the genetic code, can cause significant alterations in an individual's morphology, and these alterations may turn out to be beneficial. In a well-known example, a species of grey moths in the suburbs of London had an occasional mutation that produced an entirely black moth. So long as the tree trunks on which the moths rested were grey, the mutant black moths were eaten by birds because they were easy to see. When the tree trunks were darkened by soot from local industry, black became the advantageous color. Black moths survived and reproduced more easily, grey moths were eaten by birds, and eventually the population became entirely black. Later, when people cleaned up the air, the trees reverted to grey, and grey moths moved in from elsewhere and replaced the black ones. Thus, as we can see in this example, natural selection can be an important force in microevolution.

What is far less clear is how such microevolutionary changes can add up to the macroevolutionary changes that have produced the wide variety of plants and animals alive today. Within the phyla, we can imagine that gradual changes have produced the diversity of species that are in figure 3.2 above. But between phyla, so for instance between mammals and worms, or between birds and insects, there seem to be entirely different patterns at work, as in figure 3.1 above. Furthermore, the paleontological evidence indicates a relatively short period of time, in evolutionary terms, for the basic patterns to have diverged from one another. All of these basic patterns emerged within a period of about 20 million years, at 542 million years ago, an event that is referred to as "the Cambrian explosion." It is difficult to imagine how natural selection, which is a slow and conservative process, could have created such diversity so quickly.

Scientists in the twenteith century tried to address this difficulty with the use of population genetics. According to the "neo-Darwinian synthesis," there are four evolutionary forces: mutation, natural selection, gene flow, and genetic drift. The first two of these we have already discussed. Gene flow refers to the addition of genetic material to a population by individuals who have come from another population of the same species. Genetic drift refers to the shifts in gene frequencies that occur due to the mix and match of genes chosen through reproductive processes in successive generations. These are not necessarily adaptive changes at the time that they are made, but they alter the genome of the species anyway. Furthermore, a special case of genetic drift, known as "the founder effect," occurs when natural disasters or other types of isolation cause small surviving populations to grow into big ones. When that happens, formerly rare genes become common in the population as a whole, and the pace of change is accelerated. Thus, the evolution of the population is not just dependent on mutation and natural selection. The genetic variability needed to provide new material for natural selection can come from the outside (gene flow) and be altered quickly (genetic drift). In fact, the theory of "punctuated equilibrium" (Gould 2002) suggests that natural selection functions primarily to produce minor modifications over long periods of time in order to conserve species as they are. It is genetic drift, intensified in the tiny populations that survive natural disasters (the founder effect), that operates to produce significant changes quickly. The extinction of the dinosaurs due to the impact of a large asteroid, which cleared the way for the expansion of mammals into new niches, is an example of this process.

Still, even in punctuated equilibrium, the entirety of evolutionary theory rests on mutation as the ultimate source of adaptive variation, and mutations are accidents. They occur because genes that are in the process of reproducing themselves inadvertently alter the genetic code for the next generation. More than accidents, these alterations are actually *errors*. They are not, at the molecular level, intentionally adaptive. Scientists bent on keeping God out of the picture must explain how it is that a collection of molecular errors can turn out to be so wonderfully adaptive for species. So far, they have done this by suggesting that, given enough errors over enough time, a certain percentage of the errors will unintentionally turn out to be beneficial for the individuals who have them, and that natural selection will take over, replicating the change to the rest of the population. But this explanation rests upon a theory of chance that requires the help of mathematicians, and significantly it is the mathematicians who are suggesting that the chances of beneficial mutations producing the necessary changes are not reasonable! At the critical points at which major changes have occurred, such as the divergence between the phyla, there has not been *remotely* enough time for microevolution, as we know it, to add up to macroevolution.

It is possible that the time-for-macroevolution problem will yet be solved by scientists. For instance, about half of all "point" mutations (the ones that are the result of a single base substitution) do not alter the proteins being constructed. Such mutations can build up genetic diversity without being detrimental to the organism. Also, organisms under stress are known to have increased mutation rates, speeding up the possibility of change. Still, some of the most recent work in genetics has suggested that "the genetic code is not random" (Freeland and Hurst 1998). It appears that at the genetic level, there is a kind of "search process" going on for the genes needed to adapt successfully (David Wilcox, personal communication).

Also, we should remember that the term *mutation* is packaged with more than just scientific meaning. An entire philosophy of independent natural processes, along with a theory of accident, is included. Atheist scientists who are intent upon proving that the world is the result of chance or accident (such as Carl Sagan or Richard Dawkins) must account for the enormous statistical improbability of what has happened. There are two critical points at which the mathematical problem is the most severe: the origin of the universe and the origin of life. On the origin of the universe, the odds against a world that can support life are 1 in 10 to the 10 to the 123, a number we humans cannot even picture in our minds. The Christian geneticist, Francis Collins explains:

> Altogether, there are fifteen physical constants [necessary for our universe] whose values current theory is unable to predict. They are givens . . . The chance that all of these constants would take on the values necessary to result in a stable universe capable of sustaining complex life forms is almost infinitesimal. And yet those are exactly the parameters that we observe. In sum, our universe is wildly improbable. (2006: 74)

As for the beginning of life, the odds against the first life-form emerging spontaneously from the "primal soup" has been compared to the chances of throwing a truckload of bricks in the air and having them come down in the shape of a house. It is not just that these events are vastly improbable. Both involve the creation of highly complex forms from very simple ones. In truth, it is simply not reasonable that such high organization and complexity should be the result of a series of tiny uncoordinated accidents. The most ordinary common sense would suggest that some force or other must be guiding the process.

It is tempting for Christians at this point to use the mathematical counter-evidence to make a case against evolution in its entirety. But that would be a very selective use of the evidence. Remember that the evidence from biology (comparative anatomy and genetics) and from paleontology (fossils) strongly converges on a history of the earth marked by physical relatedness between species and a common ancestry for all of life. It appears that evolution *has* happened. But *how* it has happened is not nearly so clear.

HUMAN ORIGINS

If we accept that evolution has happened, then we must accept that we ourselves have evolved from earlier forms of life. As human beings, we share all but 1–2 percent of our genetic code with chimpanzees, the animals most similar to us. We are next closest to gorillas, then to the other primates, then to the mammals, and then to animals as against plants. That is why we are included in the scientific taxonomy of all living things with a species name, *Homo sapiens*. If we take a look at the fossil evidence, there have been a number of species in the past that had characteristics like humans, but were at an earlier stage of development. An early hominin species living in Africa, *Australopithecus afarensis*, had the following human-like characteristics: it stood upright (based on its bone structure from ankles to cranium), and it used its hands rather than its teeth to prepare food (based on its small flat teeth and manipulable digits). Yet this species was only the size of a modern chimp, and had just a chimp's brain capacity. It walked like a human, but could not think like one.

Figure 3.3: Australopithecus Afarensis Compared to a Modern Chimpanzee

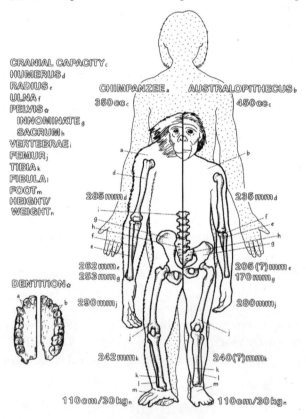

Source: Zihlman (2000: 5–17)
Artwork by Coloring Concepts, Inc.

Later species had increasing similarities to modern humans, and a history of having expanded out of their original home in Africa.

There is a common misconception that there is a "missing link" between humans and their ancestral species. Actually, there are many hundreds of fossils, establishing a variety of pre-human hominins that are intermediate between *Australopithecus afarensis* and *Homo sapiens*. Rather, the debate in science is over how to *arrange* the pre-human hominin species in an order of succession. Remember that this is always a problem for paleontologists, who are trying to connect the dots between fossils and living creatures. In that sense, the entire record is full of missing links, and scientists are involved in the massive task of linking up the ancestral tree of life, including the ancestral lines that lead to human beings.

But actually, we don't need science to establish our link to the animal world. We already know that we eat, sleep, excrete, and procreate like the other animals. Furthermore, this observed reality is acknowledged by the Bible and Christian theology. There are religions that suggest that human beings are divine—literal children of gods—or that our souls are God while our bodies are part of an illusionary and evil material world. Genesis depicts human beings as part of creation, both body and soul, and as fundamentally distinct from the Creator. Adam was made "from the dust of the ground" (Gen 2:7), a phrase that reminds us that our material existence was part of God's plan from the beginning. A Christian understanding of human beings, then, is as a creature among others in God's creation.

Still, the Bible does not indicate that we are descended from other animals. Only by reading "the dust of the ground" metaphorically (to mean, "material") can we reconcile the biblical text to the scientific evidence. Even those willing to read Genesis metaphorically can find the idea of *human* evolution uncomfortable. Perhaps the reason for this discomfort is that our relatedness to the other animals seems to threaten our uniqueness in the world and before God.

What does the Bible say about our uniqueness? First, it is important to acknowledge that, apart from God's special calling, we are *not* unique. Once again, Genesis 1 says that we are created beings, like the animals, not gods. Furthermore, according to the story of Adam and Eve in Genesis 2, we have a tendency to try to escape our creaturely limitations, and to elevate ourselves to be "like God" (Gen 3:5). Cultural anthropologists can attest to the fact that this desire to raise ourselves above nature is found all over the world. People everywhere hide their bodily functions, or alter them with "manners," to make themselves look less like animals. A great deal of effort goes into training children out of an animal-like stage of childhood into a superior human-like stage of adulthood. Calling people animal names is almost universally an insult (except for terms of endearment!). Yet, according to the Bible, our attempts to elevate our own status are sinful, and our humble acceptance of our creaturely nature is an important form of obedience to our Creator (Gen 3:22–24).

Second, however, the Bible indicates that we *are* unique because God has placed his own image within us (Gen 1:27). In chapter two, we discussed the nature of this image as a vice-regency on earth, making us stewards of creation. Stewardship means not only that we are to care for creation, but also that we have a kind of dominion or authority over it, allowing us to construct things from technology to social systems to art. We make culture as God has made us. Then, most importantly, we are able to *relate* to God in a way not possible for the other animals. It is this ability to respond to God's love with our own love and surrender that makes us truly unique and allows God to provide us with a special position in nature.

Of course, such thoughts should make us more, not less, careful in our care for creation. Ironically, those who believe humans are just another animal have no real basis for suggesting that we should be any more responsible for the earth than are rabbits or grizzly bears! We Christians, who know our uniqueness before God, have the greatest reason to be accountable to him for what is done with his garden. We are creatures ourselves. But we have been given an important responsibility to participate in God's good governance of the earth.

What remains, then, is the question of how and when God gave us the responsibility that we currently have, that is, at what point in the history of the earth did he make us unique within creation? The Bible answers this question with the story of Adam and Eve. If we are to accept evolutionary theory, we must either posit a point in time when this story took place, or suggest a metaphorical reading of the text. Thus far, Christian scholars working with evolutionary theory have not come to any agreement on this matter. But no matter how the historical question is answered, the power and beauty of God's acts in creating us and making us responsible agents on earth are preserved by the biblical account of our own origins.

DESIGN

In recent years, a new movement has emerged, called "Intelligent Design," that is composed of Christian scientists and philosophers attempting to demonstrate God's involvement in nature. They do so by pointing out evidence for intentional design in natural phenomena, especially in biology. Secular scientists have been quick to accuse those in Intelligent Design

(ID) of being warmed-over Creationists. But this is an oversimplification. ID proponents are well trained in their disciplines and usually accept some form of evolutionary theory. They hold in common the assertion that there is far too much design in nature for the sum total to be explained by a theory of accident.[6]

The idea of design is not a new one. As early as 1802, a philosopher by the name of William Paley suggested that the intricate workings of the human body, or any living thing, can be compared to a watch. A watch has two important characteristics: 1) its various parts are carefully fitted to one another to enable it to function, and 2) its functioning indicates its purpose as a time piece for someone who has designed it. The argument suggests that, likewise, biological organisms are composed of such complex and interconnected parts that they must be internally designed, and that their design indicates a purpose for their existence given to them by an external Designer (cf. Dembski 2006: 64). The contemporary Christian philosopher, Alvin Plantinga, describes the situation:

> Consider the mammalian eye: a marvelous and highly complex instrument, resembling a telescope of the highest quality, with a lens, an adjustable focus, a variable diaphragm for controlling the amount of light, and optical corrections for spherical and chromatic aberration. And here is the problem: how does the lens, for example, get developed by the proposed means—random genetic variation and natural selection—when at the same time there has to be development of the optic nerve, the relevant muscles, the retina, the rods and cones, and many other delicate and complicated structures, all of which have to be adjusted to each other in such a way that they can work together? Indeed, what is involved isn't, of course, just the eye; it is the whole visual system, including the relevant parts of the brain. Many different organs and suborgans have to be developed together, and it is hard to envisage a series of mutations which is such that each member of the series has adaptive value, is also a step on the way to the eye, and is such that the last member is an animal with such an eye. (Pennock 2001: 133)

It would seem that a plan has been considered in advance, and changes in nature, gradual or sudden, made to fit the final purpose. That is certainly

6. Collins (2006: 205) disagrees that there is a problem, suggesting, "Evolution could appear to us to be driven by chance, but from God's perspective the outcome would be entirely specified. Thus, God could be completely and intimately involved in the creation of all species, while from our perspective, limited as it is by the tyranny of linear time, this would appear as random and undirected process."

the case in the design and making of a watch. And a watch is a far, far less intricate or well-functioning object than an animal or a human being. If it takes a thinking mind to create a watch, then surely it takes a much more intelligent and competent mind to create the whole of nature as we see it.

The scholars in the Intelligent Design movement have done various kinds of work to demonstrate that there is indeed design in nature. Michael Denton has summarized the evidence for and against natural selection as the sole explanation for evolution to date (1986). William Dembski has worked out a mathematical model for eliminating the results of chance, and thereby detecting the possibility of a "specified" pattern, that is, one planned in advance (2006). Michael Behe has suggested that even at the smallest level, the level of biochemistry, life is composed of systems that are "irreducibly complex," by which he means "a single system composed of several well-matched, interacting parts that contribute to the basic function, wherein the removal of any one of the parts causes the system to effectively cease functioning" (1996: 39). Cilia, for instance, the tiny hair-like structures that enable single-celled animals to move, are composed of a circular pattern of rods which are themselves composed of molecules that fit perfectly together, and that are linked to one another and made to move with the help of over two hundred different proteins (59, 72). Cilia are a relatively minor structure in nature, and not at all exceptional. Behe notes that the world is chock-full of incredible complexity at the micro-level, and concludes:

> To a person who does not feel obliged to restrict his search to unintelligent causes, the straightforward conclusion is that many biochemical systems were designed. They were designed *not* by the laws of nature, not by chance and necessity. Rather, they were *planned*. The designer knew what the systems would look like when they were completed; the designer took steps to bring the systems about. Life on earth at its most fundamental level, in its most critical components, is the product of intelligent activity. (Pennock 2001: 254)

So, according to the scientists in the Intelligent Design movement, chance (mutation) and necessity (natural selection) are just not strong enough mechanisms to explain the complex patterns that we observe in biology.

Scientists working in astrophysics have also noticed evidence for design. The universe is amazingly "fine-tuned" to support life (McGrath 2009). For instance, at the origins of the universe, the force of the explosion of the "Big Bang" had exactly the strength needed to balance the force of gravity. If the explosion had been stronger or weaker by more than one out of ten to the sixtieth power ($1/10^{60}$), the universe would not have been formed at all. This number has been compared by Paul Davies to "firing a bullet at a one-inch target on the other side of the universe, twenty billion light years away" (Lamoureux 2008: 83). Roger Penrose has suggested that the odds against the complex organization of the universe that we see are 1/10 to 10 to 10^{123}, or one plus many more zeros than the number of particles in the universe (85). Other scientists have noted that the earth, the sun, and the solar system, are also finely tuned to support life (86). In fact, contrary to popular opinion, Charles Darwin himself noticed design in nature. In his autobiography, he wrote:

> Another source of conviction in the existence of God, connected with the reason and not with the feelings, impresses me as having much more weight. This follows from the extreme difficulty or rather impossibility of conceiving this immense and wondrous universe, including man with his capacity of looking backwards and far into futurity, as a result of blind chance or necessity. When thus reflecting I *feel* compelled to look to a First Cause having an intelligent mind in some degree analogous to that of man; and I *deserve* to be called a Theist. [Emphasis in the original.]

A few years before his death, he commented, "I have never been an Atheist in the sense of denying the existence of God."[7]

Scientists who are committed to describing nature without reference to God argue that there is counter-evidence to the notion of design as well. To begin with, there are monstrosities, accidents such as two-headed animals and worse, that are not viable. These occur throughout nature at a somewhat predictable rate, and are found among humans too. Then, there are the structures, both morphological and genetic, that appear to be vestiges of the past serving no current function, such as the appendix. And, there are the structures that appear to be modifications of earlier structures whose use has changed, such as the Panda's "thumb" which is not a true thumb at all, but a modified wrist bone (Gould 1992). The latter problem, evidence of modification, can fit with the idea of a designed process, but the former, the existence of monstrosities, is harder to reconcile. There are things in nature that appear to be accidental.

7. Both this quote and the previous one by Charles Darwin are cited in footnote 11, page 80, of Dennis Lamoureux's article, "Robert A. Lamar on Intelligent Design: An Evolutionary Creationist Critique" *Christian Scholar's Review*, XXXVII:1 (2007: 77–90). The first quote is from *The Autobiography of Charles Darwin*, 1908–1882, edited by Nora Barlow, London: Collins (1958: 92–93), and the second quote is from *The Life and Letters of Charles Darwin, Volumes 1–3*, edited by Francis Darwin, London: John Murray (1887: 304).

While it is reasonable to admit of *a role* for accident in nature, it does not necessarily follow that such a role must or can be the *only* explanation for all that we see. Despite the counter-evidence cited above, the intricacy of design in nature is by far the more overwhelming reality. Denton remarks:

> Yet, just as a few missing links are not sufficient to close the gaps of nature, a few imperfect adaptations which give every impression of having been achieved by chance are certainly, amid the general perfection of design in nature, an insufficient basis on which to argue for the all-sufficiency of chance. (1986: 327)

Denton is saying that exceptions to the rule do not disprove the rule. Furthermore, he is reminding secular scientists of their own argument for evolution. If gaps in the fossil record do not disprove the rule of common ancestry, then maladaptive accidents in nature do not disprove the rule of design. Dembski points out that secular scientists are suggesting human intelligence has arisen by an entirely unintelligent process; he comments, "The absurdity here is palpable" (2004: 23). Surely an intelligence beyond our own has made us, or why would we be speculating about our own existence?

It is possible to see signs of discomfort with the theory of accident even among its most vigorous proponents. Richard Dawkins, who uses evolution to promote atheism, defines biology as "the study of complicated things that *give the appearance* of having been designed for a purpose" (Dawkins 1986: 1) [emphasis added]. This seems an odd way to define a field of study. It suggests that the subject material is characterized by an intentional deception. In his attempts to resolve the problem of the numbers, Dawkins goes on to suggest that one in 100 billion billion against is *acceptable* odds for life having occurred on earth by accident (146). When this argument seems stretched, he suggests that the real problem is that our brains are not yet evolved to the point of understanding how such incredible odds can have occurred (162). It would seem that, as scientists have discovered more and more about the universe, a great deal of backpedaling has become necessary to refrain from including God as an explanation for both its complexity and its design.[8]

Still, Christians have work to do in developing a theology of nature that has full integrity with the findings of science. Monstrosities and the genetic

---

8. Morris (2003: 19) responds to Dawkins' suggestion that the universe is the result of a "Blind Watchmaker" by suggesting that, "It is as if the Blind Watchmaker takes off her sunglasses and decides to visit her brother Chronos. Off she sets, crossing streets roaring with traffic driven by psychotics, through the entrails of the subway system of a megalopolis, and, after catching a series of intercontinental express trains with connection times of two minutes each, she arrives at Chronos' front door at 4 p.m. prompt, just in time for a relaxing cup of tea."

record are not the greatest theological difficulty we have; that award goes to death and extinctions. Scientists estimate that 99 percent of the plants and animals that have ever existed are now extinct. This is because, as we have already seen, there have been entire worlds of living beings that have come and gone over the eons of paleo-history. At each successive "generation" of plants and animals, a few species have survived to produce the next generation. But the vast majority of them have left no descendants behind at all. Furthermore, in any particular time period, plants and animals living within the same habitat survive by putting each other out of business, so to speak. They compete for niches so vigorously that the survival of one is often at the expense of others.[9] Even in the same era, the food chain is supported by one animal consuming another animal or plant . . . death for life. In fact, at the level of the biosphere, death and decay produce the very elements needed for the continuation of life. We can hardly argue with the notion that nature is "red in tooth and claw."[10]

If God has created all of nature, and ourselves especially, for a purpose, why is there so much violence and death? And why does it appear that death is *necessary* to the continuance and further evolution of life? Is death actually a good thing, part of a cycle that ultimately benefits nature as a whole? That is the perspective of many Eastern and traditional religions, and of most secular naturalists. But the Bible is clear on this point. Death was *not* part of God's original plan for the world (Rom 5:12–14). Perhaps we can smile with the hungry cat who has found a plump, juicy mouse to eat. But we can hardly smile with the mouse as it is eaten alive, piece by piece. Living beings do not seek suffering or death under normal circumstances because they know they will be destroyed.

The Bible clearly indicates that death is an evil, one that God did not intend for us in the beginning and that he will eliminate in the new heaven and earth (Gen 3:2; Rev 21:4). So, the problem of extinctions is actually a part of the overall theological problem of evil. Christian theologians certainly have worked hard to explain the origins and existence of evil. In the main, they agree that God has permitted evil as a potentiality in the world in order to provide us with the freedom needed to choose to love and worship him. The first to abuse that freedom was Satan, who led a rebellion of the

---

9. There has been some work done by biologists to show that cooperation between species is also common in nature. Such biologists suggest that the model of competition has been exaggerated. Still, competition between species for niches can be seen regularly in habitats from the rainforest to potted plants.

10. This phrase comes from Alfred, Lord Tennyson's poem, "In Memoriam A. H. H.," in which, interestingly, he explores the need to cling to faith in the face of the ravages of human experience, especially death.

angels in heaven against God. The second was the original founding couple of humanity on earth, who chose to live apart from God, his wisdomand his counsel, rather than under his authority and provision. Death was a result of these foolish choices.

With this theological framework in mind, how can we understand the role of death in nature as it is described by science, from the food chain to massive extinctions? First, death in nature has clearly predated the existence of human beings, and by a lot! According to the geological and fossil evidence, humans have only existed for about .005 percent of the time that there has been life on earth. Did our sin bring evil to other creatures long before we were even born? Did it cause the very structure of nature to be distorted such that death became *necessary* to life? Perhaps it is most reasonable to suggest that it was Satan's rebellion that produced death in the initial instance. Gregory Boyd writes:

> To be sure, according to Scripture the creation was originally created good, and the glory of God is still evident in it (Gen 1; Rom 1:20). But something else—something frightfully wicked—is evident in it as well. Of their own free will, Satan and other spiritual beings rebelled against God in the primordial past and now abuse their God-given authority over aspects of creation . . . If this scenario is correct, then the pain-ridden, bloodthirsty, sinister and hostile character of nature makes perfect sense. (2001: 302)

Satan's rebellion took place in heaven, rather than on earth (Rev 12). But after his rebellion Satan was cast down to the earth, and since that time he has been permitted a kind of dominion over it. Jesus referred to Satan as the "ruler of this world" on multiple occasions (John 12:31; 14:30; 16:11). At Jesus' temptation, Satan offered "all the kingdoms of the world" to Jesus as if they were his own to give (Matt 4:8). Boyd suggests that Jesus acknowledged the existence of evil in nature when he "rebuked" the storm at sea in the same way that he had rebuked demons (Matt 8:26) (Boyd 2001: 318). We humans, then, are caught in the middle of a cosmic battle, torn between following Satan's disobedience and "the course of this world" (Eph 2:2), and being "made . . . alive together with Christ" (Eph 2:5). The former way leads to death, both literal and metaphorical, and the later leads to the new creation and eternal life.

There is no doubt of God's intention for the ultimate redemption of all creation, beginning with his most unique creatures, ourselves. Romans 8:19–23 says:

> For the creation waits with eager longing for the revealing of the children of God; for the creation was subjected to futility, not of its own will but by the will of the one who subjected it, in hope that the creation itself will be set free from its bondage to decay and will obtain the freedom of the glory of the children of God. We know that the whole creation has been groaning in labor pains until now; and not only the creation, but we ourselves, who have the first fruits of the Spirit, groan inwardly while we wait for adoption, the redemption of our bodies.

Here, the Apostle Paul suggests that God himself has subjected creation to "futility" or "vanity" as part of a plan of redemption that will ultimately free us from the bondage to decay, or death. That plan involves the adoption as his children of those who are willing to receive new life in Christ. These children are "the first fruits of the Spirit," the ones who will usher in the new creation.

THE ROLE OF THE CREATOR

In the main, it is not possible to be a serious Christian and suggest that there is *no* design or purpose in nature (visible or invisible). As a first principle, Christians believe that all of creation is contingent upon the Creator. That is, were God to cease to exist, the universe would cease to exist as well! This contingency implies that the so-called "laws" of nature are in some way under God's continual guidance. Plantinga writes:

> God is in constant, close, intimate *causal* contact with his creation: he continuously upholds it, and perhaps also acts concurrently with every creaturely causal transaction. We also know that he has often done things in a special way, a way in which he doesn't ordinarily do them, so that, for example, water turns into wine, or human beings emerge from a fiery furnace unhurt, or a human being rises from the dead; he is apparently not averse to working in his creation in a special way. (Pennock 2001: 224) [Emphasis added.]

So, serious Christians also believe that miracles are possible. This is important because the center of our faith rests upon a single specific miracle, the bodily resurrection of Jesus Christ from the dead.

Miracles are not surprising if we simply remember that God is at all times entirely sovereign over his creation. He can do with it as he wishes. In fact, Wilcox suggests that our dichotomy between what is natural and what is supernatural is artificial:

Many feel forced to choose between "naturalism" (materialism) and "supernaturalism" (God). This choice has been required for many because many people have lost sight of the biblical concept that God operates within nature . . . we should not have to choose between God and so-called natural causes. We can choose *both*. (2004: 49–50)

Wilcox addresses the question of causation in nature by reminding us of Aristotle's four types (42–44): 1) material cause, the raw material or substance of a thing, 2) efficient cause, the immediate force acting upon it, 3) formal cause, the plan or blueprint for it, and 4) final cause, the maker's original intent or purpose for it. The first two of these are clearly observable in nature. The third, the blueprint, can be deduced from observation, with or without an acknowledgement of God. But even the most careful description of these three types of causation, says Wilcox, is not enough of an explanation for what we see, nor can it preclude the fourth type of causation. The final cause of all things in nature is the original intent of the Creator who designed the world for a purpose.

What is that purpose? Christian theology declares the foremost purpose of creation to be to glorify the Creator, that is, to remain in perfectly harmonious relationship with him, receiving all the blessings that he has to give, and offering up gratitude in return. In his relationship with us as human beings, God uses the rest of nature as a means of communication. So, part of the purpose of nature is to make possible a relationship of love between God and ourselves, and part of the purpose of humanity is to help to reestablish God's sovereignty over his creation through proper stewardship. It is this Christian understanding of the very big picture that should be both the starting and ending points of our consideration of earth's history.

(CHAPTER 3)DISCUSSION QUESTIONS

1. What are some of the arguments you have heard both for and against evolutionary theory? What evidence is there to support or deny the theory, and how should that evidence be evaluated?

2. If evolutionary theory is correct in the main, how might Christians understand the creation account in Genesis? What does this mean for how we should properly read the Bible?

3. What are the principles that the Bible teaches us about the nature and purpose of creation, including human beings? What difference do

these principles make to how we view the findings of science, or to the decisions we must make about how to live in the natural world?

4. If you were confronted with someone who wanted to become a Christian, but firmly insisted upon evolutionary theory, what would you say?

RECOMMENDED READINGS

Collins, Francis S. 2006. *The Language of God: A Scientist Presents Evidence for Belief.* New York: The Free Press.

Darwin, Charles. 1968. *The Origin of Species.* New York: Penguin.

Gould, Stephen Jay. 2007. *The Richness of Life: The Essential Stephen Jay Gould.* Edited by Steven Rose. New York: W. W. Norton.

McGrath, Alister E. 2009. *A Fine-Tuned Universe: The Quest for God in Science and Theology.* Louisville, KY: Westminster John Knox.

Wilcox, David L. 2004. *God and Evolution: A Faith-Based Understanding.* Valley Forge, PA: Judson.

Chapter 4

Who are My People?

Deconstructing Race and Ethnicity

Two young Christian couples were having dinner, together with their children. The Smiths were a white couple, while the Jones were "mixed": the wife was white and the husband was African American. Mrs. Smith (who was white) was wearing a pair of navy blue nylon stockings. After considering the matter for a bit, the Jones' six year old boy came up to Mrs. Smith and rubbed her leg, saying, "Why are you half black?"

W hat does it mean to be "black" or "white"? For that matter, what does it mean to be "Asian," or "Indian," or "Hispanic," or "American"? Anthropologists study race and ethnicity, two different but related terms. In the main, race refers to perceived biological differences between people, while ethnicity refers to cultural differences. But, most people believe that the reason they have a common culture is because they have descended from common ancestors. So ethnic differences are thought to be rooted in biological relatedness. Anthropology started out assuming this view, inadvertently affirming a popular myth with all the power of science! It has taken more than a century and a half of careful scholarly work to debunk the connection between race and ethnicity and to demonstrate that *both* are socially constructed.

THE MYTH OF RACE

The term *race* refers to a group of people who are biologically distinct because they have a common ancestry. Any term, such as this one, references a concept in the mind, but it may or may not reference an objective reality. Thus, we must begin with the question, does "race" actually exist? Do the people of the world come in different physical types, "red and yellow, black and white," as the old Sunday school song says? Anthropologists used to think so. In the mid-nineteenth century, when the discipline was being founded, anthropologists began gathering data on human physical variation brought back to them by travelers to other parts of the world. The data indicated differences that they, as Europeans, found surprising. Skin color, height, weight, hair, and facial features varied much more than they had previously thought possible. Of course, as scientists, they were fascinated! They set to work immediately classifying the different types of people.

Initially they had some trouble identifying who was human and who was not. For instance, they thought orangutans were "wild men," based on reports of their human-like appearance and behavior. On the other hand, they thought certain groups of people in Africa looked so different from themselves that they must not be human at all. Ethnocentrism was rampant. Those populations that looked more European were assumed to be more evolved, and those that looked less European were thought to be part ape (to the very great embarrassment of the discipline now!). Eventually the matter of who was human and who was not was sorted out with the help of better data. But the ethnocentric view that white European-descended people were superior to the rest continued in science, as well as in popular culture, through the middle of the twentieth century.

In addition, some scientists speculated that physical differences reflected much deeper differences between people. They tried to link body types to personalities, moral character, and intelligence. As a result, groups were declared to be naturally smart, or naturally criminal. This caused concern over the potential impact of immigration on a country's gene pool. A new pseudo-science of "eugenics" arose, especially in Germany and the United States, to help create public policy that would prevent a population's physical and mental degeneration. In the United States, eugenicists worked to convince Congress to restrict the immigration of Eastern Europeans, who were thought to be naturally criminal, and to enact mandatory sterilization programs for those who were unable to pass intelligence tests. Stephen Jay Gould (1996) has documented the historical reasons for this misuse of science, along with its impact on society. The natural ethnocentrism of European and American scientists caused them to fudge, and even falsify, the data in their attempts to prove what they assumed to be true—that whites were naturally superior. The result was that the public became convinced that races exist, that they have different innate abilities, and that some are superior to others, particularly in terms of intelligence.[1]

Still, despite its previous errors, it was science that slowly began to debunk the idea that people can be divided into races. Franz Boas, the prominent founder of American anthropology, was one of the first to dispute the significance of biology for intelligence and for the level of cultural development (Boas 1995). Boas demonstrated conclusively that a people's behavior was *not* related to their so-called "race." Later, as the data increased in both quantity and quality, and as scientific methods of measurement improved, it became harder and harder for scientists find biological boundaries between groups. Skin color, for instance, does not come in an exact number of shades. It varies continuously from light to dark. In fact, all skin color is the result of the same pigment, melanin, which is invariably brown. This means that there are no "white" people or "black" people, only lighter and darker *brown* people! In like manner, most other polymorphisms (traits that vary normally) are distributed throughout the human species, with differences in degree, not kind.[2]

Still, when measuring single traits such as skin color failed to distinguish the races, scientists persevered in their efforts with the use of multiple traits. Perhaps skin color, height, weight, and facial features taken together would identify the different types. Not at all. In fact, multiple traits only complicated the picture due to the fact that different traits typically do not co-vary. In one study, only 6 percent of the relatively isolated Swiss people had all the traits that were thought to identify the group (Bohannan 1963: 195). In sum, the biological studies have revealed significant variability between members of the same group (as anyone can see in the differences

1. The history of intelligence studies is particularly long and complex, and is well documented in Gould's book, *The Mismeasure of Man* (1996). Nearly a century of efforts to discover intelligence differences between the "races" have failed, in part because of difficulties in defining what intelligence really is (and is not), and in part because of the impossibility of creating tests that rule out environmental effects and are truly cross-cultural. We can say with confidence that, while there are measurable differences in intelligence between individuals within the same groups, there is no evidence for the existence of group differences (see Gould's discussion of the within- and between-group fallacy, 1996:186). In sum, there is no creditable scientific evidence for the existence of any difference in natural intelligence between races or ethnic groups.

2. Blood type is another example. As late as World War I, scientists and doctors assumed that blood was different by the race and insisted on race-segregated blood transfusions. Of course, many of the patients died! There is indeed a difference in blood types (ABO), but the types are disbursed throughout populations in varying frequencies.

between siblings), but relatively little variability in the averages between groups.

Taken as a whole, the human gene pool is a very narrow one. Chimpanzees, for instance, have four times the genetic diversity of humans, and can be divided into two subspecies, common and bonobo (Kaessmann 1999). Then, the genetic variability that exists within the human species is largely spread throughout all human populations. One geneticist has suggested that if there were a global disaster, and only a small and remote group survived, that group would preserve nearly all of the genetic variability that currently exists in human populations (Lewontin in Gould 1996: 353). The genetic variability that does exist between populations (on average) is very small indeed, just 1.75 percent of our genes (Rosenberg 2002: 2381), and can be explained as the result of adaptation to local environments over the course of the migration of human beings from an original home in Africa out to the rest of the world. Finally, even the most recent studies of genetic relatedness, using the human genome project, reflect the strong interrelatedness of the whole of humanity, with waves of only slight variation from west to east across the globe.

Figure 4.1: Human Physical Relatedness

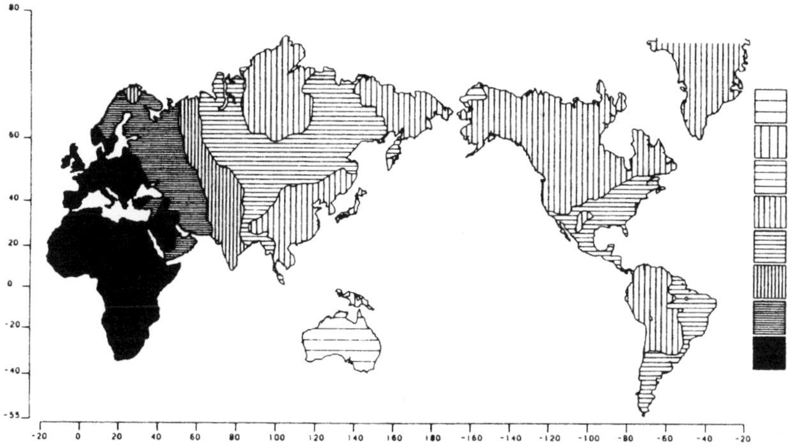

Source: Cavalli-Sforza (1994: 135)

As we see here, Europeans and Africans are most closely related to one another genetically, while Euro-Africans are most distantly related to Australian Aborigines and Native Americans.

So, the populations spread across the earth do not have distinct biological boundaries. Physically, they blend gradually into one another. This is because humans have always maintained biological contact (childbearing) with one another and because adaptation to the environment varies gradually with the environment. Skin color, for instance, is an adaptation to the amount of ultraviolet light in the environment. It is darker in tropical areas to protect from the detrimental effects of too much ultraviolet light, such as skin cancer, and it is lighter in temperate zones to permit the ultraviolet light needed for the production of vitamin D and calcium. But, as valuable as such adaptations may be physiologically, they are relatively superficial genetically, and they do not covary or form boundaries between people enough to create discrete biological types. There is, therefore, truly only *one* human race.

THE SOCIAL CONSTRUCTION OF ETHNICITY

Why, then, do people so commonly assume that races exist? Race does not exist biologically, but it does exist as a social construction. That is, people believe that it exists, and act on that belief, segregating themselves by perceived type. Ironically, this behavior can create minor physical differences between groups. In Japan, for instance, it is possible to identify a skin color difference between the highest and lowest classes simply because they have been intermarrying differentially for so long. But why should people artificially construct a concept, and then insist upon its truth value long past when it has been discredited? To understand that, we must investigate the phenomenon of ethnicity. It is ethnic group formation and maintenance that provides the powerful motivation for a persistent belief in the existence of races.

Ethnicity, as we have said, refers to the cultural differences between groups, and those differences are very real! People speak different languages, have different social structures, and view the world with different sets of assumptions. Thus it is cultural differences, rather than physical differences, that create the truly significant boundaries between people. Yet, cultural differences are entirely humanly constructed, so ethnicity is all the more a socially constructed thing. It is the product of differential patterns of social interaction, that is, of people organizing themselves into different groups, and the consequent differences in beliefs, values, and behaviors that they represent.

Fredrik Barth (1998), following Max Weber, was one of the first to identify the social construction of ethnicity. He suggested that ethnicity is the result of two things: the creation and maintenance of boundaries between social groups, and the establishment of markers of ethnic identity.

Boundaries are breaks in the pattern of social interaction. Interaction within a group is full, rich, and complex. It includes all the possible forms of relating, such as friends, business partners, colleagues, spouses, and family. Interaction between groups is simple and restricted. Public interaction, such as is found in work or marketplace environments, may take place; but private interaction, such as in residential neighborhoods, churches, or homes, is discouraged. Intermarriage is especially forbidden lest it blur the boundaries by setting up families with children that belong to two groups.

Boundaries create ethnic groups by artificially contrasting them with one another. That is to say, each group owes its existence as a social category to the existence of the others, which have been marked out as different groups for historical reasons. For instance, in America, "blacks" are contrasted with "whites"—the contrast in this case can be seen in the names themselves, which exaggerate relative skin colors. Most Americans believe that the skin color difference is the reason for the boundary, when in fact its true origin is historical. Of course, whites and blacks were from different places in the Old World, and were both physically and culturally dissimilar. But the boundary that got set up between them in the New World had more to do with economics than with ancestry. It was based on the structural relationship of slave owners to slaves, which was defended for several centuries with laws to enforce the distinction. The white-black boundary needed defending for the simple reason that even under slavery it was vulnerable to being erased by the children born to black female slaves and fathered by white male slave owners. Those children might have had a claim to inherit their fathers' estates! So a system of segregation was set into place to delegitimize them. The states codified the social practice into law by classifying all children of mixed parentage first as slaves, and later as "Negro," thereby maintaining an ethnic and "racial" boundary for social and economic purposes.

The black–white boundary in the United States is an example of how, according to Barth, all ethnic groups are constructed. Boundaries are established first by the suppression of full social interaction, creating a contrast in ethnic identity. Then markers are chosen to represent the difference, in this case, "black" and "white" skin colors. Markers are symbols that represent the group. They function as flags, causing people to rally around their own ethnicity and to avoid the boundaries with other ethnicities. Markers may be either physical, such as skin color or facial features, or cultural, such as food, dress, language, or religion. If physical markers are available they will likely be selected to represent the group. This is to some degree because they are less easily altered, but to a greater degree because physical differences help make the argument that ethnic boundaries are biologically natural and therefore part of the general order of existence. Basically, physical markers allow people to insist that they are different races, with different ancestries.

But, physical differences are not always evident between ethnic groups. In such cases, cultural differences must be identified to mark the boundaries. In America, the boundary between Hispanics or Latinos and whites is marked by language (Spanish vs. English). In Eastern Europe, the boundary between Serbs and Croats is marked by religion (Orthodox vs. Catholic). In Rwanda, the boundary between the Hutus and Tutsis is marked by the form of subsistence (agriculture vs. pastoralism). In Latin America, the various groups of indigenous peoples ("Indians") are identified by their unique forms of dress. There is usually some basis in history and tradition for these cultural institutions. But always the distinctions are exaggerated, and sometimes they are intentionally invented, to mark ethnic boundaries that might otherwise deteriorate. Hindus and Muslims in India, for instance, who function as quasi-ethnic groups, sport diametrically opposed forms of clothing, men's facial hair, and women's forehead markings. The purpose is to identify group affiliation and to maintain boundaries in the absence of observable physical differences.

In the final analysis, then, *ethnic groups exist because of each other.* Remote peoples who have had little contact with the outside world have no sense of ethnicity. They see themselves as simply human (and other people as sub-human or animals). In fact, it is only in the context of a wider sociopolitical arena that ethnicity emerges. There, it functions to provide the protection and support needed to engage in a competition for scarce resources. These include natural resources, such as access to water or land; economic resources, such possession of jobs or businesses; and political resources, such as leadership or seats in parliament. So, ethnic group formation is ultimately about social, economic, and political protection and provision in the context of large and complex societies.

ETHNICITY AS FAMILY

Still, ethnic groups are not just political instruments. They provide their members with a powerful sense of identity, rooted in a common language, culture, and history. Clifford Geertz has called this quality "essentialism," partly because of its claim to defining the deepest parts of who we are (a claim that Barth also recognized), and partly because of its ability to motivate us to selfless action to protect the group (1973: 241). Ethnicity is strong because it does not seem to be just about rational self-interest. It is about our membership in cultural groups and our identification with them. It is about who we are, and are not, collectively.

Human social identity comes first and foremost from membership in families, and arguably ethnic groups are families writ large. After all, membership within ethnic groups is supposed to be solely by birth, with all members coming from a common ancestry. Ethnic mates view one another as a kind of kin, frequently using kinship terms in their conversations. They talk about being one "blood," and call each other "sister" and "brother." In actual fact, the members of an ethnic group are mostly strangers and could not possibly trace family relations between themselves. But the notion of family functions as a metaphor to bind people together at a higher level (Lee 2002: 236).

The metaphor of the family is strengthened by the use of an origin myth. Origin myths are stories—sometimes detailed and specific, sometimes general—that recount where groups have come from, and under what circumstances they have come to be in their current places and conditions. In the case of ethnic groups, there is usually some historicity to the story, and yet it is not the whole truth. First, the members of any group have a variety of ancestries, most of which are forgotten, while only one is remembered. For instance, the Jewish people identify themselves as the descendants of Abraham and Sarah. This is historically correct so far as it goes, but have they other ancestors as well? Actually, the Bible itself makes it clear that they do. In the Old Testament, the Hebrew people intermarried with the Canaanites and other groups along the way. Since biblical times, the Jewish people have lived in diaspora all over the world where they have mixed with local populations, giving them the physical characteristics of nearly every other people on earth! These other ancestries, however, are forgotten in favor of the one that holds them together as an ethnic group, their descent from Abraham and Sarah.

Second, ethnic groups are more related to one another across boundaries than they usually admit. Not all of Abraham's descendants are currently considered Jewish. Arab peoples trace their ancestry to Abraham through his son Ishmael (rather than Isaac), which, to the degree that it is historically accurate, makes Jews and Arabs "cousins." Furthermore, there are descendants of Abraham and Sarah who have married out of Judaism, thereby joining other ethnicities. So, some who should belong to the group based on the origin story have membership elsewhere. Also, there have been converts to Judaism, including many in New Testament times, who have joined the ethnic group by taking on the religion. These people have no ancestry from Abraham and Sarah, but have contributed both physically and culturally to the contemporary Jewish people.

In point of fact, changing one's ethnic group membership, which anthropologists call "passing," is far more common than most people believe. There are multiple ways to do it. Adoption and intermarriage are the easiest to observe. For instance, an Asian child adopted into a white family in the United States will probably marry another white person (because they share a common culture) and have children who will pass as just white. But it is also possible to pass in more surreptitious ways. People may move into a new area, learn the language and culture, and deny their own past, in order to take up the new identity. For instance, second- or third-generation Koreans in Japan may be able to pass as Japanese and thereby avoid the tremendous stigma in Japan against Koreans.[3] Latin American Indians pass into the mainstream ethnic groups of their countries regularly, in part through the education system. And, every year in the United States, between 35,000 and 50,000 light-skinned blacks pass into the white community to give their children a better future (Sweet 2005: 72).[4] Sometimes whole groups pass, as when, in a well-known anthropological case, the Shan and Kachin of Burma exchange their identities as whole villages, depending on the kind of work they need to do (Leach 1965).

So, the notion that ethnic groups are families is just a metaphor, and nothing more. Origin myths are only partial accounts of ancestry at best, different ethnic groups are deeply interrelated with one another, and individuals pass across group lines regularly. Still, the metaphor of the family functions effectively to bind people into large groups that not only defend and protect their members, but also provide them with a strong sense of identity and a common culture.

ETHNIC TRANSNATIONALISM

We live in a time when people are encountering one another around the world like never before. Even if they do not meet, the media is making people aware of each other across the globe. Americans without anthropology degrees know of the Pashtuns in Afghanistan, or the Maasai in Kenya, or the Quechua in Peru simply because they listen to the news. The more people come into contact, either directly or indirectly, the more they need to identify a group of their own and to distinguish the other groups in their

3. However, the stigma in Japan is so severe against Koreans that, despite the lack of physical or cultural markers, some Japanese people will hire genealogists to discover Korean ancestry before they will hire or marry someone.

4. See also Benita Porter's book, entitled *Colorstruck* (1991), which gives an account of the lives of people who are ethnically black but have "white" skin.

social arena. Thus, under globalization, the significance of ethnicity is very much on the rise.

To understand ethnicity now, we need to look back in history to the rise of nationalism. Nationalism was a political ideology birthed in the colonial era that promoted the idea that each "people" must be free to rule themselves. In the late nineteenth and early twentieth centuries, it was successful in bringing down the colonial empires by declaring foreign rule to be illegitimate. But, the link between the various peoples, or ethnic groups, and their supposed natural places, or homelands, was not so easy to establish. The European powers, in vigorous rivalry with one another, had carved out colonies by establishing political boundaries that cut apart members of the same ethnic groups and bundled together different ones. Thus, the newly independent countries contained multiple ethnic groups with various languages and cultures. Freedom movements from Kenya to India to Indonesia had to draw together diverse peoples by convincing them that they were one nation (the word means "ethnic group") with a common history, culture, and ancestry. In actual fact, the only thing that held together the citizens of the new countries was common territory. India, for instance, had never previously been one country, and its territorial boundaries were arbitrarily established at the time of independence. The identity "Indian" was constructed by amalgamating people who spoke fourteen different languages into a single category and contrasting them with the category, "British" (which is also an amalgam). Then, this new identity was attributed to all people of the subcontinent, and India was declared their natural homeland.

The impact of nationalism was to emphasize the association of ethnicity with a place of origin. Yet now, due to globalization, residence in a common place is precisely what is being lost as a basis for ethnic affiliation. People have always migrated. But, never in human history have the diasporas of ethnic groups been so numerous or so wide. People move to find jobs, to run from wars, to escape famine, to gain political freedom, or just to join kin who have moved before them. They do not, however, leave their ethnicities behind when they move. They continue to identify as Tibetans, though they have lived for generations in southern India; as Spanish though they have lived for several centuries in Mexico; and as South African though they now live in Australia. Anthropologists are studying this phenomenon, known as transnationalism, to discover how and why people retain their ethnic affiliations when they no longer live together in a common homeland.

When they get to new countries, immigrants and refugees typically take up residence with kin or ethnic mates in known localities. For instance, in the United States, Mexican immigrants move to Los Angeles or Chicago, but not usually to New York City. Immigrants from the Sudan, who are war refugees, have been placed by the US government in various locations across the country. But studies show that within a couple of years, most have migrated to cities such as New York, Detroit, and San Diego, where there are established Sudanese neighborhoods. Such neighborhoods have networks of reciprocal relationships that support newcomers while they are finding jobs, learning the language, and generally getting established, and they maintain strong ties with home countries.

Ties with home countries take the form of frequent travel back and forth, sending money home, and even significant involvement in the politics of home countries from abroad. Immigrants who have found jobs send large portions of their paychecks back to their countries of origin to support those they have left behind. These payments, known as remittances, sometimes amount to as much as 50 percent of the GDP of poor countries. Political involvement can take the form of local ethnic associations that lobby for the immigrant group in its new country, or international associations that influence elections in home countries by providing funding for campaigns. Thus, transnational ties are far from merely romantic remembrances of the home country. They are real economic, social, and political influences that help to make up our globalized world.

Not surprisingly, given our analysis thus far, ethnicity is actually *more* salient to people living in diaspora than it is to those at home. The tension immigrants feel with the local culture, and the treatment they receive as outsiders, intensifies their ethnic identification and loyalties. But remaining tied to people who live elsewhere is not easy. Living across political boundaries is particularly difficult, since there are restrictions to the flow of communication and travel. So, international leaders arise, brandishing symbols (markers) of ethnic identity, and campaigning for the causes of the group. A case in point is the Kurdish people. The Kurds live across the borders of Iraq, Iran, Turkey, and Syria—a historical result of the colonial powers having divided up their territory. *And* they live in London, New York, and Cairo! International Kurdish leaders campaign with governments to recognize their status as an ethnic group deserving of its own state under the principle of nationalism. The same is true for Tibetans, Armenians, and many other displaced peoples. Such campaigns function to retain and reinforce international ethnic solidarity, and to prevent assimilation to local cultures.

Also, in any local environment, ethnicity is characterized by "hierarchical nesting," that is, by locating itself in relatively smaller or larger concentric circles of identification (Peoples and Bailey 2006: 355). Since it is most relevant when interacting with others across a boundary, people select the level of ethnic identification they need to suit the circumstances. The anthropologist Victor Uchendu describes his own experience:

> A Nigerian student in London or New York is more likely to identify himself as an African . . . To a fellow Nigerian, he is most likely to identify himself with his state or region; if he is speaking to his co-ethnic, he is likely to name the provincial or administrative headquarters to which he belongs. Thus identity is likely to change as the frame of reference changes. (1975: 270–1)

We all have multiple identities which are variously relevant depending on the context in which we find ourselves. In fact, ethnic classification systems are always locally constructed and only locally relevant. In Mexico, there are three broad categories of ethnicity: Spanish, *Indio* (Indian), and *Mestizo* ("mixed"). But, when crossing the border into the United States, these distinctions evaporate; all Mexicans become "Hispanic" or "Latino," and they find themselves lumped together with immigrants from the entire of Central and South America. So, despite claims to be about race, essential characteristics, and common origins, ethnicity is really about groups that are distinguishing themselves from one another in local arenas. It is a means of creating "family" at the largest possible level in order to provide identity and group membership to people in very complex and sometimes difficult social and political environments.

ETHNICITY IN THE CHURCH

If ethnicity is family writ large, what is the proper relationship between ethnicity and the church? Churches are sometimes compared to families. But they are not really supposed to be kin-based institutions, however much kinship may enter by the back door! Just as churches must be open to members of different families, they must be open to members of different ethnicities. To see this, we will begin by investigating what sort of institution the church was originally meant to be.

According to the New Testament, the church is an *ecclesium*, or "assembly," a Greek term referring to a political meeting. Under the Romans, there were people of different ancestries, languages, and cultures living together in the cities and towns of the empire. Those who had the privileged status of being Roman citizens were "called out" (the literal meaning of *ecclesium*) to assemblies to make decisions on matters of common interest (Songer 1991). So, by referring to the churches as *ecclesia*, the New Testament writers were comparing them to multicultural legislative bodies. Unlike synagogues, which were exclusively Jewish institutions, churches consisted of people of different ethnicities held together by citizenship in a common kingdom, the kingdom of God.

The multi-cultural, multi-ethnic character of the early church was problematic right from the start. Jesus had been an itinerant Jewish rabbi, and his disciples naturally assumed that the purpose of his teachings was to reform Judaism (and perhaps to liberate them from the Romans). They did not anticipate non-Jewish, or Gentile, converts. This was in part because the Jewish community had misunderstood all along what it meant to be God's chosen people. They had thought that God's election gave them a privileged status, mainly requiring them to be segregated from the pagan peoples around them in order to maintain holiness. Actually, God had made it clear that his intention was to provide "a light to the nations" *through* Israel, inviting all peoples to be reconciled to him (Isa 49:6). But, the segregationist interpretation of God's election, along with the persecution they had endured, had caused the Jewish community to turn inward to try to protect their traditional religion. That is why the Jewish members of the early church simply assumed that their new movement would be for Jewish people alone.

As the New Testament records, however, there were non-Jewish people who were followers of Jesus, and Jesus' kind treatment of them surprised everyone, as for example with the Roman centurion (Matt 8) and the Samaritan woman (John 4). Furthermore, after Jesus' death and resurrection, the Holy Spirit began to bring Gentile converts into the church quite apart from any missionary attempts to reach them. God sent visions to Peter and to Cornelius, another Roman centurion, arranging a meeting between them at Cornelius's house. Peter, who had previously resisted associating with Gentiles, said to those assembled, "I truly understand that God shows no partiality, but in every nation anyone who fears him and does what is right is acceptable to him" (Acts 10:34–5). There followed an outpouring of the Holy Spirit on Cornelius, his family, and the other Gentiles who were there, confirming God's blessing on non-Jewish converts to Christianity and their full incorporation into the church.

This event, together with the Apostle Paul's successes as a missionary to other Gentile peoples, created a crisis! How were the Jewish disciples of Jesus to understand the centuries of God's work with Israel as a chosen people if now Gentiles could receive his Spirit? One solution was to admit the Gentile converts into Judaism by requiring them to follow the Jewish law, a practice that had prior precedent. Then all Christians would still be members of the Jewish faith, held together by the same norms, culture, and identity. One of the most important markers of Jewish identity was circumcision. So, in the church at Antioch, where there were a significant number of Gentile converts, the "Judaizers" began to campaign for Gentile church members to be circumcised. Others, however, protested that circumcision was not necessary, even a hindrance, to following Christ.

As a result of the dispute, Paul and Barnabas were sent to a council at Jerusalem where the matter could be decided by the church elders (Acts 15). There Peter got up and reminded everyone that God had given the Holy Spirit to Gentiles, such as Cornelius, despite the fact that they had not been circumcised. There should be "no distinction" made between Christians of Jewish and non-Jewish backgrounds. At the same meeting, Paul and Barnabas reported that God was doing miracles among the Gentiles, even though they were not following Jewish law. James, the brother of Jesus and leader of the church in Jerusalem, quoted the book of Amos to remind those present that God had always intended to save Gentiles too: "I will set up [the house of David] so that all other peoples may seek the Lord . . . even all the Gentiles over whom my name has been called" (Acts 15:16–17; Amos 9:11–12). In the end, the council agreed to forego the requirement for circumcision and a letter was sent to the church in Antioch that set a precedent for other churches as well. It was not necessary to become Jewish in order to join the *ecclesia*, the assembly, of Jesus Christ.

Paul continued to be concerned with relations between Jews and Gentiles throughout his ministry, along with relations across other sorts of boundaries, such as between women and men, and between slaves and masters. In his letters, he always encouraged church members to be one in Christ. But the erasure of the Jew-Gentile boundary needed special clarification. So, in the book of Romans, Paul developed a theological explanation for God's unexpected acceptance of Gentiles and seeming rejection of Jews (chapters 9–11). God had hardened Jewish hearts, he said, so that salvation would come to the Gentiles, bringing "riches for the world" (11:12). Gentiles were to be the beneficiaries of the "stumbling" of the Jews (11:11). Nevertheless, he warned, Gentiles should not become proud, imagining that God somehow favored them. They too could be rejected if they did not remain in God's grace (11:17–21). Therefore, in the church, everyone should remember that "there is no distinction between Jew and Greek [i.e. Gentile]; the same Lord is Lord of all and is generous to all who call on him" (10:12–13).

The book of Romans is addressed to "all God's beloved in Rome, who are called to be saints" (Rom 1:7). It is not addressed separately to Jews or to Gentiles. In fact, Paul consistently identified churches by place, not by ethnicity. He wrote to the churches of Galatia, of Ephesus, of Corinth, and of Philippi, not to the churches of the Greeks or the Romans or the Jews. That

was, of course, because most churches already contained members of different backgrounds. But Paul heavily reinforced the notion that the Christians
of a common place should be in fellowship with one another in a common
church. He insisted that conflicts (and there were plenty of them!) should
be handled by seeking reconciliation in a spirit of Christian love, not by
segregating out. In giving these admonishments to the churches, Paul was
directing early church members to something at the core of the Christian
faith. Jesus had said that his disciples would be recognized by their love for
one another (John 13:35). Later, the Apostle John wrote that love for God
was *not possible* without love for one another (1 John 4:20). Paul made it
clear that such love was foundational to the Christian church and one of the
miraculous results of Jesus' own sacrifice: "For he is our peace; in his flesh
he has made both groups [i.e. Jews and Gentiles] into one and has broken
down the dividing wall, that is, the hostility between us" (Eph 2:14).

ETHNICITY AND CHRISTIAN MISSION

The church in Antioch was one of the first places in which Jewish and
Gentile converts began to worship together. As we have seen, the Antioch
Christians had to work out a very important disagreement, while remaining united in Christ. Significantly, it was also in Antioch that the followers
of Jesus were first called "Christians" (Acts 11:26). A term was needed to
identify those who, regardless of ethnic and cultural affiliation, declared
their commitment to the simple creed, "Jesus is Lord" (1 Cor 12:3; Rom
10:9). And, it was the Antioch church that sent out Paul and Barnabas on
the very first missionary trip. Their common commitment to Christ powerfully motivated these new believers to invite others, of other places and
other backgrounds, to become Christians too.

In the two millennia since that time, missionaries have taken the gospel, or "good news," of Jesus to "the ends of the earth" (Rom 10:14–18).
People of every ethnicity have been invited into the assembly of the citizens
of Christ's kingdom. In the process, the church has learned much about the
nature of its own faith from the transmission of the message across cultural
boundaries. Perhaps the crossing of language barriers illustrates the point
best. Right from the start, beginning with the writing of the New Testament
in Greek rather than Hebrew, Christians have been willing to learn new
languages in order to preach the gospel and to translate the Bible into the
"heart" languages of new and potential believers. That willingness to use
the vernacular has affirmed the value of the multiplicity of human cultures,
and thereby of ethnic groups as well. It has also revealed the full depth of

the Scriptures by shedding light on the text from different angles. Far from being diminished by the differences between cultures, the Christian faith has been dramatically enhanced by them (Walls 2002: 67).

In fact, we can say that Christianity "incarnates" itself into new cultures. As Jesus took on flesh and became a human being in a particular time and place, so the gospel too takes on flesh, so to speak, in cultures. It is conveyed in the language and practices of the particular people to whom it goes. After his resurrection, Jesus said to his disciples, "As the father has sent me, so I send you" (John 20:21). Thus, in imitation of Jesus, who left heaven behind for our sake and became human, missionaries have been willing to leave their homes and go to people in other places, to learn their languages and enter into their cultures, in order to invite them to faith in Christ. The result is a global church containing people of nearly every background who are united by their common membership in the kingdom of which Jesus is the Lord.

Christianity, then, strongly affirms the value of all languages, cultures, and ethnic groups. However, that does not mean that the church should be captive to these things. It is possible for local churches to become syncretized to local cultures in such a way as to betray the gospel. This danger is particularly acute when local churches are cut off from the global church that might remind them of those points at which they must diverge from their cultures as Christians. Gradually, local values and customs become overly central to church life and practice, and Christian identity starts to be conflated with ethnic identity. Commitment to Jesus gives way to commitment to culture-based traditions, such as forms of worship, and to ethnic pride. Then, inevitably, exclusion of people from other backgrounds follows, as members are more concerned with maintaining "their" church's traditions than they are in changing and growing in response to the movements of the Holy Spirit.

As an example, the oldest church in India, which was founded by the Apostle Thomas in the first century, has been engaged in a long struggle against the pervasive influence of the Hindu caste system. Thomas arrived on the southwest coast by merchant ship in the year 52 AD, and spent the next twenty years evangelizing the areas now known as Kerala and Tamil Nadu. He founded seven churches before being martyred by a Hindu king. In subsequent years, a strong community of "St. Thomas Christians" arose that maintained its commitment to Jesus as Lord in a hostile environment. Over the next few centuries, however, the connection with other Christians was somewhat sporadic, and persecution by Hindus forced Christians to become a quasi-caste within Hindu society. Then, in the colonial era, very unfortunately, Portuguese Roman Catholics persecuted the St. Thomas

Christians for their failure to acknowledge the pope. So, with its very survival at stake for so many centuries, and its relative isolation from the rest of
the body of Christ, the Kerala church grew increasingly dependent upon its
cultural identity, rigidly maintaining ancient liturgical services in Aramaic,
while uncritically adopting Hindu caste values. By the nineteenth century,
local congregations were fully segregated by the caste backgrounds of their
members, and the Kerala Christians practiced some of the worst treatment
of "untouchables" in the country. Isolation from the larger church brought
syncretism, and syncretism brought the sin of segregation.

Thankfully, this is not the end of the story for the St. Thomas Christians, nor is it for any other church. In the nineteenth century, due partly
to contact with the Anglican Church and partly to a decision to conduct
liturgies in the contemporary local language, a revival movement began that
resulted in renewed missionary activity and positive engagement with the
rest of the global church (including participation in the World Council of
Churches). Isolation and segregation had paralyzed the church for many
centuries. But contact with Christians from elsewhere brought renewed
fervor of faith and a willingness to cross local boundaries in evangelistic
outreach.

Under colonialism, churches were established in nearly every part of
the globe. Religious revivals in Europe and the United States, along with
increased ease of travel, resulted in a massive movement of missionaries to
the rest of the world. Tragically, however, the expansion of the church under colonialism was accompanied by a damaging racism that derived from
the work of scientists producing theories the colonial powers could use to
justify the oppression and enslavement of non-European peoples. The cultural climate of the time, rooted partly in military might and partly in a
dominating ethnocentrism, made the superiority of the white "race" seem
incontestable. Many Western Christians were swept up in the notion that
colonialism was part of God's plan for the redemption of the whole world
through "Christianity, commerce, and civilization."[5] While most missionaries did not accept the notion of inferior races, too many of them bought into
the supposed superiority of their own cultural backgrounds and developed
ethnocentrism against the people they had come to serve. Local Christians
were made to feel inferior in their churches at the same time that they were
alienated from their cultures by their conversions.

Of course, this was not equally true of everyone. There were missionaries who challenged inequality, and there were converts who took up

5. This was a well-known phrase at the time, popularized by the missionary and
explorer David Livingston, who actually used it to *fight* the slave trade.

positions of leadership despite the hindrances.[6] Furthermore, on the whole, missionary prejudice paled in comparison with that of European merchants and some administrators who did not have Christian values to put a check on their beliefs and behaviors. Yet, with a faith that from the beginning had welcomed people of all backgrounds, and that had always put special emphasis on God's particular care for the poor and oppressed, many Western missionaries accommodated the injustices of the colonial system much too easily.

In South Africa, syncretism with colonialism and with racism produced an utterly segregated church. Dutch and English settlers, who were bitter enemies during the Boer Wars, nonetheless identified with one another as "whites" in contrast to "blacks" (a term that lumped together Zulu, Xhosa, Bapedi, and many other groups), "Indians" (indentured laborers who had migrated to South Africa), and "coloureds" (people considered to be mixed). In order to retain their power over a country in which they were vastly outnumbered, the whites constructed an elaborate system of discrimination and exclusion that they termed Apartheid ("separateness"). Christians were forced to segregate under laws that banned intermarriage, common residence, and even integrated meetings.[7] The Dutch Reformed Church, along with many other white Christians, supported the project. In one well-known incident, Mohandas (Mahatma) Gandhi, the Indian nationalist leader, was turned away from a white church when he tried to attend a Sunday morning service. Commitment to the protection of whites had become more important than commitment to Christ and his worldwide church, and the result was the rejection of nonwhite people literally at the church doors.

Still, the church is never just its failures. Even when some of its members have compromised with evil, there have always been others who have remembered their allegiance to the gospel and stood firm. As we will see in coming chapters, it was evangelical Christians in England who began and promoted the modern anti-slavery movement. It was Catholic missionaries to Latin America who challenged the brutal treatment of Indians. And, it was missionaries to Africa and elsewhere who, by their translation of the Bible into vernacular languages, affirmed the value of local cultures in such

6. As examples, missionaries who resisted the colonial model of missions included Amy Carmichael in India, Roland Allen in China, and Bartholome de las Casas in Latin America. Local converts who picked up leadership include Sadhu Sundar Singh in India, and Samuel Adjai Crowther in Africa.

7. In the 1960s, as a protest against this arrangement, the evangelist Billy Graham, himself raised in the segregated American south, refused to hold his crusades in South Africa when he was denied the right to integrate the seating in stadiums.

a way as to fuel the rising nationalisms that ultimately brought down the colonial empires (Sanneh 1993).

The church, as a human entity, may become bound up in the sins and prejudices of the time, but the Holy Spirit never makes the same compromise. Outpourings of the Spirit have preserved the church's integrity and its faithfulness to Christ throughout the centuries of its existence. For example, in the 1930s there was an outpouring of the Holy Spirit in East Africa (Mac-Master 2006). It began when two Christians, one African and one European, met in Rwanda to pray for the vitality of the African church. African Christians were deeply divided by tribalism and mired in nominalism (a superficial Christianity). White Christians were holding on tightly to the reins of power in the church and segregating themselves off from their nonwhite sisters and brothers. During a retreat, Simeon Nsibambi and Joseph Church spent two days together in prayer, Scripture reading, and confession of sin. The renewal they received from the Holy Spirit in that meeting accompanied them back to their home congregations and then spread as a revival throughout Rwanda, Uganda, Kenya, Tanzania, and elsewhere. The revival was centered on the understanding that Jesus' sacrificial death (which is particularly poignant in pastoral societies) had made reconciliation between people of different tribes and ethnicities possible. As one of the first African bishops later put it, "It was sin which kept us concerned only with our own earthly families, our ethnic villages. The Holy Spirit showed us that Jesus' sacrifice made it possible for all of us to be brothers and sisters in the same village" (Kisare 1984: 81). African Christians who were reconciled to one another were then able to challenge white Christians for their own form of tribalism, and for their failure to live by the true gospel of full reconciliation with God and with one another.

THE AMERICAN CHURCH

The United States has a long history of racism, and that history has affected the American church. The story is as complex as it was for colonialism. Under slavery, and later under segregation, the church accommodated racism all too easily and too many Christians either vigorously defended or passively accepted the social, political, and economic status quo. Yet, beginning with the Quakers of Pennsylvania, an anti-slavery movement was born that was based firmly in Christian theology and principles. The Quakers chided the American church for allowing people to own slaves who, they said, were also made in God's image. Later, it was a Christian pastor, the Rev. Dr. Martin Luther King, Jr., who led the civil rights movement. Dr. King consistently quoted the Bible in his speeches and sermons—passages such as "let justice roll down like waters and righteousness like a mighty stream" (Amos 5:24)—and he thereby held a supposedly Christian nation to its own stated values. Still, now more than half a century later, despite the increasing integration of American society in public arenas, most churches remain segregated by ethnicity. The American workplace, after decades of affirmative action and other anti-discrimination legislation, is relatively integrated. Even the schools in America are better integrated than the churches. But, as Dr. King reminded us, 11 AM Sunday morning is the most segregated hour of the week (King 2010: 105).

Most American Christians believe that the segregation that exists in their churches is incidental to natural preferences for language, music, culture, and worship styles. This belief is not entirely false, but it is far from the full truth. People do choose to attend churches that have worship styles with which they are familiar. But, it is also true that differences in worship style emerge from the fact of segregation. Since culture always changes, those who associate with one another will develop their own styles in time. Where there is a failure to associate, the styles will diverge. So, differences in worship style are as much a *result* of segregation as a cause of it.

American Christians also think that churches are naturally segregated by the fact that they are located in different neighborhoods with different ethnic compositions. But this circumstance is no accident either. As the public arena has been forced to integrate due to legislation, many Americans have chosen to maintain segregation by moving to neighborhoods of their own ethnicity. Above all, they have been reluctant to intermarry. So while integration is the reigning value of the public world of work and marketplace in America, segregation remains the reigning value of the private world of family, home, and religion.

In point of fact, racism is far from dead in American culture. It has been delegitimized on the surface by the anti-slavery and civil rights movements, but it continues to exert influence on social relations beneath the surface. The degree of influence ranges from mild prejudice and stereotyping to hate groups, but its effects can be felt to some degree in nearly every interaction. Studies show that discrimination based on race continues to happen covertly in housing and employment, and that there is unfair treatment of minority groups by the police and the legal system. As a result, racial tensions still erupt in rioting in American cities on a regular basis.

There are legitimate reasons for Christians to meet separately by ethnicity. Perhaps the best of these is the need to speak the same language. Immigrant churches commonly use the languages of their home countries in their services. This is not only a matter of being able to communicate with one another. It is also that a person's mother tongue is a "heart" language that has the power to penetrate people's lives in a way that a second language can never do. Also, sharing the intimacies of a life walk with Christ with others whose walks are similar is a powerful experience, making people feel heard and loved and encouraging them to grow and develop as Christians. This is why self-help groups bring together people with the same problems, and small groups in churches commonly segregate by sex.

Yet, even in these special cases, segregation is not without negative consequences for the church. Immigrant churches can remain mired in traditional ways, and have difficulty with their own second- and third-generation members who are being assimilated into the larger culture. English speaking churches can imagine themselves superior due to their association with the dominant group in society, and they can lose the benefit of the testimony offered by Christians from other cultural backgrounds. Overall, there are many benefits to be had, and dangers to be avoided, by actively working to dismantle the barriers between Christians of different backgrounds and finding ways and means for them to share Christ's love with one another (John 13:35).

How can we insure that the body of Christ remains integrated—a term which means both *connected* and *whole*? Since communicating and relating across cultural boundaries is more difficult than within them, we must make intentional efforts to break down the walls that divide us. Local churches must go beyond merely welcoming other people on Sunday mornings. They must prepare to accommodate newcomers with flexibility in worship styles, languages, and shared leadership. This idea runs counter to much that has been taught in the area of church growth. In the interest of making local churches attractive to the people in their neighborhoods, pastors have been encouraged by the "experts" to appeal to very carefully identified segments of the population. Outreach has been viewed as a marketing campaign, "targeting" a specific population that is defined not only in terms of ethnicity, but also of class and of lifestyle. The suggestion is that people will join churches more freely if they are made more "comfortable" by only having to associate with others like themselves.

Undoubtedly this is true. People certainly are more comfortable with others like themselves. But the argument belies the tension between appealing to people in their own terms and remaining faithful to God's prophetic message to the world. We are called not only to be warm and inviting to those who do not know Christ, but also to challenge the evil that binds them. Christian love does not tolerate sin, in ourselves, in others, or in the society at large. Minimally, then, in accordance with the Holy Spirit's command to "show no partiality" (Acts 10:34), our church doors must always be open to people *unlike* ourselves. Maximally, we should be working hard to change both the structure and the ethos of our churches and our society to incorporate and empower people of different cultures and ethnicities. There are churches in America that have done this. Interestingly, it is in these churches that Jesus, rather than the culture, becomes most central (DeYoung 2003).

Finally, whether single- or multicultural, all local churches must remain in close contact with the global church. Among other things, this means being willing to accept the critique of the larger body of Christ. The integrity of our own faith journey depends upon it. This is all the more important for the American church because of its location in a wealthy and powerful country. It is tempting for American Christians to think only of the material aid they can give to churches in Africa, Asia and Latin America, and it is equally tempting for Christians from those places to refrain from speaking up when American Christians are syncretizing with sinful aspects of their own culture and thereby being disobedient to God. But only the global church has the *full* truth of the gospel. Thus all local churches must be willing to listen to the global church in order to hear "what the Spirit is saying to the churches" (Rev 2:11).

The Apostle John was given a vision of our common future:

> After this I looked, and there was a great multitude that no one could count, from every nation, from all tribes and peoples and languages, standing before the throne and before the Lamb, robed in white, with palm branches in their hands. They cried out in a loud voice, saying, "Salvation belongs to our God who is seated on the throne, and to the Lamb!" (Rev 7:9–10)

In the kingdom of Heaven, the "nations" (ethnic groups) of the world will all be represented, and they will stand together in the presence of Father, Son, and Holy Spirit. Then, out of pure gratitude for the salvation that God has given, they will worship him in unity (represented here as a common voice). It is that unity that we must try to approximate here on earth now.

(CHAPTER 4) DISCUSSION QUESTIONS

1. How is the myth of race perpetuated in American society? What are the full implications of Christians believing that they belong to different races?

2. In what sense is the church a "family," and in what sense does it transcend biological family principles?

3. What role does ethnicity play in our lives as human beings? How can and should ethnicity be incorporated into churches?

4. Develop various models for single- and multicultural churches, taking care to allow for both the need to associate with others whose life experiences are similar to our own and the importance of crossing cultural boundaries to create unity in Christ.

5. In what practical ways does the global church impact the local church that you attend? How does your church contribute to the global church, and how does it *listen* to what the global church has to say?

RECOMMENDED READINGS

Gould, Stephen Jay. 1996. *The Mismeasure of Man.* New York: W. W. Norton.

Priest, Robert J., and Alvaro Nieves. 2007. *This Side of Heaven: Race, Ethnicity and Christian Faith.* Oxford: Oxford University Press.

Sharp, Douglas R. 2002. *No Partiality: The Idolatry of Race and the New Humanity.* Downers Grove, IL: InterVarsity.

Unander, Dave. 2000. *Shattering the Myth of Race.* Valley Forge, PA: Judson.

Volf, Miroslav. 1996. *Exclusion and Embrace: A Theological Exploration of Identity, Otherness, and Reconciliation.* Nashville, TN: Abingdon.

Chapter 5

What About Relationships?
Social Order and Social Change

The American talk show host stood facing his panel of respondents on the stage, all married people who had committed adultery. The audience was hostile. One audience member after another bombarded the panel with accusatory comments and questions regarding their unfaithfulness. No mercy was being shown. Finally, an audience member screamed at a panel member who had been unfaithful to his wife, "Why didn't you just divorce her? Then you could have been with the other woman without committing adultery!"

Apparently, Americans think that divorce is better than adultery; that is, leaving your husband or wife is more acceptable than being unfaithful to them.[1] This is clearly reflected in the increased rate of divorce, compared to previous times. Divorces have become both easier to get, legally, and easier to justify, socially, leading people to experience divorce as always on the horizon to solve the problems of marriage. African Christians have complained of this view in Western culture since the nineteenth century. When missionaries discovered polygamy in Africa, they required new converts to abandon all but one wife despite the fact that many of the rejected wives were forced into prostitution to support themselves and their chil-

---

1. I am grateful to Jenell Paris for reading and commenting on this chapter. Her contribution as a Christian anthropologist to the difficult debates over gender roles and sexual identity in the church has been very valuable. She is not, of course, responsible for the opinions that I have expressed here.

dren. Divorce was better than multiple partners, in these missionaries' view. The missionaries were not acting on a biblical norm (the matter is not clear in the Bible, as we will see below); rather they were acting on the strong ideal for monogamy that came from their Western backgrounds. At that time, the West preferred strict monogamy, the marriage of one man and one woman "till death do you part." Since then, it has adopted serial monogamy, allowing multiple spouses, but only one at a time. So divorce (which may, in fact, sometimes be necessary) has become better than adultery, regardless of the consequences to abandoned spouses and children.

Of course, as Christians, we do not condone either adultery or divorce. Both are wrong in the eyes of God. But then so are many other things that we tolerate more easily, such as domestic abuse, social stigmatization, racism, and segregation. We know that all of these things are wrong, but we become much more outraged at some sins than others. This is because, as members of cultures, we have been trained to think in terms not only of God's laws but of society's norms and taboos. Sometimes society's norms are in accordance with God's intent for our social life, but sometimes they are not. Sometimes they can persuade us to commit evil acts against others in misguided attempts to defend morality, and sometimes they can convince us to look away while injustice is committed by those charged with maintaining the status quo.

In this chapter, we will investigate the nature of human societies both from an anthropological perspective and from a Christian one. Anthropologists view social structures as humanly constructed systems. They study them scientifically in order to understand the various ways in which social systems provide for peoples' needs and help them to adapt to their environments. But as Christians we know that our social relations have a higher purpose than just adapting to this life. We are made not just to survive in the environment, but to flourish in relationships with God and one another, in this life and in the next.

THE FAMILY IN CHRISTIAN PERSPECTIVE

Human beings are the most social creature on earth. Not only do we construct the most elaborate societies, but we establish and maintain the most complex interpersonal ties. Even our physical make-up reflects our social nature, as can be seen in the fact that there are more muscles in our cheeks for facial expressions than for chewing! Compared to other animals, human beings are very ill equipped to survive in the environment on their own and must develop means of cooperating with one another to do so. We work together to forage, or herd, or plant, and to meet one another's daily needs for food, shelter, and protection. Our personal development also requires the input of others, as we construct a sense of identity and meaningfulness. At every level, our social systems are utterly necessary to our lives.

The most fundamental unit of any human society is the family. Families come in a variety of types, but their purpose is essentially the same in all types: to be a total social institution. Total institutions provide for all of their members' needs. They are not specialized in particular functions in the way that other institutions are. Especially in pre-modern societies, families are the subsistence unit, making a living in the environment; the financial unit, holding wealth in common; the political unit, allocating power and authority; the legal unit, resolving conflicts; the educational unit, raising up and training children; the socio-emotional unit, expressing sexuality and love; and even the religious unit, conducting rites of passages and worship. As a total institution, the family is responsible for all the needs of its members, and as the most fundamental unit, it is the building block for the whole of society.

As societies grow larger and more complex, however, specialized institutions begin to take over the functions that families used to have. In modern societies, most people earn their subsistence by selling their labor for wages at a workplace away from home; are under the authority of the government, laws, and police; take their conflicts to a public court system; send their children to schools to be educated; and join formal religious institutions. The only functions that are left for the family are the satisfaction of sexual and emotional needs, the nurturance of children, and vestiges of economic ties such as forming a common household and holding a common bank account. In our own society, even these things are being eroded by economic mobility and the high divorce rate. Young children are placed into daycare centers, and married couples may have separate bank accounts or sign prenuptial financial agreements. There is a direct trade-off between reliance on complex social institutions and reliance on the family, and in modern societies the family has lost almost all of its functions, causing American families to be fragmented down to the sub-nuclear level.

As Christians, we believe that the family is part of God's design for our lives. As we saw in chapter two, it is God's intent that we live together in *shalom*, that is, in healthy, peaceful, and fruitful relationships with one another. Family is the first institution in which we are called to do this, and the one that often becomes the model for larger institutions. In Genesis chapter two, the very first family was created by God to prevent aloneness. God saw that the animals did not provide Adam with a true companion; in fact, even God's own company did not prevent Adam from feeling alone.

So God made Eve to be a partner to Adam, and eventually to have children with him. Thus God's original intent for the family was that it be a place of healthy relationships, meeting the needs of all members to live in love and fellowship with one another.

But, in Genesis chapter three, Adam and Eve disobeyed God's commandment and fell into sinful rebellion against him, losing their home in the garden and alienating themselves from God's immediate presence. Then, in Genesis chapter four, the first family paid a very high price for their fall into sin when their oldest child, Cain, killed his younger brother, Abel, out of jealousy for God's favor. There is no doubt that God intends us to live in families and that our families are supposed to provide for our deepest needs, especially the need for companionship. But equally, there is no doubt that, in point of fact, the very worst evils that human beings commit they commit also in their families. Real families, as opposed to ideal ones, provide us with the greatest joys and the deepest pains, the richest nurturance and the most abysmal neglect, the profoundest good and the most horrific evil.

This should not be surprising to us. As our primary social institution, the family reflects the full complexity of who we are as people. We are created in God's image and for his purposes, but we are also distorted by sinfulness. And that means that all of our social institutions, including families, are distorted by the same sinfulness. Thus, the solution to the problem of the erosion of family life in modern societies is not to create a false idolatry of the family, or to imagine that by defending "family values" we will preserve our children from all harm. Most of the harm that comes to children comes to them, either directly or indirectly, from the behavior of their parents! A deeper solution is needed to address not only the assault on the family from the outside, but the corruption of the family from the inside.[2]

We Christians believe that the only solution to our interpersonal problems capable of fully restoring us to God's original intent of *shalom* is the redemption that is available through Jesus' death and resurrection. Our broken and sinful state is not the end of the story. God's redemption brings

---

2. Christian psychologist Mary Stewart Van Leeuwen has said about families that, "When they are good, they are very, very good, and when they are bad, they are awful" (personal communication). Jesus' seemingly anti-family statements can be understood against this backdrop. Jesus declared that because of him, the family would be divided, "father against son and son against father, mother against daughter and daughter against mother" (Luke 12:53). He also said that, "Whoever comes to me and does not hate father and mother, wife and children, brothers and sisters, yes, and even life itself, cannot be my disciples" (Luke 14:26). Of course, Jesus' primary point is that we must forsake all else to follow him. But his inclusion of the most basic and important loyalties in society makes it clear that we are not to idealize, or worship, any human institution. All of them, like all people, "fall short of the glory of God" (Rom 3:23).

renewal not only to our personal spiritual lives, but also to our relationships with one another. Thus, our families can be redeemed when we dedicate them to Christ, to growth in Christian discipleship, and to the guidance of the Holy Spirit. By living out our redemption in our social as well as our personal lives, we can build our families up from the inside out, and that will give them the moral strength to resist society's pressures to trivialize and divide them. Then, just as we work as Christians for the redemption of individuals, we can and should work for the redemption of families, and of the larger social institutions of which we are a part, always remembering our own fallenness and need for God's redeeming grace.

It is important to remember, too, that God's redemption comes to us in the larger context of a war "in the heavenly places" (Eph 6:10–20). The real enemy of the family is not the social pressures that impinge upon it from the outside, or even the failings of family members on the inside, but the pernicious influence of the prince of darkness, who wishes our destruction. Put another way, the Christian perspective on the family is not that families are safe havens of goodness in an evil world. Rather, it is that they are a *battleground* between good and evil through which God can redeem people from their failings and build them up to become what he intended. A "good" family, then, is not one without problems or difficulties, but one in which transparency and love provide opportunity for God to "restore, support, strengthen, and establish" its members (1 Pet 5:10)—and one which welcomes outsiders into a community of God's transforming grace. In the final analysis, God's intent is that the family be part of his work of redemption in the world.

VARIETIES OF FAMILIES

Though the purpose of the family is the same in all cultures, the structure of the family is not the same. There are some commonalities. Families everywhere are created by marriages, and all societies expect married people to have children. So the relationships of husband-wife and parent-child are universal. But many societies permit the marriage of a man to more than one wife (polygyny), and a few permit the marriage of a woman to more than one husband (polyandry). These societies create additional relationships of co-wives, or co-husbands, and of half siblings.

Polygyny was a legitimate form of marriage in the Old Testament. Jacob, for instance, had two wives, Leah and Rachel, along with concubines. Kings David and Solomon both had numerous wives as part of a strategy of creating political alliances through marrying the daughters of neighboring kings. Polygyny was simply assumed to be normal, as it is even today in most tribal societies. In fact, Jewish law prescribed that a man be willing to take his deceased brother's widow as a wife, whether or not he was already married. The purpose was to support the widow and to have children for the dead man's lineage (Deut 25:5–10). Because the widow's children would compete with the first wife's children for the inheritance, living brothers sometimes tried to avoid this duty. But the right of the widow to be married to her husband's brother was defended in the Bible in the stories of Judah and his son Onan, both of whom tried to avoid their duties and were punished by God for it (Gen 38).

By New Testament times, monogamy had become the norm, largely because of the shift from tribal to agricultural and urban life. In tribal societies, men have more than one wife in order to become wealthy and have a lot of children. Polygyny makes them important in the ranked world of men. In agricultural and urban societies, the need for multiple wives fades as men gain importance from other social institutions than the family, and as widows can be cared for by their own families in a more settled context. But even in the New Testament, the only instruction regarding forms of marriage is Paul's suggestion that church leaders should be "the husband of one wife" (1 Tim 3:2; Titus 1:6)—a comment that may actually be about divorce, not polygyny! So the Bible does not clearly mandate a single form of marriage (though the example of Adam and Eve might be construed as an implicit preference for monogamy).

The varieties of the family can be seen even more clearly when looking at household construction. The West has idealized the nuclear family living in its own household. This is not because of any Christian ideal; nuclear family households were not the norm even in the New Testament. Rather, it is because of the need for job mobility in an industrialized society. In modern economies, grown children must be willing to move away from parents and grandparents in order to find work in a complex labor market, so households are reduced to just parents and children.

In farming, horticultural, and pastoral societies, subsistence work requires the cooperation of three or more generations of people. So in those societies there are "joint" households that include grandparents and grandchildren, aunts/uncles and nieces/nephews, grown sisters and brothers, cousins, and many in-laws. So strong is this larger family unit that commonly marriage relationships are given second priority to adult parent-child relationships. Local proverbs remind people of their duty to parents in old age, and warn of the danger of loyalty to spouses that might interfere with that duty. In fact, excessive commitment to one's own spouse or children may be seen as traitorous to the extended family. This is because joint families hold property in common, including herds or agricultural land, and the nuclear families within them can force the larger family to divide the property, making everyone poorer.

Which form of the household is best, nuclear or joint? Obviously there are benefits and detriments to both forms. Anthropologists sometimes refer to nuclear households as "understaffed" (Douglass 1984: 112). There are not enough adults to comfortably raise the children and get the housework done. Furthermore, the elderly may find themselves neglected, and even disrespected, as they no longer live in the home with their children and grandchildren. But joint families have difficulties too. In traditional cultures, commitment to parents, or filial piety, can be so strong that it completely circumscribes the lives of family members, leaving them unable to make choices or to respond effectively to their own spouses and children. It can even turn into ancestor worship, as the value on older generations continues on past their deaths.

There are numerous Bible passages that address the matter of excessive filial piety. Of course, one of the Ten Commandments is to "honor your father and your mother" (Exod 20:12). Yet God called Abraham to leave "his father's house" as a demonstration of his faith and willingness to put God first (Gen 12:1). Genesis 2:24 declares that in marriage, "a man leaves his father and his mother and clings to his wife," a passage that Jesus later quoted to the Pharisees as a reason not to divorce (Matt 19:5). And Paul's instructions to married couples in the New Testament presume the primacy of the marriage relationship within the family (Eph 5:21–33; Col 3:18–21). In the West, these prescriptions seem unremarkable. But in traditional societies they contain a radical element, challenging the strength of parent's authority over the family after the children are adults.

Still, nowhere does the Bible *prescribe* nuclear family households, and the benefits of joint family living can be significant. Adult women and men work together; children are cared for by multiple caretakers; and personal identity is enriched by membership in a community of people who support one another. Of course there are quarrels, but that is true of any type of family. The larger size of the joint family reduces the possibility of quarrels becoming violent, as there are always people around to step in and restrain the quarrelers. The smaller size of the nuclear family creates heavier workloads and produces high intensity relationships that can become abusive. This intensity may then cause the family to fracture into even smaller, sub-nuclear households. So while the joint family runs the risk of being too strong, the nuclear family runs the risk of being too weak.

In general, the form of the family in a culture is closely linked to the culture's economic base. Where subsistence requires the cooperation of multiple adults, joint families will form to do the work. Where mobility is needed to find subsistence, the family will split up into smaller units. Thus in the simplest societies, those that practice foraging, and the most complex societies, those that are industrialized, families tend to be small. But in the most sedentary societies, those practicing agriculture, families tend to be large, sometimes extending to four or five generations living under the same roof.

Within the household, the structure of the family is maintained by adherence to a set of social roles, that is, to society's definition of the proper behavior of one person toward another. For instance, the simple nuclear structure is built on culturally defined expectations for husband-wife relations and parent-child relations. Minimally, wives and husbands should work cooperatively for the family, and parents should rear the children. Maximally, there may be a lot of specifics for good behavior in roles, such as the expectation among the Roma (Gypsies) that wives should earn the family's primary income, or the expectation among the lowlanders of New Guinea (and among traditional Europeans) that parents should frighten their children into obedience. In joint families, there are specifics for additional roles to be prescribed, such as the expectation in Japan that children should be raised by their paternal grandmother, or in India that daughters-in-law should be subordinated to their mothers-in-law. Where co-wives are involved, there is commonly an assignment of authority to the first wife over the others, and where co-husbands are involved, the first husband may be declared the "father" of all of the children.

Many of these prescriptions have practical reasons. In agricultural Japan, grandmothers raise children because both parents are working in the rice fields during the day. In lowland New Guinea, children are frightened into obedience to protect them from the dangers of living in homes that extend out over coastal seawaters. But the prescriptions also come from larger level conceptions of the purpose of social life. Roles connect people's actions to a system of morality that is embedded in religious conceptions of the nature of the universe and the proper place of human beings in it. So, ultimately, people's behavior is evaluated in terms of their culture's beliefs about who they are and what their destiny is. These beliefs are linked to daily practices emerging from specific circumstances in specific contexts. As one anthropologist has put it, morality emerges from a particular conception of life as it is, and as it is supposed to be, and then confirms that conception by enacting it (Geertz 1973: 123).

Society depends upon the cooperation of the majority of its people. Not only must they follow the social prescriptions for proper behavior, but, to a greater or lesser degree, they must also embrace the culture's conceptions of morality in order to be motivated to cooperate. And in every society, the moral behavior of family members is considered supremely important to the total social welfare. In fact, the family as an institution may function as a model for institutions in other arenas, such as business or politics (Ong 1999).[3] Thus, it is not surprising that, even in the West where the family is relatively weak and unimportant, most people attempt to strongly defend the value of the family. A threat to family structure is a threat to the social system as a whole.

THREATS TO THE FAMILY

There are various reasons why the family may come under threat as a social institution. First, there are threats to its unity that are the result of tensions inherent in the family structure. All families have quarrels, some of which are merely due to the conflicting personalities of individuals. But some quarrels are due to naturally conflicting interests in the arrangement of roles. For instance, often the mother-in-law to son-in-law relationship has a tension in it that emerges from a competition for the loyalty of the daughter/wife that they share. In societies with age-based ranking there is a natural tension in the relationship between a woman and her husband's elder brother (who is an authority), but none in her relationship with her husband's younger brother (who is like a son). Often, people blame the individuals involved when conflict erupts. But an anthropological perspective reveals that it is the family structure that is creating the problem, making the tensions inevitable. In such cases, there may be cultural prescriptions for roles, such as avoiding or joking, that help to ease tensions. The "proper" thing for a son-in-law to do in many cultures is simply to avoid his mother-in-law, even leaving the room when she comes in. Prescriptions for how to handle structural tensions help to maintain the peace.

Secondly, however, some threats to family unity are neither the result of personal differences nor of natural tensions in the structure. They are the result of social change, or even of societal breakdown. The high divorce rate in the United States is partly due to two types of change: 1) economic mobility, encouraging both men and women to put careers first and to pursue them separately if necessary, and 2) new social roles, creating tension over

3. Ong suggests that capitalist business is done differently in Asia than in the West because of a model of the family that stresses the subordination of women to men, the sacrifice of individual desires to family welfare, and the power and benevolence of the patriarch, the "mandarin." The family in Asia, she says, is an institution for upward mobility, and business is conducted by means of these family principles.

who is going to do the work in the home (housekeeping, childcare, meeting emotional needs, etc.). These changes are rooted in a deep shift in the American conception of the purpose of life, from valuing sacrifices made for family to valuing individual self-fulfillment.[4] This shift makes family life a matter of personal convenience, rather than calling and commitment, and results in children being shifted around between divorced parents who are pursuing their own dreams first. Thus, the most serious threat to family life in America is simply the high value on self-fulfillment and individualism.

Recently in American culture, the most controversial social change has been the legitimization of new forms of the family, especially the same-sex family. Christians are in legitimate disagreement over this phenomenon, and to some extent only time will tell the full effects of the new arrangements. But, for now, I will present here a case against this legitimization based on the argument that same-sex desire (along with a lot of other forms of sexual desire) is not God's intent, nor a "normal" circumstance (the word means both the usual case and what should be the case) for human sexuality.

We have already seen that there is diversity in the forms of the family found around the world. That diversity is not, however, unlimited. In all societies, families have complementary gender-based roles, restrictions on sexual activity, and provision for children. Occasionally, traditional societies will permit unusual arrangements, such as the transgender and same-sex households of the *hijra* of India, or the *berdache* of plains Native American societies (Lang 1998: 353). But even in these cases, transgender and same-sex households are an exception to the rule of families built on male-female relations.

In traditional societies the family is a total institution through which all of society's functions are mediated. Thus, society as a whole is built on opposite-sex relations and on the importance of having children. In modern societies, however, the family is only one institution among many that provide for people's needs. As a result, the family has become increasingly less necessary for society's various functions, and is left resting on the thin and insecure basis of emotional attachment. Americans, for instance, believe they should marry entirely for love, choose freely whether to have children or not, and be able to leave their families if they are not happy. So the promotion of alternative, highly choice driven, forms of the family is emerging in a context in which the family as an institution has become *optional* (Paris 2011: 42). It is not only the same-sex community that dissociates sex

4. In fact, work itself has shifted from being a sacrifice for family to being an opportunity for self-fulfillment. This is most true of middle-class families in the service industries. Working class families, who have jobs that are far from self-fulfilling, still view work primarily as necessary to feed the family.

from having children, or promotes individualistic choices in marriage—the whole of American culture is doing that. In contradiction with our own deepest human needs, we are valuing personal freedom over social responsibility in relationships.

This circumstance is a dramatic swing of the pendulum from a former time in which personal freedom and choice, especially in the area of sexuality, was subordinated to strong cultural norms about correct moral behavior. Unfortunately, American society then was more than a little severe in its treatment of deviance from the norm. Jokes, scorn, ostracism, beatings, and even murder were our society's punishments for same-sex behavior. All societies identify normalcy and deviance, rewarding the former and punishing the latter. But they vary as to how much deviance they will tolerate, and how severely they will punish it. For instance, women caught in adultery have been killed by stoning in Afghanistan, while they are only mildly chided for it on the island of Dobu (in Melanesia). Children who disrespect their parents are severely shamed in East Asia, while they are largely tolerated or ignored in the West. Men, who around the world are expected to provide economically for their children, may be fined for paternal neglect, or allowed to casually avoid their responsibilities. So, while some sanctions are necessary to produce social conformity in any society, the severity of the punishment can be a social problem in itself when it involves responses so harsh as to cause more harm than the behavior it intends to reject or prevent. Arguably, this was the case in American society with regard to deviance from sexual norms.

Understandably, then, the gay rights movement emerged as a backlash against American society's harsh treatment of sexual deviances. Yet, this new movement wanted more than just to stop society's harsh responses. It aimed to fully legitimize same-sex relations and to make them parallel to heterosexual relations in marriage. To do this, it has put forward the notion of "orientation": a cultural concept which packages together the direction of sexual desire with personal identity. Ironically, the former element, the direction of desire, is presented as an innate characteristic, while the latter, personal identity, is presented as a matter of choice. So the paradoxical argument is that people cannot change the direction of their sexual desire, so they must be allowed to choose to "be who they are."

In point of fact, there is a very wide variety of sexual experiences possible for human beings, including "orientations" (in the sense of persistent desires and romantic love) for children, animals, and even inanimate objects. Furthermore, change in the direction of desire does sometimes occur, as in the case of a prominent lesbian activist who discovered to her own chagrin that she was in love with a man (Claussen 1999). Still, sexuality is complex and deeply rooted in us all, and it does not simply respond to a command to change. All we need do is remember our own struggles with sexual thoughts to know that this is the case. To the degree that orientations exist, they are a complex mix of good and bad, healthy and unhealthy, desires found in all of us. Simply legitimizing them will not remove our struggles with our own sexuality, and may entitle people to sexual behaviors that are harmful to themselves and others.

The twin notions that sexual desire determines personal identity, and that identity is a matter of choice, should be problematic for Christians. Jenell Paris, a Christian anthropologist who has studied the gay community, demonstrates that in fact neither of these notions is correct. Paris begins by identifying the fact that terms such as *heterosexual* and *homosexual* are taxonomic categories that force everyone to identify themselves as one or the other. Even the addition of third or fourth categories, such as "bisexual," is based on the same principle of organizing experience into a limited number of options and requiring people to choose.[5] Paris explains further that:

> Well into the twentieth century, there was no word at all for what most considered healthy and normal sexuality . . . Then, as contraception became more accessible and reliable, sexual identities became linked almost entirely to sexual feelings, as they are today. Reproduction, family and religion have become optional components of sex (though vital for those who choose them), and sexuality has taken on new meaning as an essential force that exists not between persons but within each individual, one that is expected to provide personal identity and happiness. (2011: 42)

The problem is that using sexual identity categories "implies that what you want, sexually speaking, is who you are," says Paris (43), when in fact, "Sexuality . . . is better understood in light of our beloved created nature, not in light of sexual desire. Identity comes from God, not sexual feelings" (51). Sexual desire, then, should not be the central component of anyone's identity. When we locate sexuality inside of ourselves and link it too closely to individual identity, we miss God's primary purpose for sex, which is to provide a deep and rich way of relating to one another across gender lines.

Why, then, do some people wish to avoid opposite sex relations? There is anthropological evidence that the factor most likely to create third

---

5. See Valentine 2002. David Valentine is a secular gay anthropologist who documents the confusion transgender people feel when trying to fit their various experiences into the taxonomic categories offered to them by the sexual rights movement, and thereby construct an identity for themselves.

or fourth gender categories in a culture is not a naturally occurring innate sexual orientation, but a deep rejection of the usual gender *roles* (Lang 1998: 347–48). Such a rejection is more likely to take place in societies where gender roles are dramatically opposed to one another, with high hostility between the sexes and a strong subordination of women. In Brazil, for instance, the expectation of hyper-masculinity or machismo in men, together with an intense subordination and hyper-feminization of women, results in an unusually high number of men choosing to live in transgender roles. These men are rejecting their society's ideal for aggressiveness in males. On the other hand, in New Guinea, those cultures that have less rigid gender roles and less hostility between the sexes also have less same-sex behavior (Mead 1963: 270). So, it may be that the emergence of same-sex families in the West is actually symptomatic of overly rigid and embattled culture-wide prescriptions for sex, gender, and family roles, a kind of fallout from the "war between the sexes."[6]

If this is the case, it means that the real threat to family life in America is located in the tense relations between men and women generally, producing a high divorce rate and far too many sub-nuclear families. The loss of stability in children's lives, as they flip-flop between divorced parents in accordance with court mandates is especially problematic, producing whole generations who have not known the security that comes from belonging to a family that provides them with both female and male adult caring, support, and correction. With this in mind, perhaps the best way that Christians can defend the family is simply to live differently themselves. A recent study has demonstrated that Christians in America divorce, watch pornography, and commit domestic abuse at the same rates as other Americans (Sider 2005). So, an important first step for Christians will be to begin to take seriously the self-sacrifice and commitment to the family that Christian morality requires of them.

CHRISTIAN SOCIAL JUSTICE

As societies grow in size, they grow in the complexity of their internal organization as well. Extended families become tribes, tribes become ethnic groups, and ethnic groups become nations. Meanwhile, nonkin-based

6. This circumstance was predicted by Betty Friedan, in *The Feminine Mystique.* In 1963, Friedan suggested that the absence of fathers from the suburban home, and the frustrations of mothers who were trapped at home, would produce an increasing incidence of homosexuality in boys, as well as promiscuity in both sexes at younger and younger ages (1983: 274–76).

associations, beginning with age sets and moving eventually to schools, courts, banks, political parties, and governments, develop to handle the complexity of the system with the necessary specialization. In the West, this growth in complexity has been accompanied by a division of society's functions into two arenas, public and private. The public arena is the world of work, marketplace, and politics; the private arena is the world of family and religion. In chapter one, we saw that scientific beliefs hold center stage in the public arena, while religious beliefs are relegated to the private arena where they are viewed as matters of opinion. Here, we can see that, very unfortunately, morality has also been split. Personal morality, which includes sexual behavior and forms of the family, is allocated to the private arena and therefore a matter of opinion. Social morality, which includes fairness and the common good, is debated in the public arena from which religious opinions are excluded. There, despite the political rhetoric, solutions are commonly found according to principles of expediency or pragmatism rather than a true agreement on what is morally right and good (Bellah 2007; Smith, 2010).

In the Bible, the morality that defines what is right and good in relationships between people is called "justice." Justice is an essential element of the *shalom* that God intends for our lives in community. We cannot claim to be good based on personal purity without behaving justly toward others, especially the poor and oppressed. Marshall notes that "the main vocabulary items for sexual sin appear about 90 times in the Bible, while the major Hebrew and Greek words for justice . . . occur over 1000 times" (1989: 10–11). In the Old Testament, justice is commonly paired with righteousness, as when the Psalmist says that God, "loves righteousness and justice" (Ps 33:5). It is also associated with God's salvation, as when Isaiah declares, "Thus says the Lord: Maintain justice and do what is right, for soon my salvation will come, and my deliverance be revealed" (Isa 56:1). God is instructing the Jewish people to anticipate his salvation by acting rightly toward one another. Furthermore, salvation here refers not just to the personal salvation we experience as individuals, but to the Day of Judgment, when God will set right all that is wrong with the world.

It is important to note that even in the Old Testament, God's justice is less about following laws than about faithfulness in relationships. Initially, God established a covenant (mutual promise) of faithfulness with Abraham. Genesis 15 tells the story. First God promised Abraham many descendants, and when Abraham believed God, "the Lord reckoned it to him as righteousness" (verse 6). So Abraham's righteousness rested not on his keeping of the law (which had not yet been given), nor on his own moral purity (which was tainted), but on his willingness to *believe* God, an act of trust. Then God demonstrated his own faithfulness by engaging in an ancient promissory rite. He had Abraham cut a number of animals in half, and passed between the halves in the form of a smoking fire pot and a flaming torch. According to the culture of the time, by doing this God declared a curse of death upon himself, should he fail to keep his promise. God, the Almighty Creator, bound *himself* in a promise to Abraham to demonstrate his own faithfulness.

There are a number of reasons why a covenant of faithfulness is a better basis for justice than is the law. First, human laws tend to favor the powerful, and so cannot bring about justice for the powerless. In fact, some of them are quite simply unjust, placing power on the side of immorality. Second, even God's laws can be circumvented, as was demonstrated by the Pharisees in the New Testament. Jesus' condemnation of the Pharisees was not because they were attempting to be righteous by following the law, but because they were using the law to evade true righteousness (Matt 23). Finally, a covenant of faithfulness is more binding than the law could possibly be. A clear example is marriage, in which the faithfulness due from each partner to the other goes far beyond the following of a simple set of rules.[7]

Why, then, did God provide his people with a law at all? When God called Abraham to follow him, he intended to found a new community of justice, in the form of faithfulness, that would be a light to the world (Romans 3–4). As Israel became a nation, however, the law became necessary to cope with people's rebelliousness. God gave the Ten Commandments to Moses at a time of quarreling and disobedience, of breaking faith with God and with one another. Coming out of a terrible period of slavery, the Israelites did not trust each other, their leader Moses, or even God. The Ten Commandments gave them a minimal definition of good behavior. Later, after they settled in Canaan, the Israelites wanted to be like their neighbors. So they built upon God's law a full set of normative practices, added judges, and to God's dismay, even a king (1 Sam 8). In anthropological terms, Israel was evolving from a pastoralist tribal society, based on an ethic of egalitarianism, to an agricultural stratified society, based on differences in power and wealth. The result was a new set of structural injustices that were never intended to be part of God's community of *shalom*.

God responded by sending the prophets to remind the Israelites of the covenantal nature of the relationships that should exist between them.

---

7. Jesus himself acknowledged the inadequacy of the law when responding to the Pharisees on the matter of divorce. The law allowed for easy divorce, but Jesus told them that it was only "because of your hardness of heart [that Moses] wrote this commandment for you." Jesus then presented a higher standard for faithfulness in the covenant of marriage, saying, "what God has joined together, let no one separate" (Mark 10:2–8).

The prophets held the high classes and the ruling authorities accountable for their treatment of disadvantaged groups. Oppression, which is the *legal* domination of one group by another, was commonly the subject of the prophets' strongest condemnation. Amos declared:

> Alas for those who lie on beds of ivory, and lounge on their couches,
>
> and eat lambs from the flock, and calves from the stall,
>
> who sing idle songs to the sound of the harp,
>
> and like David improvise on instruments of music;
>
> who drink wine from bowls, and anoint themselves with the finest oils,
>
> . . . You have turned justice into poison,
>
> and the fruit of righteousness into wormwood. (Amos 6:4–7, 12b)

Though they were simply enjoying the ordinary pleasures of wealth and power, the higher classes had turned "righteousness into wormwood" by living lives of idleness and indulgence, and "justice into poison" by ignoring the hard lives of those living in poverty.

Amos drew a parallel between the slavery that the Israelites had experienced under the Egyptians, and the injustice they were now committing against their own people. He warned that God's judgment was the same in both cases (4:6–13), and described the disgust with which God viewed the Israelites' worship under these conditions:

> I hate, I despise your festivals, and I take no delight in your solemn assemblies.
>
> Even though you offer me your burnt offerings and grain offerings,
>
> I will not accept them . . .
>
> Take away from me the noise of your songs;
>
> I will not listen to the melody of your harps.
>
> But let justice roll down like waters,
>
> and righteousness like an ever-flowing stream. (Amos 5:21–24)

Here, Amos implied that the sins committed by the Israelites against one another were also sins committed against God himself, a theme found throughout the Bible (cf. Gen 4:8–16; 2 Sam 12:13; Ps 51:4; Mic 3; 1 Cor

8:12). We cannot mistreat one another and imagine ourselves to be right with God.

It is important to note that in the Bible the decision to treat people justly is not a reward for their righteousness. That is, the prophets did not suggest that the poor and powerless were to receive justice based on whether or not they deserved it. They were to receive justice simply as a matter of course from those in power. This is because the rulers and authorities that God permits on earth are to act as he would. And, as we have seen, God is faithful to us even when we are unfaithful to him. In fact, we humans only receive justice because it is an attribute of God's own nature; it is "a description of what God is like and of how God relates to the world" (Marshall 1989: 32). For God, justice *"is all about relationships . . .* Justice means doing all that is necessary to create and sustain healthy, constant, and life-giving relationships between persons" (Marshall 1989: 35) [emphasis in the original]. Thus, in our relationships with one another, and especially in situations of power and responsibility, we must follow God's own example and be faithful to others even when they are not faithful to us.

In the Old Testament, justice largely meant good treatment of one another in the context of covenantal relationships. In the New Testament, Jesus established an even deeper motive for justice by emphasizing the role of love in bringing about true *shalom*. When asked to sum up the law and the prophets, he quoted, "You shall love the Lord your God with all your heart, with all your soul, and with all your mind . . . [and] you shall love your neighbor as yourself" (Matt 22:37–40). He told the crowds that followed him to love even their enemies (Matt 5:38–48), and he said to his disciples: "I give you a new commandment, that you love one another. Just as I have loved you, you also should love one another. By this everyone will know that you are my disciples, if you have love for one another" (John 13:34–5). So, Jesus' new commandment, that we love one another, sums up the law and the prophets, must be extended even to our enemies, and is the sign by which everyone will know that we are his followers.

The word *love* is used very freely in our culture. It generally refers to personal tastes, ironically causing us to focus on what we want for ourselves! But true love is focused on the needs of others. The Apostle Paul describes the behavior:

> Love is patient and kind. Love is not jealous or boastful or proud or rude. It does not demand its own way. It is not irritable, and it keeps no record of being wronged. It does not rejoice about injustice but rejoices whenever the truth wins out. Love never gives up, never loses faith, is always hopeful,

and endures through every circumstance. (1 Cor 13:4–7, New
Living Translation)

True love is selfless behavior based on a deep desire for the highest good of
the other. Jesus' death on the cross was the supreme example of this kind of
love. "No one has greater love than this," he said, "to lay down one's life for
one's friends" (John 15:13).

Selfless love is very difficult to achieve. It goes completely against the
grain of our human nature to sacrifice ourselves for others. Furthermore,
American culture is very self-oriented, encouraging us to think about what
we want and to pursue it aggressively, from consumer goods to jobs to marriage partners. At best, American culture recommends caring for our own
needs first, and then for others out of the remainder of our resources. But
this is an *unacceptable* principle for a Christian! When Jesus was watching
people give money to the temple treasury, he commended a poor widow to
his disciples, saying, "Truly I tell you, this poor widow has put in more than
all those who are contributing to the treasury. For all of them have contributed out of their abundance, but she out of her poverty has put in everything
she had, all she had to live on" (Mark 12:41–44).

The point is an important one because well-meaning people in circumstances of privilege commonly imagine that justice can be accomplished
without any cost to themselves. They are willing to help out of the excess
of their wealth, but not to the detriment of their own privileged positions.
Worse, when people believe that "putting number one first" is legitimate,
they commonly feel justified in using other people for their own purposes.
Reinhold Niebuhr suggests that the root of all injustice is exploitation, the
inverse of love (Lebacqz 1986: 85). Most Christians do not think of themselves as exploiting others. But exploitation can be a very subtle sin, ranging from a polite indifference to the needs of people who are providing us
with goods and services through the market, to a real hostility toward those
who do not meet our demands. The danger is especially acute in a large
society. In small societies, relationships are face-to-face, making it harder to
use other people without seeing their pain. But in large societies, there are
many impersonal relationships and indirect ties, making it much easier to
take advantage of the people we never see.

We Christians, however, are not absolved of responsibility for injustice
just because we cannot see the faces of the people we are hurting. That is
part of the message of the book of Amos. Unfortunately, in America, many
Christians have imagined that a life of personal purity is all that is needed
to satisfy God's demand for holiness. These Christians fail to remember the
many, many injunctions in the Bible to care for the needy and oppressed.

On the other hand, some have imagined that if they fight for just social causes they can permit unlimited freedom in their own or others' personal (especially sexual) lives. They fail to remember that the Bible clearly calls us to purity, and that our personal behavior is *always* a social matter. This divide in the church is a syncretistic accommodation to the divide between the political "left" and "right" in the culture. A truly Christian view of justice addresses both personal purity and structural justice, linking them together to create a world in which God's self-sacrificing faithfulness to us is reflected in our self-sacrificing faithfulness to one another.

SOCIAL CHANGE THROUGH THE CHURCH

It is through the witness of the church that God brings both morality and justice to society. By our behavior toward one another, and by our service to others, Christians are to show the world what it looks like to live according to the principles of love for God and one another. Of course, we fail at this every day. But that fact does not change Jesus' command to be known as his disciples by our love. When we love one another and our neighbors rightly (Luke 10:25–37), we *become* the church in its witness to Christ in the world.

One might think that demonstrating Jesus' love would make Christians popular in their own cultures. Sometimes it does, especially initially. But the church is, by its very nature, a counter-cultural institution, and the love that it demonstrates must critique the self-interested and unjust practices which society thinks are "necessary." Many people mistakenly associate love with a weak acceptance of whatever the other does. But as Martin Luther King, Jr. has said: "What is needed is a realization that power without love is reckless and abusive, and that love without power is sentimental and anemic. Power at its best is love implementing the demands of justice, and justice at its best is love correcting everything that stands against love."[8] Christian love, then, is a tremendously powerful force, dismantling systems of injustice by challenging people's natural self-centeredness and reorienting them to God and to each another. The social change that this kind of love produces causes a backlash, as people with vested interests begin to lose their privileges. The backlash should not surprise us. Jesus' own ministry of love resulted in his martyrdom. We who follow him should expect the same treatment.

Unfortunately, rather than face the backlash for taking a truly counter-cultural position, Christians often choose the easier road of accommodating

8. From "Where Do We Go from Here?," an address delivered to the Southern Christian Leadership Conference, on August 16, 1967.

the culture. At a truly shameful period in the history of the American church, Dr. King wrote:

> Nowhere is the tragic tendency to conform more evident than in the church, an institution that has often served to crystallize, conserve, and even bless the patterns of majority opinion. The erstwhile sanction by the church of slavery, racial segregation, war, and economic exploitation is testimony to the fact that the church has hearkened more to the authority of the world than to the authority of God. (2010: 15)

Imagine the seriousness of the sin of a church that is ignoring the authority of God in favor of the authority of the world! Surely this is the ultimate failure for Christians.

Thankfully, the Spirit of God is not stopped by our opting out of his will! As Esther was told when she hesitated to risk her life to save her people, "If you keep silence at such a time as this, relief and deliverance will rise for the Jews from another quarter, but you and your family will perish. Who knows? Perhaps you have come to royal dignity for just such a time as this" (Esth 4:14). We have a choice. If we fail to take the risk of living as true Christians in a hostile environment, God will find another way to accomplish his purposes without us. But if we follow God's call to represent his love and justice, we will experience the joy of participating in the manifestation of his kingdom on earth, despite any suffering we may endure.

Dr. King knew that he had been called by God to speak for justice in his own place and time in history. He endured a tremendous backlash, including over twenty arrests for peaceful protests, having his house bombed, and receiving countless death threats for himself and his family. In the end, he paid the ultimate price for following God's authority rather than the world's when he was assassinated. Yet he did not lose! Toward the end of his life, King wrote:

> The agonizing moments through which I have passed during the last few years have also drawn me closer to God. More than ever before I am convinced of the reality of a personal God. True, I have always believed in the personality of God. But in the past the idea of a personal God was little more than a metaphysical category that I found theologically and philosophically satisfying. Now it is a living reality that has been validated in the experiences of everyday life. God has been profoundly real to me in recent years, in the midst of outer dangers, I have felt an inner calm. In the midst of lonely days and dreary nights, I have heard an inner voice saying, "Lo, I will be with you." (2010: 163)

As Jesus promised, he will be with us to the end of the age when we choose to follow him (Matt 28:20).

The good news is that, despite failures, the church *has* witnessed to God's justice through history. Here, we will consider three Christian-inspired social movements to make the point: the anti-slavery movement in the West, the anti-caste movement in India, and the women's movement worldwide. In all three cases, committed Christians stood up for social change, despite significant backlashes, and persisted till those changes were made. And in all three cases, the proposed changes emerged directly out of the application of Jesus' command to love others. Slaves, untouchables, and women have been in circumstances of systematic oppression, and the challenge to these systems has come from the witness of the church to Christ's unbounded love for all people.

First, the global slave trade developed under colonialism for the purpose of providing plantation labor worldwide. It was certainly one of the most brutal systems in human history. Hunters on horseback trapped people like animals, shoved and stacked them into ships like cargo where a significant number of them died in transit, threw them overboard if they were sick, and sold them like cattle to plantation owners who regularly beat them to make them work. Many Christians at the time took this situation to be normal, or remained ignorant of the sources of their own material benefits. Yet it was also Christians, living out the implications of their faith, who objected to slavery, and eventually succeeded in getting it banned. One of the first major figures in the movement was Bartolome de las Casas, a seventeenth-century Dominican priest. Las Casas had been a slave owner himself in the New World. But after witnessing the horrific abuse of the Native American Indians, he began to speak out against their mistreatment both in the Americas and back in Europe. Initially, he tried to reform the system, rather than abolish it. But when his efforts resulted in yet another massacre of Indians, Las Casas turned his back on his former life, joined the Dominicans who had already taken a stand against slave-holding, and spent the rest of his life as a missionary and abolitionist.

Later, in England, the anti-slavery campaign was taken up by William Wilberforce and Thomas Clarkson, among others, all of whom were members of a group of evangelical Christians committed to abolition. Both Wilberforce and Clarkson reported having received direct personal calls from God to oppose slavery. Wilberforce campaigned in parliament for over forty years before anti-slavery legislation was successfully passed for the British Empire. In America, the Quakers were active in the anti-slavery movement. They too had initially owned slaves. But under the leadership of John Woolman, who preached with great conviction that slaveholding was not Christian, the Quakers came to lead the movement for abolition, partly through participation in the Underground Railroad.

It is easy to look back and applaud those who took a stand against something we now view as obviously wrong. But we need to remember that, at the time, these Christians were viewed by their governments and by many ordinary people, including other Christians, as subversive. Las Casas was driven out of Mexico and accused of being a traitor to his home country, Spain. Wilberforce was viewed as an agitator, even a revolutionary, though his other opinions on government were generally conservative. Later, here in America, Martin Luther King, Jr. was put under surveillance by the FBI during the civil rights movement. We now recognize all three of these Christians as having represented biblical justice to entrenched systems of injustice. But at the time they were viewed as troublemakers who were endangering the smooth running of society.

Society's argument against social change is always that it is impractical, even impossible. The entire economy of the American South rested on the plantation system, and the plantation system needed slaves. Thus, the strongest argument against abolition was that it was not feasible for an entire society to give up the holding of slaves; the economy would crumble! In truth, this fear was not unfounded. An economy built on a system of exploitation will certainly have to make costly adjustments when justice is instituted. Unfortunately, fearful of the price they would have to pay, there were many Christians who not only defended slavery, but tried to use the Bible to do so (Swartley 1983). Some even picked up guns and fought on the side of injustice. But in the end their efforts failed. As Dr. King put it, "the arc of the moral universe is long, but it bends toward justice."[9] So, while it may be impractical to change our systems in the short run, it is impossible to sustain them over the long run when they are built on false or evil principles.

In the second example, the relevant social issue for the church in India has been caste. Caste distinctions, which originally come out of Hinduism, separate Christians from one another, and rank some above others based on believed differences in inherent worth. This situation has a long history. As we saw in the last chapter, the very first converts to Christianity were the result of the missionary efforts of the Apostle Thomas in the first century. Those early Indian Christians endured tremendous persecution, and ended up capitulating to many Hindu social practices. As a result, over the centuries, the St. Thomas churches became entirely segregated. In daily

9. From "Where Do We Go from Here?," an address delivered to the Southern Christian Leadership Conference, on August 16, 1967.

life, high-caste Christians engaged in the same abusive practices toward low-caste Christians as were the norm in Hindu society, including heavy stigmatization, physical beatings, and exclusion from village life.

When Catholic and Protestant missionaries first arrived, they wanted to convert Hindus to Christ without disturbing their social life, so they made every attempt to adapt the church to caste practices. Gradually, however, as they realized the effect of caste on church life, they came to view it with increasing severity. High-caste converts were insisting on having separate churches, or on a dividing wall within the sanctuary, to keep them separate from low-caste converts. Christians were marrying their daughters and sons to Hindus rather than across caste lines. Most significantly, the Lord's Supper could not be held in common. Eating together symbolized equality, and high-caste church members did not want to place themselves on a level with untouchables. It was on this last matter that missionaries finally took a stand, insisting that all converts must be willing to take communion together. Some high-caste Christians were so incensed at this that they reverted to Hinduism. But low-caste people were so moved by the church's stand in their favor that they converted out of Hinduism into Christianity in droves. As one new convert put it, "Christ has given me a turban [i.e. respect] in the place of dust" (Webster 1992: 53).

Once again, it is much easier to see injustice at a distance, whether in time or in space. For Western Christians, the evils of caste are obvious and require immediate social action, while those of racism or poverty are simply "the way life is." But, as a point of comparison, caste has always been far more truly necessary to Indian society than slavery was to colonialism or the American South. It is a total way of life, enveloping all relations between people, and providing an interdependent productive village economy. Because of caste, everyone has a place, work to do, and the right to exchange for what they need. Mahatma Gandhi made an attempt to reform the system by demanding good treatment of those at the bottom of the hierarchy while leaving the basic structure intact. But as we have seen, reform is not enough if the system is built upon principles of oppression. The powerful love of Jesus requires us to dismantle unjust systems by refusing to conform to them and being willing to pay the price ourselves of the change. Yet there is a kingdom reward for our sacrifice. It is instructive that where Indian Christians have accommodated caste, the church has stagnated; where they have rejected it, the church has grown by leaps and bounds.[10]

10. A case in point is Paul Dass, founder of the micro-enterprise PeopleKraft. Dass is a high-caste (Brahmin) convert to Christianity who has begun a small handicraft factory to employ low-caste and untouchable people. As the employees are working, Dass sits on the floor working with them. He reminds them that, as God's handicraft, they

Finally, around the world, women have benefitted from the introduction of the love of Jesus to local cultures. This may be surprising to some Western Christians who are under the impression that feminism is a secular movement that is opposed by the church. But, in point of fact, the Christian view of the value of all people, including women, contradicts the treatment of women in most cultures. Especially in traditional societies, women are subordinated to men beyond what even the most conservative Christians would approve. They are viewed as inferior not merely in rank, but also in worth. The belief in women's inferior worth can be seen in the statements that are made about them, in the depictions that are made of them, and in their exclusion from social institutions (Ortner 1974: 69).

Among tribal peoples, for instance, women are commonly considered polluting to men, and are carried off in raids and beaten as a matter of course. In fact, South American Yanomami women are told that their beatings are a sign of their husbands' love! (Chagnon 1977: 83). In India and China, women are restricted to their homes so severely that they cannot freely associate with one another as friends. They are also blamed for their own stigmatization, such as with the Hindu belief that people are born women because of sins they committed in a previous life. Proverbs and stories reveal and legitimize the situation. Jewish men used to recite "Blessed are you, O God, for not having made me a Gentile, a slave, or a woman," and a proverb from North India states, "The unfortunate one's son dies; the fortunate one's daughter dies" (Chowdhry 1997: 305). This latter sentiment is so widely held that female abortion and infanticide is a significant social problem in multiple areas of the world.

In such cultural contexts, Paul's statement that "there is no longer male and female for all of you are one in Christ Jesus" (Gal 3:28) is truly revolutionary. The stories of Jesus' treatment of women are remarkable for the seriousness with which he responded to them, never demeaning them or considering them less worthy of his notice. Thus, as the church has spread, Christianity has insisted on women's full worth as human beings, and even conservative missionaries have campaigned for better treatment of women in traditional societies.

In India, for instance, William Carey, a nineteenth-century evangelical Christian missionary, passionately objected to the traditional practice of encouraging women to commit *sati*, or suicide by burning on their husband's funeral pyres. The Hindu teaching was that a woman's most immediate "god" was her husband. If he died before her, she should follow him in death

---

themselves are even more beautiful than the crafts they are making. Seven churches have been founded as a result of his ministry.

as a sign of her devotion. Christian teaching encouraged respect for husbands, but not idolatry, and it strongly forbade any kind of suicide. So Carey, together with the Hindu reformer Ram Mohan Roy, campaigned against *sati* and was successful in convincing the government to ban it. Carey also campaigned successfully against female infanticide, and other missionaries started the very first schools for girls in India, despite the fact that Hinduism had banned women's literacy. As with slavery, evangelical Christians played a significant role in bringing about social change for women.

Ironically, the importance of defending women in traditional societies was far more clear to Western Christians in the nineteenth century than it has been since. Though Western societies were themselves male-dominated at the time, reports of the treatment of women in other places shocked Europeans and Americans. In fact, "The position of women in different cultures was commonly used by Western observers as an indicator of the general status of society" (Okkenhaug 2004: 5). Okkenhaug, an historian of nineteenth-century missions, describes the situation:

> Images of women's intellectual deprivation, domestic oppression and sexual degradation were used to justify missionary work in Africa and Asia. Within the mission movement this is a universalist theme; men and women share a common humanity, and christianization entails a restoration of women's humanity. Western women had a moral duty to uplift the non-Christian women and in many societies, for example in Asia and the Middle East, women could only be reached by women. Thus Western women went out to do Christian work in far away places. (2004: 3)

Under colonialism, Westerners had fewer qualms about evaluating other cultures' practices than they did later. So, programs to protect and promote women developed in association with the exploding Protestant missionary movement, which sent so many women out as missionaries that by the end of the century, they "greatly outnumbered men" (Neill 1990: 256). Those who stayed at home formed women's associations for the financial and prayer support of the work being done elsewhere. Okkenhaug (2004: 1) calls this mission work "the first global women's movement."[11]

How is it, then, that many Western Christians now, especially Americans, feel the need to emphasize the subordination of women as an important biblical ideal? Mary Stewart Van Leeuwen, a Christian psychologist and theologian, suggests that we have misinterpreted key verses in the Bible that refer to women. In her book, *Gender and Grace*, Van Leeuwen points

---

11. See also Dana Robert's article on the role of women in mission (2006).

out that Genesis 3 explains the universal subordination, and devaluation, of women *not* as God's original plan for creation, but as a result of humanity's fall from grace (1990:44). We all remember that, when Adam and Eve disobeyed God, God declared that Adam would be cursed with hard work, and Eve with pain in childbirth. But we commonly forget that there was a second curse for Eve, ". . . yet your desire shall be for your husband, and he shall rule over you" (Gen 3:16). This was no declaration of God's intent for a perfect family or societal order. It was punishment, in the form of natural consequences, for Eve's failure to obey God. It would henceforth be in Eve's nature to *falsely* subordinate herself to her husband and to permit him, rather than God, to rule over her. For his part, it would be in Adam's nature to, "let [his] dominion run wild, to impose it in cavalier and illegitimate ways, not only on the earth and on other men, but also upon the person who is bone of his bones and flesh of his flesh—upon the helper corresponding to his very self" (45).[12] Around the world, the most common form of abuse in families is husbands mistreating their wives. Even where abuse is not present, the belief in male dominance serves to disqualify women's opinions and abilities from making a full contribution to society. The result is a loss not only of women's freedom, but of society's benefit from women's input.

Van Leeuwen reminds us, however, that because of Christ's death on the cross for our sin, the curses of Genesis have been lifted (1990: 35). The effects of this new reality for gender relations were seen in the church immediately after Pentecost:

> After Pentecost, the church baptized men and women alike. Before it was considered at best unnecessary and at worst scandalous for women to study the Scriptures beside men in the synagogue. Now they broke bread and participated in worship services with the men. Before, women's freedom of movement was rigidly constricted because of the rabbinic assertion that public contact between non-married women and men was bound to produce lust. Now women assumed positions of leadership even in mixed gatherings and were acknowledged and praised by Paul at various points in his letters (1990: 35).

While, of course, the effects of sin are still with us, the new freedom we experience in Christ allows God's original purposes for balanced loving relations between women and men to flourish.

12. Van Leeuwen suggests that women permit men to dominate them partly in order to avoid the full responsibility of dominion that God has given to all of us. That is, women "avoid taking risks that might upset relationships," and thereby escape the requirements of adulthood, including the necessity of exercising dominion responsibly (1990: 46).

None of this implies that we should attempt to eliminate all of the differences between the sexes. God certainly did intend that men and women should live in relationship to one another, especially in marriage. In fact, "human beings . . . need a sense of female/male complementariness to be complete and to image God fully" (Van Leeuwen 1990: 213). That is, neither sex is able to fulfill God's purposes for humanity without the other. Justice for women, then, is not necessarily same treatment, but equal value. The way that this is accomplished, says Van Leeuwen, is through *flexibility* in gender roles (139). All societies assign gender-based roles. But societies that allow, and even encourage, flexibility between the roles promote greater harmony between the sexes than do those with strictly segregated roles.

Such societies also provide better care for children. Flexibility in gender roles is good for children primarily because of the importance of *fathers* in child-rearing. The British anthropologist, Raymond Firth, described his surprise at men's involvement in children's lives in Tikopia (a small Polynesian island). While there is a general expectation that mothers will be primarily responsible for babies (due to the requirements of breastfeeding), Tikopian fathers are deeply involved in caring for their children right from birth. Firth watched as fathers would easily agree to watch small babies when their wives wanted to go fishing. Other men supported fathers who were doing childcare by taking the situation seriously and not making scornful jokes about it (Firth 2004: 127). The result was a respect and relative harmony between the sexes (compared to England!) that benefitted children.

Certainly, God has created us to be male and female. Such a difference, woven as it is through the whole of nature, is not insignificant. Furthermore, it has been the normal case for cultures to have gender-specific roles. But God has assigned dominion over creation to the whole of humanity, both women and men (Gen 1:28). It is by working together, under God's authority, that we are to exercise this dominion. So, far from disturbing the natural order, justice for women restores God's original plan for loving and responsible relationships in communities of *shalom,* and for care for the earth.

(CHAPTER 5) DISCUSSION QUESTIONS

1. What biblical principles are most relevant to a Christian understanding of the purpose and nature of the family? How should the church respond to the different forms of the family in different cultures?

2. How does the history of the global church inform our understanding of sexual identity, the social construction of gender, and male-female

relations? How can we take a fresh look at biblical passages on these matters, and what will that reveal?

3. How do we determine truly *biblical* principles of social justice, and distinguish them from our culture's principles? How do we enter into our society's dialogue on the matter and present a Christian perspective there?

RECOMMENDED READINGS

Claiborne, Shane. 2006. *The Irresistible Revolution: Living as an Ordinary Radical.* Grand Rapids: Zondervan.

King, Martin Luther, Jr. 2010. *Strength to Love.* Minneapolis: Fortress.

Paris, Jenell. 2011. *The End of Sexual Identity: Why Sex is Too Important to Define Who We Are.* Downer's Grove, IL: InterVarsity.

Van Leeuwen, Mary. 1990. *Gender and Grace: Love, Work and Parenting in a Changing World.* Downers Grove, IL: InterVarsity.

Chapter 6

Can We Be Christians and Still Make a Living?

Life in the Global Economy

The American tourist in India gazed sadly out of the bus. A small crowd of obviously poor people were begging for small change. How could she sit in comfort and not help? She checked her purse. All she had were larger denominations of rupees, nothing smaller than a Rs. 100 bill (about three American dollars). She pulled a bill out and handed it to a woman in the crowd through the window, indicating that she should share it with the others. The women, however, grabbed the bill and ran away, causing the others to become angry. In a flash, the crowd began yelling, pounding on and rocking the bus. As the bus driver pulled away quickly, the tourist felt all the more keenly the desperation of the billions of poor in the world, and her own helplessness to do anything about it.

What should the tourist have done?[1] Not giving the money seemed hard hearted; yet giving the money nearly caused a riot! The tourist had not asked to be born a wealthy American any more than the Indians in the crowd had asked to be born desperately poor. Furthermore, no one

---

1. I deeply appreciate the helpful comments and critique provided by Drs. Lindy Backues and Mike Mtika on this chapter. Both have long experience and professional expertise in the areas of Christian mission, social transformation, and community development.

could accuse these poor of being lazy. The tourist knew from previous experience how hard they worked just to keep their families fed. Their circumstance of poverty was clearly not their own fault. For that matter, her own circumstance of wealth was not to her credit. Something in the larger order of things had created a concentration of wealth in some places and a deficit in others. By crossing over the boundaries, the tourist had brought wealth into contact with poverty, revealing the terrible disparity.

Poverty is certainly the most serious economic problem of our time. Of the more than 7 billion people on the earth, over 2 billion are poor (about 1/3 of the earth's population)[2] and more than 3/4 billion are desperately poor (living in "extreme poverty" on less than $1.90 per day).[3] Almost half of child deaths under the age of five are related to being malnourished,[4] and there are an estimated 17,000 children dying of hunger each day.[5] But statistics only give the bird's eye view of the problem. The ground level view reveals the degree to which poverty enslaves people. Mothers lock their children in homes to go to work during the day. Family members take turns eating on different days. A ten-year-old child in Africa says, "When I leave for school in the mornings I don't have any breakfast. At noon there is no lunch, in the evening I get a little supper, and that is not enough. So when I see another child eating, I watch him, and if he doesn't give me something I think I'm going to die of hunger" (Narayan 2002: 35). Hunger and easily contracted illnesses make it difficult for parents to do the work they need to do to feed their families. The work they do is physical day labor, without benefits such as vacations, medical compensation, or retirement. Poor people also suffer the indignities of abusive treatment from those above them, including those who are supposed to protect them such as the police. Barriers such as illiteracy, corrupt officials, and social exclusion prevent their best efforts to get out of poverty from succeeding. A poor person from Eastern Europe says, "Poverty is a lack of freedom, enslaved by crushing daily burden, by depression and fear of what the future will bring" (Narayan 2002: 37).

2. *Human Development Report 2013. Sustaining Human Progress: Reducing Vulnerabilities and Building Resilience.* New York: United Nations Development Programme, 3.

3. *Taking on Inequality: Poverty and Shared Prosperity 2016.* Washington, DC: The World Bank, 3–4.

4. International Food Policy Research Institute. 2016. *Global Nutrition Report 2016: From Promise to Impact: Ending Malnutrition by 2030.* Washington, DC, 25.

5. United Nations Secretary General, Ban Ki-moon, in 2009 interview with CNN. http://edition.cnn.com/2009/WORLD/europe/11/17/italy.food.summit/. Accessed 3/23/17.

The magnitude of the global problem of poverty is certainly ironic in a world in which more wealth exists than ever before in human history! Just 200 years ago, food production was largely done by small subsistence farming, and technology did not include many ordinary things we take for granted now, such as plastics, stainless steel, or synthetic fabrics. Of course, population growth has skyrocketed since then, eating into the gains made by new forms of technology and economic organization. But even taking population growth into account, the world has more wealth per capita now than ever before. In one estimate of worldwide annual income, the $500 per capita that had been steady through centuries shot up to $6000 per capita after 1850 (Sachs 2005: 28).

So why are there so many desperately poor and starving people? At one level, the answer is simple: the wealth is concentrated in the hands of a minority and the majority are unable to access it. According to a World Bank study, the richest 1 percent of the world's population has an income equal to the bottom 57 percent (Milanovic 1999: 50). Even if we adjust for the different purchasing power of money in different countries, the top 20 percent has more than 70 percent of the world's income.[6] The global distribution of income is illustrated below:

Figure 6.1: Global Income Distribution

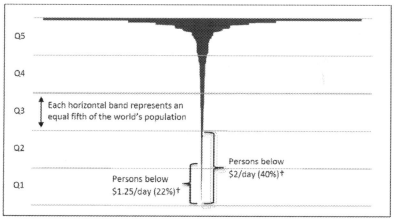

Source: UNICEF[7]

---

6. *Global Inequality, Beyond the Bottom Billion,* by Isabel Ortiz and Matthew Cummins. UNICEF Policy and Practice working paper. April 2011, 7.

7. "Global Income Distribution by Population Percentiles of the Population in 2007 (or latest available) in PPP constant 2005 international dollars." *Global Inequality, Beyond the Bottom Billion,* by Isabel Ortiz and Matthew Cummins. UNICEF Policy and Practice working paper. April 2011, 21.

The massive difference in wealth between rich and poor can also be seen in the nature of the health problems that people have, as is illustrated below:

Figure 6.2: Overweight versus Malnourished People in the United States and India

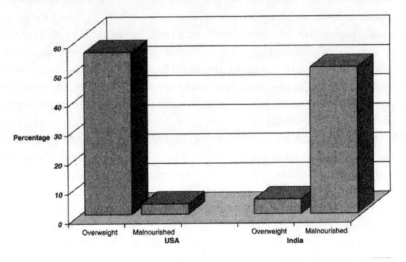

Source: McMichael (2004: xxxv)

In fact, even the leftovers of the rich (who would include all who are reading this book) might make a life-giving difference in the lives of the poor. Kofi Annan, former Secretary-General of the United Nations has pointed out that:

1. Europeans and Americans spend $17 billion per year on pet food— which is $4 billion more than would be needed to provide basic health and nutrition for everyone in the world.

2. Europeans spend $11 billion per year on ice cream—which is $2 billion more than would be needed to provide clean water and safe sewers for everyone in the world.

3. Americans spend $8 billion per year on cosmetics—which is $2 billion more than would be needed to provide basic education to everyone in the world.[8]

The world has not always had such an unbalanced distribution of wealth. Economist Jeffrey Sachs says, "The gulf between today's rich and

8. "Kofi Annan's Astonishing Facts!" by Barbara Crossette. *New York Times,* September 27, 1998. http://www.nytimes.com/learning/general/featured_articles/ 980928monday.html. Accessed on 3/28/17.

poor countries is . . . a new phenomenon, a yawning gap that opened during the period of modern economic growth" (2005: 28). And, unfortunately, all indicators are that the situation is getting worse, not better. It is true that there is an emerging middle class in developing countries like India and China. But the tremendous disparity between the rich and the poor is worsening globally. To cite just two of a multitude of statistical studies: the ratio of the income earned by the top 5 percent of the world to the rest *increased* from 78/1 to 114/1 between 1988 and 1993 (Milanovic 1999: 50), and the ratio of the wealthiest 1 percent to the median in the United States increased from 125/1 to 190/1 between 1962 and 2004.[9] In a World Bank-sponsored study involving 60,000 interviews of poor people in 60 countries, the bank concluded that "a majority of them feel they are worse off and more insecure than in the past" (Narayan 2002: ix). Traditionally, the poor have relied on their networks of family and friends to survive in difficult times. But now, even that source of security is eroding. With the increasing reach of the market into traditional communities encouraging young men to leave to find work in cities, "the social fabric—poor people's only 'insurance'—is unraveling" (Narayan 2002: 4).

As mentioned above, world population growth is a factor in the current crisis of poverty. But it is not the main cause of poverty as relatively wealthy people are inclined to think. In the 1960s and 1970s, people working in economic development from the Western world strongly urged poor families, at home and abroad, to have fewer children. They were under the assumption that children are a financial liability, eating up (literally) a poor family's income. But in much of the world children are laborers and a source of income to their families as early as six years old. Thus, especially considering high infant mortality rates, it makes solid financial sense for poor families to have as many children as they can. Without welfare, social security, medical help, or retirement benefits of any kind, it is crucial for parents to have enough children to survive their harsh conditions and to provide for them in old age. So, in point of fact, population growth may well be the *result* of poverty, rather than its cause. Evidence in favor of this view can be found in the fact that when parents' incomes rise, they commonly take their children out of the labor market and put them into school. Then, because the children have become a financial liability rather than an asset, parents choose to have less children and family sizes shrink naturally. In general, the higher the income level, the lower the fertility rate of the family.

9. Economic Policy Institute. http://www.epi.org/economic_snapshots/entry/webfeatures_snapshots_20060823/. Accessed on 3/30/17.

Figure 6.3: Fertility Rates by Per Capita Income

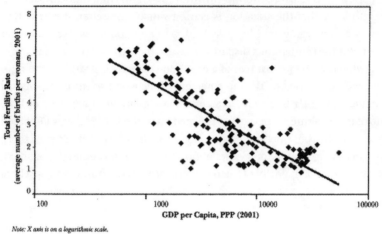

Note: X axis is on a logarithmic scale.
Source: Calculated using data from World Bank (2004).

Source: Sachs (2005: 65)[10]

What then is the cause of such high global poverty rates? This chapter will analyze the world economic system to look for the roots of the problem and to suggest a Christian approach to finding solutions.

THE GLOBAL ECONOMIC SYSTEM

The divergence between rich and poor people is found in every country and in every part of the world, and it is also found between countries. There has been a debate among scholars as to whether poor countries are merely being left behind in the race toward economic prosperity or whether they are actually being *made* poor by the global economic order. Those of the former view (including most economists) assume a theory of progress, and expect that the solution lies in helping poor countries to catch up to the rest by being incorporated into the global system. Those of the latter view (including most anthropologists) assume traditional ways of life were viable prior to their encounter with the modern system, and expect that the solution lies in protecting poor countries from the voracious effects of outside interests

10. "Figure 1: Fertility and Economic Development" from *The End of Poverty: Economic Possibilities for Our Time* by Jeffrey D. Sachs, copyright © 2005, 2006, 2015 by Jeffrey D. Sachs. Used by permission of Penguin Press, an imprint of Penguin Publishing Group, a division of Penguin Random House LCC. All rights reserved. All third party use of this material, outside of this publication, is prohibited. Interested parties must apply directly to Penguin Random House LCC for permission.

on their resources. The debate centers on the nature of the world economic system. Is it a system that yields benefits for everyone in the long run? Or is it a system that marginalizes and disempowers the many for the benefit of the few? Does it create wealth by invention or by exploitation? Is the wealth within the system flowing up or down?

On the one hand, there can be no doubt that there has been tremendous progress in the specialization of labor and the production of new technologies resulting in the creation of massive amounts of new wealth. Furthermore, some of that wealth and technology *has* "trickled down" to people at the bottom. For instance, the plastic pots that women use to carry water on their heads in developing countries are lightweight and durable compared to the clay pots of the past, and the invention of cell phones has provided a means of making a living for street children who rent them out to others. The construction of infrastructure, from roads and electric lines to telecommunication satellites, benefit rich and poor alike. Also, the introduction of business and/or industry can provide employment that is better paid than the previous forms of subsistence, such as when the urban unemployed find work in a factory, or when rural subsistence farmers start small businesses in newly forming markets. All this would suggest that *some* wealth does flow down through the system.[11]

On the other hand, there is plenty of evidence that a great deal of wealth is flowing *up* through the system as well. This is clearest in the case of natural resources. Since industrialization, the worldwide economic production system has needed increasing quantities of natural resources to fuel its operations. These resources range from minerals such as oil, coal, and diamonds to agricultural products such as jute, cotton, and lumber. As a result, over the past 250 years, land has been seized from indigenous peoples, from Native Americans to African and Australian aborigines, to gain access to their resources. John Bodley, in his book *Victims of Progress,* documents the high level of violence with which this seizure has taken place. "Conquest through colonization by commercially organized societies," he says, has "destroyed millions of indigenous peoples and countless cultural groups" (Bodley 2008b: 1). Those that remain fight a constant battle against

---

11. According to the World Bank, the global poverty rate has fallen dramatically in recent years. Between 1990 and 2013, the percentage of desperately poor people (as opposed to more moderately poor) has dropped from 35 percent to 11 percent. This is very good news indeed! However, the gains made are very regional, and arguably not due to the benefits of the global economy. The largest gains were made by socialist China, and to a lesser extent by previously socialist India. Sub-Saharan Africa, which is the most open to the global market, remains the site of the greatest extreme poverty. http://www.worldbank.org/en/topic/poverty/overview. Accessed on 3/30/17.

encroachment on their land by more powerful peoples backed up by their governments.

Furthermore, natural resources that were previously used for subsistence needs have been diverted to production for markets. Land used to grow food crops such as rice, beans, and maize has been converted to the production of cash crops such as coffee, sugar, and fruit. Even the uses of agricultural products are changing, such as the shift from producing corn for food to ethanol. Governments typically support production for sale because it means increased tax revenues and foreign exchange (currency, such as US dollars, that can be used to pay debts). Local elite accumulate land, either legally through purchase or illegally through land grabs, in order to reap the rewards of producing cash crops. As land becomes consolidated into fewer and fewer hands, subsistence farmers lose their source of livelihood and must become wage laborers, with no security for the future. Finally, as the economy shifts to the production of higher end goods, the production of subsistence goods declines and prices of essentials rise. Most significantly, food prices rise because less and less land is producing food, and wealthy people can easily afford to pay more for it. The consolidation of land and the rise of food prices squeezes the poorest people the hardest, driving them down into desperate levels of poverty. Bodley says:

> Costs are systematically shifted downward to those least able to pay, while rewards flow disproportionately to the wealthiest and most influential corporations and individuals, and from poor to rich countries. Just as the earlier politicization process made the needs of governments more important than the interests of households and villages, the commercialization process now makes the needs of giant corporations and anonymous investors more important than the well-being of either governments or communities. (2008b: 20)

In sum, markets do not encourage the production of what poor people want and need; they respond to the desires of those with money to pay, producing sugar rather than rice, coffee rather than beans, and ethanol rather than maize. Far from being a democracy, the market system is a plutocracy; it is governed by the wealthy.

There have been many well-intentioned efforts to assist poor people and poor countries to "catch up" with the global economy. The large-scale efforts have been in the form of international aid channeled through the World Bank and monitored by the International Monetary Fund (IMF). This "aid," however, is in the form of loans at market rates of interest, making it not just assistance to the borrowers but investment for the lenders.

Since the money is given directly to governments, some of it gets hijacked by wealthy elite or used for expensive government projects. Then, it must be repaid through taxation and other coercive economic policies. When repayment becomes difficult, the IMF demands cuts in government programs and services to increase the repayment rates, and the result is an *increase* in poverty.

For example, during the 1970s–1980s, there was a massive international effort to assist poor countries through IMF-sponsored loans. The world's richest countries were experiencing a glut of money in need of investment opportunities (George 1988: 30). Experts in the West believed that international aid could be both a means of investment for the rich and a way out of poverty for the poor. But over the next thirty years, the results for poor countries proved disastrous as they fell ever more deeply into debt. The rich countries benefitted by the repayments (loans were continually renewed), and massive amounts of wealth flowed *up* through the system. To illustrate the point, between 1982 and 1990, poor countries received 927 billion dollars in loans. But, during that same period, they paid back 1.3 trillion dollars, a net flow of wealth of 418 billion dollars from poor countries to rich ones (Bodley 2008a: 254).

Nowhere is the upward flow of wealth more evident than in the financial markets. People and institutions with money to invest search for opportunities to make more money. The bottom line on the decision is made simply by a calculation of the risk involved as against the possibility of a return (profit). Since the decision generally rests with hired financial investors, there is little or no investigation of the impact on local people and/or environments, either of investing or of withdrawing the money. Short-term investments can be especially destructive, pouring in money and destroying previously existing businesses by outcompeting them, and then suddenly withdrawing it and leaving the local economy devastated. Those who had money to invest walk away with more; those who needed to borrow are left with less.

In general, financial markets can be quite volatile. The values of stocks and other financial products (such as loans) shoot up and plummet down due to short-term strategies (trying to make a lot of money quickly) and even to irrational beliefs and prejudices. In 1997, the country of Thailand, which was heavily indebted to the IMF, tried to avoid bankruptcy by devaluing its currency.[12] The financial crisis from this event spread through

12. Devaluing currency means altering the exchange rate of the country's currency against the USD (United States dollar). This makes the home country's goods cheaper for foreign purchase, increasing exports, and other countries' goods more expensive, decreasing imports. The result is increased sales and decreased spending for the

southeast Asia. As a result, Western investors withdrew their money not only from Asia, but also from Russia and Latin America, areas not at all linked to the Asian markets. Even Argentina, a modern and highly market oriented country, was hit by the withdrawal of finance and had to default on loans from the IMF (Weisbrot 2007). Investors, it seemed, were lumping all "third world" countries together and declaring them to be too risky.

Even in ordinary times, financial investors have a strong tendency to follow the herd, investing just because stock prices have edged up a bit, and selling off a few minutes (or seconds!) later because prices have begun to fall. Short-term investments are often computer driven, with slight changes in stock prices triggering automatic purchases or sell-offs. This is a very long way from the considered investment that might "trickle down" to benefit local people by providing jobs or business opportunities. The journalist, Naomi Klein, says that the global market "thinks like a drug addict."[13]

Thus, there are at least two serious problems with the global economic system: 1) the preference it gives to the demands of the rich over the needs of the poor, and 2) the volatility of the markets. The market crash of 2008 has reminded us that the entire financial system can collapse, as wealthy institutions pay the price for high-risk speculation, and a subsequent loss of confidence causes everyone to withdraw their money in an effort to protect their own futures. Crises in the financial system cause a downturn in the rest of the economy as businesses can't get loans and begin to lay off their employees. Laid off employees can't purchase things in the markets at the same levels as they used to do, so sales begin to fall, causing further distress for businesses and yet more lay-offs. These crises are not at all a new phenomenon. They have been well documented since the beginning of the global capitalist order.[14] When they occur, they produce a downward spiral that is difficult or impossible to control.

Anthropologists typically analyze modern problems by comparing to earlier forms of human life. In this case, earlier forms of economic exchange can reveal much about what is wrong with the global economy, some of which parallels biblical principles as well.

---

country, which saves money that can be used to pay down debt.

13. "The Possibility of Hope," 2007 documentary extra to the film *Children of Men*, on DVD. Universal Pictures.

14. See Karl Marx's description of the crises of the 19th century (1990: 583–84, 802). Marx thought financial markets were merely a form of high-stakes gambling (1981: 608–9).

PRINCIPLES OF RECIPROCAL EXCHANGE

For the bulk of human history, we have lived as foragers in the natural environment. There are a few foraging communities left, and anthropologists have taken care to study their economic life. Foragers do no food production, so their experience is of a profound dependence on the environment to provide them with what they need. In fact, it could be said that their first reciprocal relationship is with nature; nature provides them with food and other resources, and they give back a respect that acknowledges their dependence upon it. That acknowledgment is in significant contrast to the strong sense of control over the environment that other groups have. Food producers manipulate the environment to grow what they need, and have a corresponding cosmology that emphasizes human dominance over nature. They are also far more likely to go to war, as their belief in human dominance fosters attempts to control one another. Foragers are not perfect—they are fallen human beings in need of God's grace just as the rest of us are. But their sense of dependence on the environment makes them good ecologists and strong advocates for peace (Turnbull 1987).

Social life is predominant in foraging societies. All economic concerns, vital as they are, are subordinated to the building and maintenance of social relationships. Foragers hold very little private property and have a strong value on sharing—so much so that taking someone's things is "borrowing," not "theft," even when the items are not returned. They believe that generosity is an important personal characteristic, and selfishness a serious character flaw. So, whatever people's feelings may be (and foragers expect people to be naturally selfish!), they must subordinate their own desires to the consideration of others' needs.

Most remarkably, foragers have an economic system that rests entirely on gift giving. That is to say, all goods and services that flow through the economy are exchanged as gifts, not purchased or sold. Gift giving is based on a fundamentally different principle of exchange than buying and selling. This might seem obvious, but on close examination, we will see that the difference does not lie where most people think it does. Most people think that the difference between gifting and purchasing lies in the notion that the gift is "free," that there is no necessary repayment involved. But even a brief consideration of the matter will reveal that actually nearly all gifting is deeply obligatory. Gifts are usually given to known people, most often relatives, on specified occasions such as birthdays or holidays. There is a strong expectation that return gifts will follow on either the same or the next specified occasion. A simple test to confirm this would be to refuse to give any return gifts . . . ever! Such a person would gain a reputation for stinginess and be considered anti-social. Thus, an initial gift can be viewed as a kind of a loan, one that needs to be repaid, sometimes even with interest, as when rivalries develop to give bigger and bigger gifts. People everywhere will *say* that there is no need to repay, but in actual practice most gift giving is fraught with expectations, obligations, and even danger! (Mauss 2000).

What is at stake with gifting? In order to discover this, we must examine the *meaning* of a gift. First, gifts are not just for the purpose of meeting people's needs, which can be done through simple sharing. Gifts have a symbolic value that goes beyond utilitarian purposes. We can see this in the fact that gifts are given with markers of their special nature, such as wrapping paper and bows, and cards expressing warm thoughts. People may make speeches to mark the importance of the occasion, and even public announcements regarding the value of the gifts themselves.[15] Furthermore, while receivers can say openly that they do not need what is being offered when someone is sharing, they risk hurting or offending the givers if they reject a gift. The gifts themselves are commonly not as useful as we would like. Yet, when a gift is not wanted, the unfortunate receiver is expected to smile and thank the giver anyway . . . and then look for secret ways of disposing of it!

What then is the meaning of a gift? According to anthropologists, a gift is a symbol marking the existence of a social relationship. That is why the rejection of a gift gives offense—it symbolizes a rejection of the relationship. When gifts are given and received, the underlying message is of a concern for the welfare of the other. In fact, it is care for the physical needs of the other, their economic wellbeing, that is being symbolized most directly. Food is the most commonly given gift around the world, carrying the message, "I am feeding you at my own expense; I value your welfare more than my own." So, the gift symbolizes our interdependence and reminds us that we cannot survive alone. We need others in the community to care for us, as we care for them. Though they are among the most self-sufficient peoples on earth, foragers acknowledge their dependence upon one another, just as they do their dependence on the natural environment. Through an economy entirely composed of gift giving, they symbolically mark the priority of social relationships over material things, of the social fabric over economic necessity, and of concern for others over self-interest.

The message of the gift is polar opposed to the message naturally embedded in market exchange, where the pursuit of one's own economic interest comes first. Ironically, it is purchasing that is truly free. A customer who

15. This is considered in poor taste in many cultures, such as our own, but in some cultures the monetary value of the gift is announced openly, and is a source of pride (or shame!) to the givers.

chooses not to buy can walk away, with no offense taken. So, the freedom of markets is specifically the freedom to pursue one's own interest without regard for the welfare of others. Self-interest, which is considered selfish and destructive in foraging societies, or even in our own private family lives, is completely legitimized in purchase and sale. A purchaser who does not look out for the lowest price, or a seller who does not try to get the highest price, is foolish, not generous. The true difference between gifting and purchasing, then, is not in the relative freedom to exchange (which is in the reverse direction that we think it is), but in the *purpose* of the exchange: social in the case of gifting, and economic in the case of market exchange.

Reciprocal economies focus on the construction and maintenance of the social fabric. That is, they put social life ahead of economic life. But that does not mean that these societies are better than ours in every way. Social life can be distorted by pride, greed, selfishness, and revenge. The gifting rivalry mentioned above demonstrates this. In gift rivalry, gifts still symbolize relationships, but now they are relationships of competition and jealousy, not of love and care for one another. In some societies, gift rivalry approaches a kind of warfare, as chiefs declare their own glory by giving enormous gifts to other chiefs in attempts to humiliate them. These gifts must definitely be repaid, and with interest, lest the receivers admit defeat in the competition.[16] Societies such as these, with "prestige economies," institutionalize gift giving rivalry, and value the accumulation of wealth just for the purpose of gaining and maintaining power over others. Thus, while the pursuit of money (material gain) is the principle sin of market economies, the pursuit of prestige (social gain) is the principle sin of reciprocal economies.

To understand how this can happen, we must take a close look at the act of gift giving once more. In the moment of giving, the giver always earns a little prestige and the receiver is always a little humbled. In fact, this is part of the reason that return gifts are given; to right the balance between giver and receiver, thereby restoring equality to the relationship. If the balance is not righted, and the gifts flow in only one direction, the giver becomes socially superior to the receiver permanently. As the old saying goes, "charity always wounds." Specifically, charity wounds the pride of the receiver. People who want to avoid the wound may set up a kind of a reverse power struggle, with each trying to outdo the other in giving (not receiving). Our sometimes humorous attempts to pay restaurant bills are an example. Why do people vie with one another to pay the bill? The answer may be partly that

16. The classic example of this type of gift-giving rivalry is the potlatch, a feast held by the Kwakiutl chiefs of British Columbia explicitly in order to "flatten" one another (Cronk 2012).

they are avoiding the humble position of the receiver, and are making a bid for the prestigious role of the giver. Of course, they may also be symbolizing their care for one another in true reciprocal style. But this does not change the fact that, socially, the giver always wins and the receiver loses prestige.

It is possible, however, that both parties may be content to allow gifts to flow in one direction more than the other. If the receiver is content to remain inferior to the giver, or is required to do so by society, a hierarchical relationship will be established. The relationship itself may be either positive or negative in character. Americans have a strong value on equality, and therefore tend to assume that egalitarian relationships are naturally positive and hierarchical relationships are necessarily negative. But if we define good relationships, based on our discussion in chapter two, as ones in which *shalom* is nurtured, then there clearly can be hierarchical relationships that are positive, such as between parents and children. In hierarchical situations, return gifts are still given to mark the relationship, but they are of lesser value. This is the case in our own relationship with God. God has initiated a relationship with us (which was previously broken) by giving us the gift of his Son for our salvation. We have the choice to reject this gift and thereby reject a relationship with him. But if we accept the gift, we must reciprocate it if there is to be a relationship at all. We do so by giving everything that we have, our very selves, back to God. Still, the gift of ourselves is no match for the value of the gift of God's Son. So a hierarchical relationship of benevolence is established, with God as the generous giver and ourselves as the humble receivers.

This is certainly not to say that all hierarchical relationships are positive. In fact, there is an inherent danger that the superior person or party may abuse power, a problem that ranges from child abuse to social oppression. Yet, as we have seen, egalitarian relationships can be filled with jealousy, competition, and rivalry. The social fabric weaves together all of the various complexities of who we are as human beings, sometimes supporting us in communities of *shalom,* but sometimes trapping us in social bondage. Recall Mary Stewart Van Leeuwen's comment about families in the last chapter (footnote 2), "When they are good they are very good, and when they are bad they are awful." The social fabric is absolutely necessary to our existence, but it is not in and of itself a panacea for all of our problems as human beings.

PRINCIPLES OF MARKET EXCHANGE

Still, the problem with market exchange is that it threatens to destroy the social fabric altogether. Why should this be so? It is not just that self-interest is legitimized; it is also that pursuing your own interests is completely necessary to functioning effectively in the system. A real consideration of people's needs can threaten a business's viability, causing it to lose out in the competition with other businesses. Thus business owners commonly find that they must distance themselves from family and friends, and even from their own ethnic groups, to avoid constantly having to cut prices or give away goods for free to people with whom they have social relationships (Foster 1974). Their social obligations make defending their business interests difficult. So market exchange must be conducted *as if* between strangers even when the parties know one another. More than this, metaphorically speaking, the market arena must be set apart from the rest of society in order to protect it from the pressing demands of social relationships.

It is also necessary to protect social relationships from the operating principles of the market. Imagine that *all* things were for sale! What would be the impact on society if sex could be legally purchased as a service, or children as a commodity? The answer is that the intrinsic value of these relationships would be lost. Thus, to protect the social fabric, especially in the area of kinship, there are restrictions on market exchange in every culture. In fact, when markets move into a culture, initially only the most marginal products of the economy are bought and sold, such as crafts or surplus produce. Productive assets, such as cattle or land, are still shared, inherited, and given as gifts. Increasingly, though, the convenience of market exchange, along with the possibilities for gaining new wealth, encourage people to begin buying and selling more and more things. In peasant societies, wealthier people begin to buy up the land of those who have fallen on hard times, causing land consolidation. They do this because they can increase their own wealth through access to markets, something that was not previously possible. Then, fewer and fewer families own the land, and more and more people end up as low-wage laborers. A divide emerges between those with accumulated productive assets and those who are living hand to mouth.

During the colonial period, there was a worldwide expansion of markets turning more and more goods into commodities (for purchase and sale). People who had lost their land, their primary productive asset, had to sell their labor, causing mass migrations to cities and around the world. In fact, people themselves became a commodity under slavery. This was the first stage of globalization, and it was marked by carrying the market principle to its logical extreme. Through a long and arduous process, the world's societies agreed that the slave trade was immoral, and they banned it. But slavery has not been entirely eradicated. Bonded labor, which is an arrangement just short of slavery, is still rampant around the world, especially for children, and underground slavery for sexual and domestic purposes continues to this day.[17]

Even when the market principle is limited by banning the conversion of certain goods into commodities, society can be negatively affected by the open promotion of self-interest. In the broader culture, a value on promoting your own interests in competition with others encourages the growth of individualism (thinking of yourself as an individual first, rather than as a member of a group), materialism (imagining that your material well-being is more important than your social well-being), and consumerism (working primarily to accumulate material goods). Actually, in market-based systems, materialism is more than just a desire for material goods. It is a means of measuring people's success, and even their value, in society. We can see this in the fact that people are treated with respect because they have wealth, rather than because they have integrity or character, or because they are compassionate and care for others.

Furthermore, the self-sufficiency that individualism encourages denies the value of any form of dependency, including dependency on God and the community. People view themselves as fully in command of their own destinies, and believe that their success or failure is entirely in their own hands. The result is a loss of faith in God to provide for ordinary daily needs, and a weakened commitment to family, friends, and society. Robert Wuthnow demonstrates that most Americans realize the danger, and think that their culture's values on individualism and materialism are a result of selfishness and the breakdown of community (1994: 178). Yet these same Americans continue to pursue higher and higher salaries and greater and greater consumption, failing to recognize the inconsistency between what they say they believe and the way in which they are living.

Market exchange, then, causes society to put the pursuit of economic needs first. As the world's leading market-oriented economy, America represents this lifestyle to the rest of the globe, encouraging others to pursue wealth over relationships too. Even in places as group oriented as China, extended families are now breaking down into nuclear ones, as young professional adults pursue their careers and no longer have time to care for children or the elderly. Around the world, social systems are giving way to economic systems as the primary means of organization. That is why the

17. See the work of the International Justice Mission at: http://ijm.org. Accessed on 4/4/17.

social fabric is under threat. We are all choosing material comfort over so-cial enrichment.

BIBLICAL PRINCIPLES OF THE ECONOMY

As Christians, it is important for us to remember that God created the world material. He also created us material, with bodily form, and declared his work "very good" (Gen 1:26–31). Greek Gnosticism viewed the physical world as an evil limitation on the spiritual world, and Eastern religions such as Hinduism deny the body in favor of a purification of the soul. But the Hebrew Scriptures declare that the material world is inherently good. In fact, Jesus indicated that our material needs, such as to eat and drink, are a means of wholesome dependence on God when we trust him rather than ourselves to provide (Matt 6:25–33).

Furthermore, as Christians, we believe that human beings have a God-given responsibility to care for the material world and for ourselves within it. We are stewards of creation. Stewardship is precisely *non*-ownership; it is the very opposite of *private* property. God owns the earth completely, and we are his vice-regents with the duty to administer and the right to use the resources he has provided. Our role is not to garner parts of the earth to be our very own. But rather, we are to care for it as a whole, and to be account-able to God for it.

The Christian environmentalist Calvin DeWitt suggests that creation is God's *oikos*, or household, the root of the word "economy" (cf. Acts 7:49–50) (1).[18] Our household, says DeWitt, which is the economy, must fit appropriately into God's household, which is creation. DeWitt compares economic growth to human development, and suggests that "proportioned growth and balance is the rule" (4). When human cellular growth is uncon-trolled it becomes a cancer and kills the host. So, likewise, when economic systems are allowed to grow uncontrollably they damage and even destroy the earth. When rightly managed, however, human economies can serve the purpose of stewardship, as is implied in the Greek word, *oikonomia*, which means household management. DeWitt recommends five principles for good management of economies: 1) engaging in earth keeping, or care of the natural environment, 2) observing the Sabbath, not only for ourselves but for animals and the land, 3) appreciating God's blessing and creation's

18. "Creation Care and Evangelical Relief and Development" by Calvin B. DeWitt. Occasional paper #4 of the Association of Evangelical Relief and Development Agen-cies (AERDO). http://www.aeseonline.org/aeseonline.org/Creation_Care_%26_Re-lief_and_Development.html. Accessed on 2/23/18.

fruitfulness by enjoying the natural world and making a healthy living in it; 4) providing relief for those in need, such as the poor, who sometimes damage the environment in their efforts to stay alive, and 5) breaking the chains of injustice and oppression that prevent people from experiencing the freedom to become good stewards of the earth (7–11).

As stewards, we are not to imagine ourselves independent either of God or of one another. The importance of acknowledging our dependence on God is a strong theme throughout the Bible and there are many warnings against excessive self-sufficiency (Deut 32:15; Hos 13:6; Luke 12:13–21). Acknowledging our mutual interdependence as human beings is also important, and produces the communities of *shalom* that God intends for us. In contrast to the American value on self-sufficiency, the Bible values reliance on God and others, and consideration of our responsibility for those in need.

In chapter five, we saw that the Bible roots justice in communities of faithful relationships. In economic terms, this means never imagining that our wealth is entirely our own, or that we have no responsibility for others. In Isaiah 58, the prophet declares that Israel's worship is worthless to God because of their self-interestedness:

> Day after day they seek me
> and delight to know my ways,
> as if they were a nation that practiced righteousness
>   and did not forsake the ordinance of their God . . .
> Look, you serve your own interest on your fast day,
>   and oppress all your workers
> Look, you fast only to quarrel and to fight
>   and to strike with a wicked fist.
> Such fasting as you do today
>   will not make your voice heard on high. (Isa 58:2–4)

Isaiah then identifies what Israel needs to do differently and what the rewards will be from God for doing it:

> Is not this the fast that I choose:
>   to loose the bonds of injustice,
>   to undo the thongs of the yoke,
> to let the oppressed go free,
>   and to break every yoke?
> Is it not to share your bread with the hungry,
>   and bring the homeless poor into your house;
> when you see the naked, to cover them,
>   and not to hide yourself from your own kin?

Then your light shall break forth like the dawn,
   and your healing shall spring up quickly;
your vindicator shall go before you,
   the glory of the Lord shall be your rear guard.
Then you shall call, and the Lord will answer;
   you shall cry for help, and he will say, Here I am. (Isa 58:
6–9)

According to this passage, then, God will answer our needs when we answer the needs of others. The prophet Amos gives us a warning:

Hear this, you that trample on the needy,
and bring to ruin the poor of the land,
saying, "When will the new moon be over
so that we may sell grain;
and the Sabbath,
so that we may offer wheat for sale? . . .
The time is surely coming, says the Lord God,
when I will send a famine on the land;
not a famine of bread, or a thirst for water,
but of hearing the words of the Lord. (Amos 8:4–5, 11)

Amos says that those who grow wealthy at the expense of the poor will discover a greater need than wealth, the need for "hearing the words of the Lord," and that God will refuse to satisfy this greater need because the wealthy have trampled on and ruined the poor. The prophet Ezekiel declares, "This was the guilt of your sister Sodom: she and her daughters had pride, excess of food, and prosperous ease, but did not aid the poor and needy" (Ezek 16:49). So Sodom was destroyed not just for sexual sins, but for economic ones. When we fail to help those in need, God himself takes up their cause and demands justice (cf. Ps 35:10; Ps 140:12; Isa 41:17).

    As we have seen, most Americans are willing to be generous with *excess* wealth, what they have left over after all their bills are paid and their own needs satisfied. But few Americans recognize that the satisfaction of their own "needs" may be nearly limitless. Famously, when the oil magnate, John D. Rockefeller, was asked how much money was enough, he responded, "Just a little bit more." Rockefeller was one of the richest men in the world at the time, and surely understood the irony of his own statement. (In fact, he became one of America's first great philanthropists.) But that statement reflects the reality that most Americans, who are very well off by the world's standards, chronically feel underprivileged. The nineteenth-century French scholar, De Tocqueville, commented, "In America, I have seen the freest and best educated of men in circumstances the happiest to be found in the world; yet it seemed to me that a cloud habitually hung on their brow, and they seemed serious and almost sad even in their pleasures. The chief reason [is that they] are forever brooding over advantages they do not possess" (2000: 661).

This misperception is a direct result of Americans' value on economic success. That value causes them to continually focus on those above, rather than those below, themselves. By a simple shift to looking down the economic scale, instead of up, Americans can begin to realize their tremendously privileged position, and the injustice it represents. Bringing about economic justice will certainly require some sacrifice on the part of those who are relatively wealthy. But the Bible states clearly that such sacrifice honors God and is rewarded by him. Proverbs 14:31 says, "Those who oppress the poor insult their Maker, but those who are kind to the needy honor him," and Proverbs 19:17 says, "Whoever is kind to the poor lends to the Lord, and will be repaid in full."

In order to create communities of *shalom* that care for the poor and needy, we must begin by ordering our economic lives around biblical principles. One of these principles is the principle of the Sabbath. At Mount Sinai, God told the Israelites though Moses:

> "You shall keep my sabbaths, for this is a sign between me and you throughout your generations, given in order that you may know that I, the Lord, sanctify you. You shall keep the sabbath, because it is holy for you; everyone who profanes it shall be put to death; whoever does any work on it shall be cut off from among the people . . . It is a sign forever between me and the people of Israel that in six days the Lord made heaven and earth, and on the seventh day he rested, and was refreshed." (Exod 31:12–14, 17)

No work was to be done on the Sabbath on pain of excommunication from the community, and even death! (Exod 35:2). The time was to be spent in worshipping God and resting. By forcing the Israelites to stop working every seventh day, God was reminding them of the dangers of self-sufficiency and of the importance of dependence upon him.

Historically, the Judeo-Christian principle of the Sabbath is the reason that Sunday is a day of rest for the entire world. Even the global economy observes a partial rest on Sundays, such as by closing the stock markets and businesses. But this is less true than it used to be, and the pressure is on to develop a 24/7 economy in which not even the need for sleep at night is respected. We are all working furiously to achieve material success by our own hands. John Rempel reminds us that,

The Sabbath is the first step in reversing the Fall, in placing the world back into God's hands. In the Fall we tried to take the world into our hands, insisting we knew better than God what makes life good. This flight from God leaves us with an overwhelming realization that now the only meaning in life is one we create. The basis of human existence is no longer who we are—children of God—but what we make. Capitalism sees people as doers: On weekdays they are producers; on weekends they are consumers. And most of us conclude that life has passed us by if we are not engaged in one or the other. (2000: 6)

To counter-act the global culture on this point, Rempel recommends that we live out the Sabbath by observing the following rules on Sundays: 1) don't work, 2) don't shop, 3) don't worry, 4) squander time, by which he means, "do something for no other reason than that it expresses creativity or brings pleasure," 5) worship God, and 6) welcome someone into your life (7). Observing the Sabbath in this way would go a long way toward helping to repair the social fabric if we were to practice it seriously!

In the Old Testament, the Sabbath principle was extended to include even longer periods of rest. After the Israelites settled in Canaan, they became agriculturalists. Each tribe was allocated land for its sustenance (except the priestly tribe of Levi, which received towns) (Josh 1:13–22). God declared that the land itself should be given a Sabbath rest every seventh year (Lev 25:1–7), and he specified that this rest was to also benefit the poor: "For six years you shall sow your land and gather in its yield; but the seventh year you shall let it rest and lie fallow, so that the poor of your people may eat; and what they leave the wild animals may eat. You shall do the same with your vineyard, and with your olive orchard" (Exod 23:10–11). Furthermore, all debts were to be forgiven in this seventh year (Deut 15:1–2). Thus, the seventh year functioned as a leveling mechanism, providing relief to the poor and preventing the rich from accumulating too much wealth.

Care for the poor was also provided by the gleaning laws. In Leviticus, God instructed landowners to leave behind part of their harvest: "You shall not strip your vineyard bare, or gather the fallen grapes of your vineyard; you shall leave them for the poor and the alien: I am the Lord your God" (Lev 19:10). "When you reap the harvest of your land, you shall not reap to the very edges of your field, or gather the gleanings of your harvest; you shall leave them for the poor and for the alien. I am the LORD your God" (Lev 23:22). Notice that these injunctions extended even to "aliens," or immigrants (cf. Deut 24:19–21; Lev 19:33–34). The Bible says that God "loves the strangers, providing them food and clothing" (Deut 10:18; 24:17).

Every fiftieth year was a "year of Jubilee" in which all land that had been sold was to be returned to its original owners (Lev 25). The practical reason for this law was to prevent any one individual, family, or tribe from buying up most or all of the land, and making others permanently landless. But the relational reason was to remind the Israelites that they were in any case stewards, and not owners, of the land. God declared, "the land shall not be sold in perpetuity, for the land is mine; with me you are but aliens and tenants" (Lev 25:23). Though the land was allocated to families and tribes, it was never to be owned absolutely; that right belonged to God alone, who could give it or take it away at will. Thus, God declared even his own people to be "aliens and tenants" on the land, removing all claims to exclusive possession of it.

There is a parallel here to our ownership of wealth, along with a positive lesson. As we have seen, all that we own belongs to God; we are only stewards of the material world. Living by that reality prevents us from imagining ourselves to be self-sufficient—and it provides us with a great *freedom* from the bondage of possessiveness. St. John of the Cross describes the difference between the person who depends upon God for the satisfaction of material needs and the one who tries to hang on tightly to material goods:

> One person rejoices in all things—since his joy is dependent upon none of them—as if he had them all; and another, through looking upon them with a particular sense of ownership, loses in a general sense all the pleasure of them all. This former person, having none of them in his heart, possesses them all, as Saint Paul says, in great freedom. This latter person, inasmuch as he has something of them through the attachment of his will, neither has nor possesses anything; it is rather they that have possessed his heart, and he is, as it were, a sorrowing captive.[19]
> (1958: 407)

Ironically, by trying to possess material goods absolutely we become slaves to them, while by letting go we gain a sense of owning the whole world![20]

A second principle by which we must order our economic lives as Christians is that we should put God's kingdom work first, before our material concerns. Jesus put it this way:

> Therefore I tell you, do not worry about your life, what you will eat or what you will drink, or about your body, what you will

19. I have lightly edited this quotation from the original for clarity and gender inclusivity.

20. St. Francis of Assisi also understood this principle and lived by it. See the story of his life by G. K. Chesterton (1987).

wear. Is not life more than food, and the body more than clothing? Look at the birds of the air; they neither sow nor reap nor
gather into barns, and yet your heavenly Father feeds them. Are
you not of more value than they? And can any of you by wor-
rying add a single hour to your span of life? And why do you
worry about clothing? Consider the lilies of the field, how they
grow; they neither toil nor spin, yet I tell you, even Solomon
in all his glory was not clothed like one of these. But if God so
clothes the grass of the field, which is alive today and tomorrow
is thrown into the oven, will he not much more clothe you—you
of little faith? Therefore do not worry, saying, "What will we
eat?" or "What will we drink?" or "What will we wear?" For it
is the Gentiles who strive for all these things; and indeed your
heavenly Father knows that you need all these things. But strive
first for the kingdom of God and his righteousness, and all these
things will be given to you as well. (Matt 6:25–33)

Jesus did not ask us to give up our earthly needs. Rather he commanded us
to trust God for them so that we can freely turn our attention to God's larger
purposes for us and for the world. Eastern religions require severe austeri-
ties to purify the soul from the contaminating influences of the body's attachment to this world. In Hinduism, for example, anyone who wishes to
be a saint must restrict their intake of food, water, and even air. In Jainism,
an offshoot of Hinduism, starving yourself to death is the supreme act of
religious piety. But Jesus taught that the true path to freedom from earthly
concerns was to focus on the work of God's kingdom and to humbly allow
God to care for our physical needs.

The early church lived out this principle by developing communities of
shalom that cared for widows, orphans, and the poor. They did this so consistently and so effectively that the Roman Emperor Julian, who was trying
to eradicate Christianity, wrote to a pagan priest, "Nothing has contributed
to the progress of the superstition of these Christians as their charity to
strangers, the impious Galileans provide not only for their own poor but
for ours as well" (Keller 2010: 124). Some Christians gave up their personal
possessions entirely for the sake of the church. Luke reports, "Now the
whole group of those who believed were of one heart and soul, and no one
claimed private ownership of any possessions, but everything they owned
was held in common . . . [and] there was not a needy person among them,
for as many as owned lands or houses sold them and brought the proceeds
of what was sold" (Acts 4:32, 34). Actions such as these reflected a primary
commitment to the work of the kingdom of God through the church, and a
deep trust in God's care for those who rely upon him.

The assurance of God's provision for those who trust in him is made repeatedly throughout the Bible. When they were wandering in the wilderness, God provided a double portion of manna to the Israelites on the sixth day so that they could rest on the seventh (Exod 16:22–26). When they were to give the land a rest in Canaan, God provided for them in the year prior to the Jubilee: "Should you ask, 'What shall we eat in the seventh year, if we may not sow or gather in our crop?' I will order my blessing for you in the sixth year, so that it will yield a crop for three years" (Lev 25:20–21). And, in the passage above, Jesus reminded the crowds who were following him that, "Your heavenly Father knows that you need all these things" (Matt 6:32). Thus, by observing the Sabbath and putting God's kingdom work first, we can begin to experience the trust in God's provision that will free us from the bondage of slavery to our material needs.

CHRISTIANS AND THE GLOBAL ECONOMY

At the larger level, by remembering God's kingdom and observing the Sabbath we are ensuring that the economy is properly *subordinated* to the greater purposes of life. With a healthy independence from concern for our own material needs, we can contribute to economic life in ways that are constructive, rather than destructive, of the social fabric. Christians down through the centuries have participated in improving their societies and economies. Today, they are involved in a variety of economic activities that reveal a commitment to a different agenda than just what works to produce wealth for themselves. These activities include relief and development, service oriented business, and economic advocacy.

Some of the largest relief and development agencies in the world were begun by Christians, such the Red Cross, Oxfam, World Vision, Food for the Hungry, Compassion International, and others. World Vision in particular has developed theories, methods, and strategies for addressing the problem of global poverty. Drawing on the work of Robert Chambers, Bryant Myers suggests that poverty consists of a web of interrelated needs that must be addressed holistically.

Figure 6.4: The Web of Poverty

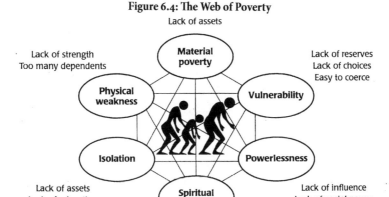

Lack of assets

Lack of strength
Too many dependents

Material poverty

Lack of reserves
Lack of choices
Easy to coerce

Physical weakness

Vulnerability

Isolation

Powerlessness

Lack of assets
Lack of education
Excluded from system

Spiritual poverty

Lack of influence
Lack of social power
Exploited by powers

Broken relationships
with neighbor and God

Source: Myers (2011: 116)

Like the strands of a spider's web, dysfunctional relationships of multiple types are woven together into a "poverty trap" from which it is very difficult to escape. For instance, children from disrupted homes find it difficult to do well in school; lack of education makes it difficult to get a good job; lack of a good job makes it difficult to provide healthcare for the family; stresses on family life make caring for children difficult; and demoralization about one's own life makes it difficult to participate in local religious or political movements that might help change the larger circumstances. Christians in development realize that a holistic approach to poverty alleviation is needed to reconstruct communities of *shalom* where they have been destroyed by poverty. Myers says, "poverty is the result of relationships that don't work, that are not just, that are not for life, that are not harmonious or enjoyable. Poverty is the absence of *shalom* in all its meanings" (2011: 143).

There are, of course, many, many Christians involved in the business world as well, both as business owners and as employees. The markets evaluate businesses purely by the degree to which they maximize profits for owners and shareholders. But Christians should evaluate businesses not just by their profitability, but by the contribution they make to the communities in which they operate. The true value of the goods and services produced, beneficial employment for people in need of work, and charitable giving are all important factors in a kingdom-oriented business. This larger view of business can be found even in the secular world, where mission statements are written to identify the company's purpose beyond simply meeting the financial bottom line. Some Christian-owned businesses have explicitly incorporated their Christian values into their mission statements. As an example, ServiceMaster, a cleaning and restoration agency with over 30,000 employees, has as its first commitment, "to honor God in all that we do." The founder of ServiceMaster, Marion E. Wade, "viewed each individual employee and customer as being made in God's image—worthy of dignity and respect," and established rules and procedures ensuring that all staff would be well treated on the job.[21] Many Christian businesses give charitably to the church, and some form agencies such as the Mennonite Economic Development Associates[22] that assist others to start their own businesses and thereby come up out of poverty. Businesses that are service oriented can significantly impact society in ways that restore relationships rather than destroy them.

Christians can also join movements for economic justice, or advocacy. For instance, there are Christians involved in the fair trade movement working to properly compensate growers and producers of goods. Fair trade is based on a model of economic cooperation, rather than competition, making it more suitable to the maintenance of the social fabric. The World Fair Trade Organization lists ten principles for fair trade: 1) creating opportunities for economically disadvantaged producers, 2) transparency and accountability, 3) practices that demonstrate "concern for the social, economic and environmental well-being of marginalized small producers," 4) payment of a fair price, "one that has been mutually agreed by all through dialogue and participation," 5) ensuring there is no child or forced labor, 6) commitment to nondiscrimination, 7) ensuring good working conditions, 8) providing capacity building, meaning "the organization develops the skills and capabilities of its own employees or members," 9) promoting fair trade, and 10) respect for the environment.[23] The idea of a more cooperative form of trade may seem unrealistic in the face of the demands of global competition. But there are now about three thousand fair trade organizations operating in over seventy countries and improving the lives of more than a million workers and producers.[24] These organizations recognize the need to accommodate the realities of the market, but encourage the development of a holistic and ethical approach to business that remembers the lives of the human beings involved.

21. See https://www.servicemaster.com/company/about/history. Accessed on 4/6/17.

22. See http://www.meda.org/web/. Accessed on 4/6/17.

23. See http://www.wfto.com/index.php?option=com_content&task=view&id=150 6&Itemid=293. Accessed on 4/6/17.

24. See http://www.wfto.com/about-us/history-wfto/history-fair-trade. Accessed on 4/6/17.

At the macro-level, then, Christians with a kingdom-oriented view of business should support government policies that encourage economic co-operation, as well as a healthy competition. Governments can misuse their trust and abuse the people and institutions they are meant to protect. In fact, they commonly back the wealthy who are already benefitting from the markets. But part of the purpose of government is to protect the marginalized, to produce cooperation between interest groups, and to help maintain conditions that are beneficial to the social fabric (such as by promoting civil society). Development economist Jeffrey Sachs (2005: 327) remarks:

> Economists from Adam Smith onward have recognized that competition and struggle are but one side of economic life, and that trust, cooperation, and collective action in the provision of public goods are the obverse side. Just as the communist attempt to banish competition from the economic scene via state ownership failed miserably, so too would an attempt to manage a modern economy on the basis of market forces alone. All successful economies are mixed economies, relying on both the public sector and the private sector for economic development . . . Without *cooperation*, a collection of national economies will not provide efficient levels of investment in cross-border infrastructure, knowledge, environmental management, or merit goods among the world's poor. [Emphasis added.]

Thus, according to Sachs, the economy itself needs the cooperation between people that governments can provide.

In fact, completely unfettered markets are so volatile that they are dangerous for everyone. Sachs demonstrates this point with a comparison of national economies that are relatively open versus closed to the global market:

Figure 6.5: Average Growth Rate of Eight Open versus Forty Closed Economies

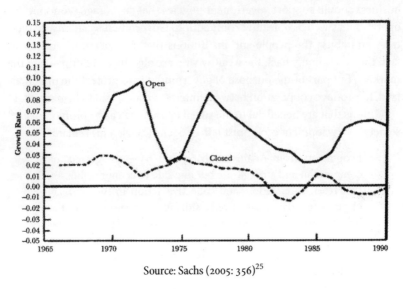

Source: Sachs (2005: 356)[25]

Markets that are open to the global economy (that is, unprotected by their governments) have higher growth rates, but are much more volatile. Those that are partially closed to the global economy have lower growth rates, but are more stable. For the poor, who are living on the margin of a sustainable life, stability is more important than growth. If the economy takes a turn for the worse, it is not luxuries goods that they must give up, but basic necessities such as food and shelter.

The Nobel prize-winning economist Amartya Sen has suggested that government policies that focus on an equitable distribution of wealth, rather than just on its production, can help to provide a viable life for everyone. He demonstrates this with a comparison of the gross national product (GNP, the per capita amount of wealth produced by a country in a year) of selected countries with their life expectancy at birth:

Figure 6.6: GNP versus Life Expectancy

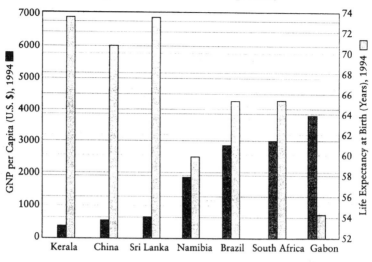

Source: Sen (1999: 47)
Artwork by Mark Stein

Note that the state of Kerala in India has achieved a remarkably high life expectancy on a very minimal GNP, while Gabon in West Africa has a truly dismal life expectancy despite a much higher GNP. Kerala, with a long history of good social policies, including education, healthcare, and political participation, is ensuring that everyone benefits from its wealth. Gabon, which is rich in oil reserves, is permitting an elite few to benefit while a significant portion of its population suffers in poverty and its environment is heavily polluted by the oil industry. It is selling out the majority of its people, along with its own economic future (the oil reserves are declining), to the interests of a wealthy minority who can afford to relocate elsewhere. The difference between these two situations is in their different government policies. In the next chapter, we will investigate the purpose and formation of governments, along with a biblical understanding of the role that they should, and should not, play. Here, the point is that Christians must advocate for economic policies that favor a just distribution of wealth, assistance to the poor and marginalized, and the maintenance of the social fabric.

Through relief and development agencies, service-oriented businesses, and advocacy, Christians *are* contributing to economies in holistic ways that reflect the values of the kingdom. Can you be a Christian and still make a living? Certainly. But, as followers of Jesus, we must pursue kingdom goals ahead of our own material success, and we must actively promote the interests of those who are not benefitting from the global economic order. In

his speech accepting the 2002 Nobel Peace Prize, former president Jimmy
Carter said,

> At the beginning of this new millennium, I was asked to dis-
> cuss, here in Oslo, the greatest challenge that the world faces.
> Among all the possible choices, I decided that the most serious
> and universal problem is a growing chasm between the richest
> and poorest people on earth . . . Tragically, in the industrialized
> world there is a terrible absence of understanding or concern
> about those who are enduring lives of despair and hopelessness.
> We have not yet made the commitment to share with others an
> appreciable part of our excessive wealth.[26]

As Christians, we have a special responsibility to invest time, money, and
energy in the construction of a just economic system, both locally and
globally, in accordance with our commitment to building communities of
shalom.

(CHAPTER 6) DISCUSSION QUESTIONS

1. In what ways is the influence of the global economy felt in your own
   home neighborhood? How might that influence be felt differently in
   another type of neighborhood?

2. What further insights into the dynamics of gift giving do you have
   based on your own relationships? How does reciprocity establish and
   maintain social ties?

3. What other biblical principles are there that should be considered when
   constructing a Christian perspective on economic life?

4. What are some examples of good social policies that will enable the
   wealth of a country to be evenly distributed?

5. What is one small thing that you could begin to do now, as a holy habit,
   that would help make the economy, local or global, more like the kingdom of God?

RECOMMENDED READINGS

Bodley, John. 2008. *Anthropology and Contemporary Human Problems*. Lanham, MD:
    Altimira.

26. Nobel Prize. http://nobelprize.org/nobel_prizes/peace/laureates/2002/carter-
lecture.html. Accessed on 4/6/17.

Myers, Bryant. 2011. *Walking with the Poor: Principles and Practices of Transformational Development.* Maryknoll, NY: Orbis.

Narayan, Deepa, et al. 2002. *Voices of the Poor: Can Anyone Hear Us?* Oxford: Oxford University Press.

Sachs, Jeffrey D. 2005. *The End of Poverty: Economic Possibilities for our Time.* New York: Penguin.

Sen, Amartya. 1999. *Development as Freedom.* New York: Anchor.

Chapter 7

Can We Be Christians and Still Love our Country?

Politics and the Kingdom of God

"What should we have done?" asked the American Christian student of his professor. The United States had invaded Iraq a second time. Many American Christians thought the invasion was warranted. Saddam Hussein was clearly a dictator, brutalizing his own people—even his few allies thought so. Furthermore, he was threatening the world with weapons of mass destruction. Yet when the invasion was over no such weapons were found, and the American public discovered the uncomfortable truth—that Iraq was a small poor country, apart from its oil wealth, and *very* difficult to stabilize.

The student's question seemed reasonable at first glance.[1] Not to have intervened with a brutal dictator would have been uncharitable to the people suffering in the country, and possibly irresponsible to the rest of the world. Yet the question, "What should *we* have done?" contained a significant assumption, one that needs some critical thinking. The student did not mean "we Christians." In context, he clearly meant, "we Americans," . . . what should we *Americans* have done? In framing the question in this

---

1. This chapter was read by Robin Lowery and Sharon Gramby-Sobukwe, both of whom gave me excellent insights into political processes and the complexities of a Christian position with regard to war. Neither is responsible for my views, of course, but I sincerely thank them both for helping me to think these matters through.

way, the student was identifying himself for the moment as an American, rather than as a Christian. No doubt, if asked, the student would have acknowledged that his Christian identity must come first, but he probably thought that in matters of politics his American identity was more relevant . . . or he simply conflated the two. For Americans, the relevant institution in a situation like this is the government, so the student's question was really, "What should the American government have done?" But if he had asked, "What should we *Christians* have done?" the relevant institution would have been the church, and the question would have meant, "What should the Christian church have done?" This question would have required everyone to remember the church in Iraq, and to speculate on how the global church might have supported the Iraqi church in its efforts to witness to Christ under a dictatorship.

We Christians are always citizens of two countries, an earthly one and a heavenly one, the kingdom of God. Christians down through the centuries have been citizens of a great number of different earthly states and empires. The Apostle Paul was a Roman citizen, and willing to use his citizenship to his own advantage (Acts 22:22–29). But his primary allegiance was always to Christ and the church, and in the end Paul was put to death for his faith by his own Roman government. States are sovereign authorities and rarely willing to accommodate another political authority in the lives of their citizens. Thus, throughout the history of the church, Christians have had an uneasy relationship with the states in which they have lived (Troeltsch 1992). Remembering the Bible's instruction to honor the authorities that God has put into place (Rom 13:1–7), Christians have been good citizens of their respective countries, contributing constructively to the social and political order. But, also remembering the Bible's teaching that the "principalities and powers" of this earth have only temporary power, and will be judged for it at the end of time (1 Cor 15:24), Christians have opposed the evil deeds of their governments and insisted on following God first.

Why do American Christians think first of their government to solve global problems? They do so partly because it is easy to imagine that the government has the real power, and that the church is merely a private voluntary association, lacking in the ability to make a difference in the world. But, Lesslie Newbigin reminds us:

> The Church is an entity which has outlasted many states, nations, and empires, and it will outlast those that exist today. The Church is nothing other than that movement launched into the public life of the world by its sovereign Lord to continue that which he came to do until it is finished in his return in glory. It

is his promise that the gates of hell shall not prevail against it. In spite of the crimes, blunders, compromises, and errors by which its story has been stained and is stained to this day, *the Church is the great reality in comparison with which nations and empires and civilizations are passing phenomena.* (1989: 221) [Emphasis added.]

The United States of America is less than 300 years old, and it will pass away. The church is over 2,000 years old and has survived innumerable governments, many of which were hostile to it. Furthermore, it is a *global* institution, and one guided by the Holy Spirit. Thus, we Christians have the potential to do more for the good of the world as members of the church than we do as citizens of our various countries.

THE ANTHROPOLOGY OF POWER

States and governments are institutions that organize and execute power. As with other subjects, we will begin by examining what anthropologists know about power from a cross-cultural survey of political systems, and especially from small-scale, traditional systems rather than large and complex ones. Then we will apply what we learn to our own situation and examine it from a Christian perspective.

First, power is commonly defined as the ability to get others to do as you wish. The means for exercising power vary from gentle persuasion, to covert manipulation, to overt coercion or force. Anthropologists distinguish broadly between the use of legitimacy and coercion in the exercise of power. Legitimacy is convincing people of the rightness of what you propose, or of your right to propose it if you hold an office. Since persuasion is used, people who cooperate under legitimacy do so voluntarily. Coercion, on the other hand, is forcing people to cooperate whether they agree with you or not. It is exercised by threats of punishment and restraints on behavior. Since it is difficult to persuade everyone to cooperate all the time, most attempts to exercise power combine legitimacy and coercion. But the two types of means are significantly different in nature and can have different results. People will endure much hardship and sacrifice when they believe they are serving a just cause. But when they are not persuaded of the cause, and especially if they are forced, they almost always resent the exercise of power. Sooner or later that resentment boils over into rebellion (which rejects the leadership) or revolution (which overthrows the entire system). Thus, all those in power, even dictators, must constantly reinforce their legitimacy with the public lest their use of coercion create dangerous levels of resentment.

A stable arrangement for the exercise of power is a political system. The smallest political system is actually the family, with parents having power over children. This example reminds us that the exercise of power can be benevolent. The Bible speaks frequently of God as our Father in order to elicit the notion of a loving authority. But human political systems are, at best, always a mix of good and evil. As we saw in chapter five, the exercise of power in the family can be abusive. And certainly larger political systems can be abusive as well. Of political systems, as of families, it can truly be said, "When they are good they are very, very good, and when they are bad they are awful!"[2]

The value of political systems is in the internal order they create. The Enlightenment philosophers thought that governments are formed because people agree rationally, by "social contract," to submit to an authority that will protect their rights. This benevolent view of political systems has some merit, as governments have often looked out for the interests of their peoples. But, anthropologist Elizabeth Colson (1974) suggests another reason for the formation of political systems, the fear of neighbors. Colson sees evidence for this fear in the fact that belief in witchcraft (or sorcery) is most common in societies without established legal systems (cf. Whiting 1950: 36, 87). Witches are people who harm others supernaturally out of envy, jealousy, or the desire for revenge. In societies with witchcraft beliefs, people never know who is a witch or whether they may have offended one. Furthermore, they know that they may be accused of being a witch if they are uncooperative or anti-social. So most people try to be polite and generous with one another in order to avoid either being attacked by a witch or accused of being one.

Political systems, which include both legitimized authorities for protection and legal institutions for recourse when a crime is committed, relieve people of the fear of their neighbors. They work so well, in fact, that in modern suburbs people commonly do not even *know* their neighbors. There is, however, a price to be paid for this form of safety. People must hand over some of their power to the government, in the hope that the government will care for them without demanding too much of them. Governments can demand a lot. For instance, they may appropriate property for the common welfare, or just for the use of rulers, and they commonly demand taxes and military service, which takes peoples' lives. Furthermore, since governments are built on the appropriation of power, they have a natural tendency to increase their power at the expense of the people they rule, says

2. Mary Stewart Van Leeuwen uses this phrase to refer to family dynamics (personal communication).

Colson. So, the price to be paid for safety is in the increasing loss of political autonomy, or freedom. Still, most people are willing to pay this price rather than face the fearful circumstance of no system at all, or a return to the tiresome attempt to keep the peace with neighbors themselves (Colson 1974: 45).

Political systems are built on a social order that is composed of rules for behavior. There are two types of rules involved: norms, which are rules enforced by informal means, such as praise or criticism, esteem or scorn, or even just smiles or frowns; and laws, which are rules enforced by formal means, that is, by predetermined sanctions carried out by established authorities (Hoebel 1978). Even in the largest political systems, it is norms that guide most people's behavior most of the time. Norms are the product of a set of commonly held values and a vision of the common good undergirding civil society. They are deeply rooted in the social fabric, and constitute a culturally specific agreement about what is good, right, and proper. So norms, which by definition have high levels of legitimacy, are especially effective at establishing a stable order.

As an example, there is a norm in America (and even more so in Europe, but unlike elsewhere) that requires people to form a line when waiting for something. They do this without speaking about it, unless someone tries to get ahead of the line. If that happens, the norm will quickly be revealed by the reaction to its breach, from complaints to fisticuffs. Though elsewhere in American society you can purchase your way to the front of the line (metaphorically speaking), in an ordinary street line, you are likely to end up in the gutter. The strength of this norm is in the American conception of fairness. In the back of their minds, Americans are envisioning an ideal society composed of equal individuals. So fairness requires a norm for "first come, first served." By way of contrast, in India, where the ideal for society includes membership in groups and a legitimized hierarchy, fairness requires that the most important people be served first! Thus, rather than making a line, people form a crowd and wait to be called upon. Social norms, not laws, are dictating people's behavior in both cases.

The simplest political systems operate exclusively with the use of norms. Their small size makes it possible to achieve social conformity without the establishment of laws or the use of much coercion. Bands and tribes have leaders who function largely as facilitators, and they use consensus to reach agreement. Kinship is the primary organizing principle, so the norms for behavior toward family members dictate much of the political process. Because all relationships are face to face, people's personal circumstances are always taken into account when judging their situation. On the other hand, it is difficult for people to evade the consequences of their own behavior.

Just as in our families and small town communities, on the whole social pressure works well to produce cooperation.

As political systems grow, however, power gets centralized and coercion is increasingly used to control those who will not cooperate. Thus, chiefdoms and states have leaders with the authority to make binding decisions, backed up by the use of coercive institutions such as the police, courts, and jails. Citizenship becomes the organizing principle, treating people solely as individuals (ignoring their group memberships or social backgrounds), and demanding their primary allegiance to the state. Coercion is used not only on people when they commit crimes, but also on groups when they gather to demonstrate or riot, and on religious, political, and ethnic movements when they resist assimilation. In this way, a formal system of political control is superimposed on the informal system of social control, resulting in an expanded order. Through human history, political systems have been enlarged to include more and more people, and to create more and more elaborate structures.

THE ANTHROPOLOGY OF WAR

Political systems must negotiate their relationships with other political systems. Negotiations commonly include agreements or treaties, the reciprocal exchange of goods, and even intermarriage to solidify relations with the strength of kinship bonds. Always looming on the horizon, however, is the possibility of war. Societies vary significantly with regard to their willingness to engage in violent conflict (Ember and Ember 1994). Some, such as the Trumai of central Brazil or the Lepcha of the Himalaya mountains, make every effort to avoid war. They view violence as disruptive of the natural as well as the social order. When negotiations with their neighbors fail, these societies simply submit to their circumstances or migrate to avoid the clash (Fabbro 1978). Other societies, such as the Kapauku of highland New Guinea or the Yanomami of Venezuela, not only approve of war, but encourage it. They are easily provoked, and commit acts of aggression to demonstrate prowess. Boys are praised for fighting one another, manhood is linked to killing enemies, and women chide men who are reluctant to avenge the community's honor.

War is a culturally patterned response to conflict between political systems. A small sample of the legitimized reasons for it include: raiding for women and for revenge (among the Jivaro of Ecuador), stealing horses and gaining prestige (among the Blackfoot of the American plains), taking land and promoting leaders (among the Zulu of southern Africa), getting

revenge and enhancing internal solidarity (among the Maori of New Zealand), and blood feuding (among the Albanians of Eastern Europe) (Bohannan 1967). These reasons fall into a number of categories: economic gain
(women, horses, and land); personal prestige (of the warriors or leaders);
and group pride (revenge and blood feuds). In each case, the culture ap-
proves of the use of violence to meet what is considered to be a critical need.

Is violence really necessary to fill these needs? At one time, anthropologists assumed that there must be functional reasons for war. Purposes
from resource competition to population control were investigated. Now,
however, most would concede that war is destructive beyond any short-
term benefits it may have. Economic gain is often temporary, and rivalries
for prestige or national pride escalate into mutual destruction. Rather than
functional, war is more likely a trap that people fall into, and from which
they find it difficult to escape. Stanton Tefft has described the "war trap"
in three cases: the Mae Enga of Papua New Guinea, the Dassanetch of
Southwest Ethiopia, and the Maori of New Zealand (1992). The Mae Enga
have a very high population density, and historically they have attacked one
another to gain land. But, says Tefft, the victors lost men to the war and
gained women, thereby exacerbating the overpopulation problem that had
caused war in the first place. Dassanetch men were divided into age sets, and
younger men especially tried to establish their personal power and prestige
by raiding other groups. They did so even when opposed by older men in
authority, who preferred to keep the peace. The result was instability for the
whole community. The Maori had a tradition of attacking one another for
land, like the Mae Enga. When they gained muskets from Europeans, they
engaged in an arms race that resulted in so much war they neglected their
subsistence farming. The result was famine, disease, and near mutual an-
nihilation. Tefft suggests that, in all three of these cases, people fell into war
traps "as a result of actual or perceived rewards, symbolic reinforcement,
ignorance of the long term effects of various actions, miscalculations of the
risks, and vicarious satisfactions" (1992: 43). That is, they pursued perceived
short-term gains to their own real long-term detriment.

Unfortunately, once warring had begun, these groups could not see
any other way to resolve their problems than to continue it. "To the victims
of the trap," says Tefft, "the existence of superior alternatives is often much
less obvious than it is to those outside" (1992: 43). In particular, the felt
need to avenge previous deaths, along with the fear of future violence from
enemies, causes people to arm themselves and commit acts of aggression in
"self-defense." This shortsightedness is especially clear in tribal cultures with
endemic warfare. Clans are in a continual state of shifting alliances as they
attack and counter-attack one another to avenge the deaths of the previous

raids. The culture legitimizes the violence by awarding men high honor for bravery and scorn for reluctance to fight. Peacemakers are accused of being cowardly, even traitorous, and the result is a perpetual state of conflict from which the culture cannot emerge (cf. Ritchie 2000).

The impact of endemic war on a culture is devastating. Of course, the most obvious consequence is that young men and boys are killed, sometimes to the near extinction of the group. But there are other more subtle and pervasive consequences too. One of these is that the encouragement of violence necessary to prepare men to kill outsiders also affects their relationships with insiders, that is, with family, friends and other members of their own group. Ember and Ember have demonstrated that, statistically, a culture's involvement in warfare increases its own homicide rate (1994: 642). They suggest that boys who are trained to be aggressive in anticipation of military service are more prone to commit murder because, "Once you learn to kill an enemy, you may find it easier to hurt or kill anyone" (643). That is surely why so many soldiers come home to commit violent acts against their own families, the ones they were supposedly protecting. Once it starts, violence becomes an increasingly easy solution to all relational problems.

There are also studies demonstrating that acts of state violence encourage the commission of crimes. A cross-cultural survey by Archer and Gartner (1987: 118–39) has shown that the abolishment of capital punishment results in a decreased homicide rate. Rather than act as a deterrent, capital punishment sets an example for killing that is adopted by the culture's members with one another. In fact, cultures that encourage any form of violence end up encouraging all forms (Ross 1985: 553). They become characterized by a constellation of types of violence, including violent sports, family abuse, capital punishment, endemic war, and crime (Ember and Ember 1994: 622).

Why does this happen? According to Marc Howard Ross, it is not just that violence tends to spill over from one arena to another, though this is certainly the case. It is that the glorification of violence associated with war creates a "disposition," or "*culturally* learned and approved method for dealing with others" that pervades the whole society (Ross 1985: 564). Ross makes the point that, "objective situations don't cause overt conflict, it is the *interpretation* of such situations that is crucial" (564) [emphasis in the original]. Cultures that breed the disposition of violence cultivate beliefs that a) war is necessary, b) the alternatives are foolish or impossible, and therefore c) under certain circumstances, there *must* be a violent response. They then glorify those who are willing to make the necessary sacrifices to defend the defenseless in circumstances that are believed to be a last resort.

If war is a trap, what is the solution? One possibility, the one especially favored by more violent cultures, is to force an end to it by outgunning the enemies and coercing them into submission. Under colonialism, "pacifying" other groups meant threatening, and if necessary using, such superior firepower that they acquiesced to being ruled by a foreign power. Surprisingly, the endemic warfare that these other groups were enduring was sometimes so severe that even the irritations of political oppression became a welcome option:

> In the pacification of tribal peoples, it is frequently found that the presence of an external authority relieves them of the necessity for continued fighting. Not infrequently they abandon the game of confrontation and counter-confrontation with a sense of relief, and they turn to more productive pursuits. (Goldschmidt 1989: 26)

This is exactly what Colson would have predicted. People are willing to put up with oppressive political systems if they gain safety from conflict and violence. Still, establishing political order with the use of coercion creates resentment over time, and this resentment can bubble over into a return of violence, as it did in the independence movements.

The other solution to war is to establish a legitimate (commonly agreed upon) set of rules for fairness and good relations. The process is not easy, of course, because disagreements about what is fair, rooted in people's limited perceptions and natural self-centeredness, not to mention their differing cultural values, make the negotiations difficult. Still, cultures throughout history, even the most violent ones, have attempted to make peace through agreements to avoid the devastating effects of war. Treaties have been enacted to address problems, reparations have been made to compensate for offenses, and forgiveness has been offered for the effects of the violence itself.

As an example, in the period after World War I, Albania was in a state of lawlessness and had regressed to a system of revenge killings. In some parts of the country, however, people were able to stop the cycle of violence by enacting a customary form of asking for and receiving forgiveness:

> Accompanied by six to eight men, the man originally at fault, with his hands tied behind his back, went unexpectedly on a festive evening to his enemy's house. The host, as in duty bound, said, "Come in!" and invited them to sit down. They refused to do so until in sign of forgiveness he untied his enemy's hands. He never refused, for he said, "Better forgive and forget one dead man than quarrel with ten living ones." If he had not granted their request, the murderer's escort would never have visited his house again. That night the invited guest ate a meal at the involuntary host's house, and the next day the man forgiven

carried them all off to his house, where he provided a meal with meat pasty and sweets. (Hasluck 1967: 405)

In this example, the violent offender had to make himself vulnerable to the victim (or victim's family). The men who accompanied him protected the offender and pressured the victim to make peace. Forgiveness was offered in the symbolic act of untying the offender's hands and peaceful relations were reestablished by an exchange of food taken at one another's homes. Significantly, the community held *both* parties responsible for reconciliation and provided a clear procedure to follow. The result was the cultivation of a disposition of peace-making in the midst of lawlessness and war.

CONTEMPORARY WORLD POLITICS

Thus far, we have focused on political systems that are small and mono-cultural. Larger political systems encompass multiple cultures, or ethnic groups, and must negotiate between them. In these systems, the goal is to create a country by developing a sense of citizenship that cuts across ethnic groups and binds them together. Currently, the world is composed of about 195 such countries. Anthropologists call these countries "nation states" be-cause they are the result of a particular history. As we saw in chapter four, under colonialism, empires were formed in which vast numbers of people were ruled by representatives of foreign governments. The independence movements that broke up colonialism established a global political philoso-phy of self-rule, with each *nation* having its own *state*. Since the word *nation* refers to an ethnic group, the idea was that every ethnic group should have its own country and its own government. But, as the anthropologist David Maybury-Lewis points out, there are over 5,000 nations in the world (ethnic groups) and just under 200 states (countries).[3] So, in reality, contemporary states are composed of *multiple* nations, or ethnicities, each of them vying with the others for control of the government.

This circumstance has caused a splintering of post-colonial countries into smaller and smaller pieces as one nation after another has demanded its right to self-rule. After India declared its independence from England, Paki-stan declared its independence from India, and then Bangladesh declared its independence from Pakistan. Even now, within each of these countries there are separatist groups that would subdivide the states further. The

---

3. Film series, *Millennium: Tribal Wisdom in the Modern World,* episode "The Tightrope of Power." Biniman Productions Limited, Adrian Malone Productions Lim-ited, KCET, and BBC-TV, in association with the Global Television Network, and with the participation of Rogers Telefund and Telefilm Canada.

political philosophy of nationalism, which was supposed to create a world of self-governing societies living in peace with one another, has instead created the most violent century in human history (Ferguson 2006). First, the two world wars broke up the colonial empires at a devastating human cost, and then an epidemic of bloody civil wars followed that is continuing to this day.[4] In all, an estimated "mind-boggling" 167–188 million people were killed by war in the twentieth century (649). That is certainly not to say that colonialism was better, or that we should return to it. Colonialism was very violent, especially in the beginning, and it was supported by false notions of racial and cultural superiority. Even in peaceful times, it was maintained by institutionalized violence in the form of oppression. Yet the violence did not stop with the success of the independence movements.

Anthropologist Clifford Geertz suggests that the problem lies in the fact that modern states must be constructed with two opposing principles (1973: 234–254). The first, "essentialism," postulates a common history for the country, and tries to create an identity based on a perceived common heritage. Following this principle, common ancestry, culture, and ethnic identity must be valued. The second, "epochalism," attempts to incorporate modern political conceptions of the state, including ideals such as self-rule, democracy, and citizenship. Following this principle, people must give up their various ethnic and cultural backgrounds in order to give allegiance to the government. Thus, leaders who are attempting to create a nation-state must build a common national identity by stressing a shared language, history, and culture, without allowing people's different languages, histories, and cultures, that is, their ethnicities, to divide them. Their hope is that "the nationalists would make the state, and the state would make the nation," says Geertz (1979: 240). But the task has proved a difficult one, to say the least. In some places, such as east Africa and eastern Europe, essentialism is winning out over epochalism, as the value on heritage is so strong that ethnic groups are able to tear apart states. In others, such as the United States, epochalism is winning out over essentialism, as the state becomes so strong that ethnicity is almost completely marginalized.

Furthermore, there are global forces at work in the constitution of any nation-state. In theory, all countries are sovereign over their own people under the philosophy of nationalism. But, in reality, there is a distribution of political and economic power between countries that affects sovereignty. Soon after the colonial empires broke up, two superpowers arose, the United States and the Soviet Union, and they engaged in the deadly standoff

4. In 1987, the Carter Center estimated that 90 percent of the armed conflicts in the world were internal to the countries in which they occurred. http://www.cartercenter.org/documents/1142.pdf, 5. Accessed on 4/11/17.

known as the Cold War. The "Cold" War was not without bloodshed. The superpowers fought bitterly by arming, and sometimes joining, the opposite sides of civil wars in Africa, Asia, and Latin America. Eventually the Soviet Union broke up, leaving a single standing superpower, the United States. Most Americans are relatively unaware of just how dominant the United States is on the world scene now. Especially since the attacks of September 11, 2001, Americans have imagined that they are in a vulnerable and endangered position. But a brief glance at the relative sizes of the world's militaries reveals the degree to which the United States dominates the world scene, and perhaps sheds some light on why America was attacked on 9/11 in the first place.

Figure 7.1: World Military Spending

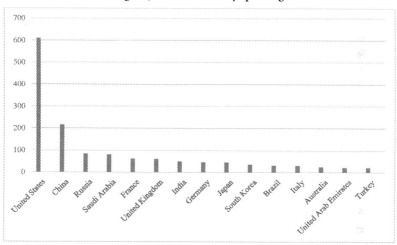

In Billions of USD, 2014
Source: SIPRI[5]

Clearly, the United States military is the largest in the world by far. China is second, but at one-third the size. Even if the entire rest of the world were to coordinate their activities, they would barely be able to contest America's military strength.

Very unfortunately, especially since the attacks of 9/11, many Americans have been inclined to think in "us or them" terms with respect to the rest of the world. The anthropologist Brian Ferguson identifies this kind of

5. Based on statistics from "Trends in World Military Expenditure, 2014" by Sam Perlo-Freeman, Aude Fleurant, Pieter D. Wezeman, and Siemon T. Wezeman. The Stockholm International Peace Research Institute (SIPRI) Fact Sheet, April 2015. http://books.sipri.org/product_info?c_product_id=496#. Accessed on 4/11/17.

thinking as the first step to war. "Opponents are constructed in conflict. In war, a line must be drawn between 'us' and 'them', otherwise one would not know whom to kill" (2009: 42). The second step is for leaders to promote war. It is commonly in leaders' interests to do so, especially if they are concerned for their own political positions. "Leaders favor war because war favors leaders . . . War often forces a coalescence of groups in a way that makes the management of people more possible" (44–45). Then, as we have seen, war becomes a kind of habit:

> Once a given society is internally adapted for war, making war becomes much easier—a necessity, even, for the reproduction of existing social relations. Commentators have often compared war to a disease, but a more apt analogy is an addiction. We should ask how far the United States has gone in this direction. (2009: 40)

Certainly the attacks on 9/11 were unjustified, and the suffering that Americans endured was very real, including about 3,000 deaths. Yet, in the US-led invasions of Afghanistan and Iraq that followed, over 6,000 *more* Americans were killed in combat,[6] and a further 550,000 were disabled.[7] The financial cost to the United States in the first ten years after 9/11 was nearly 4 trillion dollars. The human cost in Afghanistan, Pakistan, and Iraq (which did not actually sponsor the 9/11 attacks) included 137,000 civilians and almost 8 million refugees. In all, an estimated 225,000 people, or one quarter million, lost their lives in the American retaliation for 9/11.[8] And, as the theory of the war trap predicts, the circumstance that originally caused the violent response was exacerbated rather than resolved, as Islamist terrorists scaled *up* their attacks worldwide.

The United States has engaged in nearly constant war since its birth, from the battles against Native Americans, through the chronic interventions in Latin America under the Monroe Doctrine, to the fueling of countless civil wars during the Cold War, and now to the ongoing "War on Terror" of the twenty-first century. According to an estimate by the cultural

6. The Department of Defense has listed 6,387 military casualties for Iraq and Afghanistan as of March 12, 2012. http://www.defense.gov/news/casualty.pdf. Accessed on 3/13/12.

7. This figure, and the following statistics on the War on Terror, are based on a Brown University study conducted in 2011 by a team of economists, anthropologists, political scientists, and legal experts, entitled the "Costs of War Project." http://news.brown.edu/pressreleases/2011/06/warcosts. Accessed on 4/11/17.

8. This number, from the Brown University study cited above, includes all military personnel, contractors, and civilians. http://www.watsoninstitute.org/news_detail.cfm?id=1536. Accessed on 3/13/12.

geographer, Zoltán Grossman, there have been 146 "interventions" by the United States military, both inside and outside of the country, between 1890 and 2011—an average of more than one per year for over a century.[9] Furthermore, the United States is the largest merchant of war worldwide, with $10 billion of $30 billion in international arms sales in 2011 coming from American companies.

Figure 7.2: Top Suppliers of Global Arms

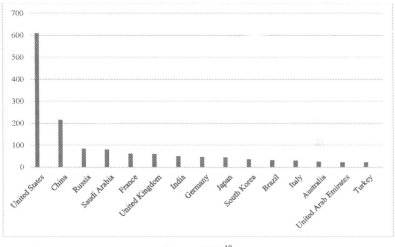

Source: SIPRI[10]

Included in these sales are supplies of weapons to poor countries, where money is sometimes diverted by despotic governments from badly needed social services to fighting neighbors and subduing their own people.[11] All in all, it would seem that Americans are deeply in the grip of the war trap, a disposition so thoroughly engrained in the culture that most Americans are unaware of the negative impact of their own government's actions abroad.

9. http://academic.evergreen.edu/g/grossmaz/interventions.html. Accessed on 4/11/17.

10. Based on "Trends in International Arms Transfers, 2011" by Paul Holtom, Mark Bromley, Pieter D. Wezeman, and Siemon T. Wezeman. The Stockholm International Peace Research Institute (SIPRI) Fact Sheet, March 2012. http://books.sipri.org/product_info?c_product_id=443. Accessed on 4/11/17.

11. In 2010, the US ranked first in arms transfer agreements (49 percent of them) and arms deliveries (39 percent) to developing countries. These figures are based on US government statistics in a report for the Congressional Research Service, entitled "Conventional Arms Transfers to Developing Nations" by Richard F. Grimmett, Specialist in International Security, September 22, 2011, 27. http://www.fas.org/sgp/crs/weapons/R42017.pdf. Accessed on 4/17/17.

It is worth remembering that falling into the war trap would be impossible were it not for a certain cultural logic based on group identity. The anthropologist Raymond Kelly reminds us that war requires us to kill people who are actually *substitutes* for the guilty parties:

> Substantial cultural elaboration is required to make the killing of an unsuspecting and uninvolved individual "count" as reciprocity for an earlier death, and to make it morally appropriate as well as emotionally gratifying and socially meaningful . . . This entails not only an ideology of the group, but also the kind of internalization of a group identity illustrated by the statement "I *am* an American" (as opposed to "I live in America" or even "I am a citizen of the United States of America"). The substitution of one person's death for another, a substitution that is central to war and feud, is rendered intelligible by elucidating these underlying concepts. (2000: 6)

It is only with an internalized identity as a member of a group that one can act in retaliation for another group member's death and kill someone from the other group in substitution for the original offender. To the degree that we remember our identities as individuals we will be less willing to sacrifice our own lives or to take the lives of others. And to the degree that we remember our membership in other groups, such as families or religions, we will be forced to *choose* which of these memberships comes first. War is only possible when people put their citizenship first, over other loyalties. Without a primary allegiance to the country, killing anonymous members of other countries would make very little sense.

All of this is not to say that there are no noble motivations for involvement in war. People can be truly convinced that war is necessary and that they are giving self-sacrificing and honorable service to their nation, defending it against threats. For instance, the American military academies stress ethics in warfare, peacekeeping as a goal, threat as deterrence, and a positive role for the American military in nation building around the world.[12] Also, some high-ranking American military personnel have been well aware of the dangers of war and have been the first to warn against engaging in it too easily, such as President Eisenhower and Secretary of State Colin Powell, both of whom were generals before they took political office. Yet, there is a logic to all of this that rests on loyalty to one's own country, as against other countries, that we as Christians must investigate.

12. Robin Lowery, personal communication.

CHRISTIANS IN THE NATIONS

Citizenship has always been problematic for Christians. For the first 300 years after Christ, Christians were heavily persecuted by their government, Rome. They met to worship in secret and developed a coded language to communicate, lest they be arrested and killed as Jesus and the apostles had been. Rome was a large and multicultural empire, and it maintained its control by mandating worship of the emperor and of the official gods of the state. When Christians and Jews refused to worship at state shrines, they were accused of treason and put to death for it. Most Christians refused military service. The leaders of the early church, such as Tertullian and Origen, condemned participation in war, partly because it involved killing and partly because it mandated a vow of allegiance to the state (Latourette 1999: 243; Troeltsch 1992: 123). St. Hippolytus of Rome, wrote:

> A soldier of the civil authority must be taught not to kill men
> and to refuse to do so if he is commanded, and to refuse to take
> an oath. If he is unwilling to comply, he must be rejected for
> baptism. A military commander or civic magistrate must resign
> or be rejected. If a believer seeks to become a soldier, he must be
> rejected, for he has despised God.[13]

Thus, the persecution of the church forced believers to acknowledge that allegiance to God and allegiance to the Roman government were in tension with one another.

In 313 AD, the Emperor Constantine put a stop to the persecution of Christians. Constantine had converted to Christianity because of a vision of the cross he saw before winning an important battle, the one that made him emperor of Rome. Believing that the Christian God had assisted him to win, he had the symbol of the cross placed on the shields of his army. As emperor, Constantine declared religious freedom and generally supported the church. But when theological disagreements threatened the unity of the empire, he cajoled and coerced the Christian bishops to agree with one another by making himself the central negotiator between them. Though he acknowledged God's sovereignty, Constantine's commitment to the sovereignty of the empire caused him to incorporate the church as an institution *under* the state's authority. Later, Christianity was officially made the state religion, with the result that it was used to sanction all of the empire's activities, including its military actions. So, from this time forward,

---

13. This translation is by Kevin P. Edgecomb at: http://www.bombaxo.com/hippolytus.html. Accessed 4/17/17. It is based on a more literal translation by Gregory Dix (1968: 26).

Christians participated increasingly in government and military, and developed theologies to justify their participation. It had become much easier to serve *both* God and country.

After the Western Roman Empire broke up, the European church was caught in an uneasy balance of power between popes and kings. The cross continued to be placed on shields for more than a millennium, as the various Christian kingdoms fought one another in the name of Christ. In the Eastern Empire, Byzantium, the king was declared to be a "messenger of Christ" in an attempt to resolve the problem of competing authorities by aligning the government directly with God. But elsewhere in the world, most notably in Persia, India, and China, Christians continued to be heavily persecuted for their unwillingness to worship the pagan gods of the state. Ernst Troeltsch suggests that, throughout history, Christianity has always had "a disintegrating effect upon all undiluted nationalism and upon every form of exclusively earthly authority" (1992: 82). Even in the best of circumstances, faithful Christians have refused to give an unlimited allegiance to their countries. In the worst, they have preferred martyrdom to state idolatry.

Ultimately, the tension we Christians feel with the state is because we acknowledge that Jesus' words, "all authority in heaven and on earth has been given to me" (Matt 28:18), reflect the true circumstance for power in the created world. Ephesians (1:20–22) declares that Jesus is seated with God in the heavenly places, "far above all rule and authority and power and dominion, and above every name that is named, not only in this age but also in the age to come." There is no power in heaven or on earth that is not subordinated to Jesus' reign over all that God has made. Furthermore, Jesus' words continue in Matthew (18:19–20), "Go therefore and make disciples of all nations . . . teaching them to obey everything that I have commanded you." Paul continues in Ephesians (1:22–23), "and he has put all things under his feet and has made him the head over all things for the church, which is his body, the fullness of him who fills all in all." Thus, through our discipleship and through the church, we Christians have been granted some of Christ's authority to be used in our capacity as citizens of the kingdom of God. And that kingdom is a heavenly kingdom relativizing the power of all earthly kingdoms.

It is tempting to think that we can handle this situation by a kind of dual citizenship, one to God and one to country.[14] But that solution denies

14. Sometimes Jesus' statement, "Give to the emperor the things that are the emperor's, and to God the things that are God's" (Mark 12:17) is used to defend this strategy. But the theologian Luis Lugo reminds us that, in this instance, Jesus was not making a definitive statement about church-state relations. Rather he was responding

the reality that, despite being ordained by God to keep order (Rom 13:1–7), the nations of this earth have all fallen into sin, and abuse the power that they have been granted (Col 2:8–15). Thus, wherever the kingdom of God is actively present, we can expect conflict with the state, along with other human institutions. Lesslie Newbigin writes:

> This hidden presence [of the kingdom] creates crisis and conflict. The powers that be, both in their outward form as the established religious and cultural and political structures, and in their inward reality of the principalities and powers of this age, are challenged and fight back. (1989: 104)

In actual practice, the nations of this earth are not willing to acknowledge a power higher than their own in the lives of their citizens. Certainly some are more accommodating than others of people's religious beliefs. But when those beliefs imply actions that contradict the goals of the state, the state will repress them—and blame the religions for any resulting violence. For our part, if we Christians do not choose to give priority to our heavenly citizenship over our earthly one, we will compromise our allegiance to the one true king, who is Jesus. We must be ready to choose, as Peter did, to "obey God rather than any human authority" (Acts 5:29).

For Christians who live in countries with persecution the fact that they have to choose is obvious.[15] But for Americans, the choice is more difficult to see. The American government was founded on Christian principles and has largely supported the creation of a separate space for the church and for religious expression. Furthermore, American religious freedom is based on a Christian conception of the limitations of the power of the state. (There is no suggestion, for instance, that the president is divine.) Yet this acknowledgement of a role for the church has been in part a compromise that permits the government to retain the final power in areas most relevant to itself, such as law and order, and military service. Thus, American Christians can find themselves compromising their kingdom citizenship in favor of their national citizenship, either by compartmentalizing their duties to God and to country (when, in fact, God has authority over *all* areas of life),

---

to the Pharisees' attempt to trick him by reminding them that money, imprinted with the image of the state, belongs to the state, while people, imprinted with the image of God, belong to God. "While Jesus clearly intends to affirm his followers' obligations to the state, even a pagan state, the main thrust of his statement is to underscore the fact that these obligations are rooted not in the presumed ultimacy or autonomy of human political institutions but in the absolute sovereignty of God, the creator and sustainer of all things" (Lugo 1996: 5).

15. For information on contemporary persecution of Christians, see the Voice of the Martyrs, at www.persecution.com. Accessed 4/17/17.

or by simply assuming that the United States is a representative of God's will and has his blessing.

Compromising allegiance to the state is a constant threat to Christian faith everywhere. But it is especially deadly in a nation as powerful as the United States. Under Saddam Hussein, the Iraqi church enjoyed a good deal of privilege. Hussein protected Christians from Muslim extremists, and Christians largely cooperated with the dictatorship, failing to stand for justice because their own lives were not threatened. But Iraq was a small country, and the failures of its church did not affect many people elsewhere. By contrast, the Roman Empire was the regional power of its day. So, when Roman Christians allowed the church to be put in service of the state, the result was Christian participation in the expansion efforts of the empire, affecting many other peoples in surrounding areas. Now, America is the political Rome of its day, with uncontested military might. Certainly, the American government is far more tolerant and generous with its own people than Saddam Hussein was, or even the Roman government. But its foreign policy has included a long history of violent and self-serving military interventions in other countries.[16] So, when American Christians give the allegiance to their country that belongs to God the impact on the rest of the world, and on the global church, can be very damaging.

Military service is especially problematic, as the following stories will illustrate: Arthur Glasser, a missiologist who was once a chaplain in the Marines, tells his story of coming across a dead Japanese soldier after a battle in WWII (Pierson 1993: 4). There was a New Testament lying on the ground next to the body. Glasser realized that the man had been a Christian, and that brothers in Christ, Japanese and American, had been killing one another that day. The evangelist Tony Campolo tells the story of two soldiers, one American and one German, who met on a battlefield after the Americans had won the battle (personal communication). The Americans were looking for wounded enemies to kill, and the German soldier was sitting exhausted under a tree. When the American soldier approached him, the two discovered they were both Christians. They sat together for some time, talking and sharing pictures of their families. Finally, the American got up, "did his job" as a soldier and killed the German, and went on with his work. As these stories demonstrate, in military service, soldiers must kill based on

16. For a listing of these military interventions, see the Congressional Research Service report, "Instances of Use of United States Armed Forces Abroad, 1798–2015," R42738, by Barbara Salazar Torreon, October 15, 2015. It is true that the United States has come to function as a global police force, sometimes in the interests of other nations. But an examination of this report will reveal how the defense of its own interests distort that role and the resulting actions.

national identity alone, regardless of the common commitments they share, one of which may be faith in Christ.

Christians disagree legitimately about whether they should serve in their nations' militaries or not, and they have disagreed since the first century. Yet, this very disagreement reflects the discomfort that Christians have always had with allegiance to governments. The quandary arises because of the need to restrain evil. Where injustice has been committed, or law and order has broken down, it seems logical that force must be used to rectify the situation. In America, World War II is commonly cited as an example to make the claim that "we" should be willing to go to war to stop the spread of evil. Not to do so is not only to fail to defend ourselves, but also to fail in our responsibilities toward others who are endangered or suffering. Especially when the offending people and institutions are themselves using force, it does not appear that there is any other option than to respond in like kind.

But perhaps we should always stop and consider our position when we imagine that there is "no other choice." Throughout history, there have been Christians who have stood firm for justice while refusing to join in the cycle of violence, trusting in God for the consequences. This does not mean they were passive—far from it! Many died martyrs' deaths for speaking "truth to power," leaving behind the witness of their lives. The Apostle Stephen, St. Francis of Assisi, and Martin Luther King, Jr. are well known examples. A lesser known example is Festo Kivengere, sometimes called "the Billy Graham of Africa." Kivengere lived as an evangelist and Anglican bishop in his home country of Uganda under the brutal dictator, Idi Amin. Amin, "the Hitler of Africa," conducted a reign of terror in the 1970s that included torture, public executions, mass killings, and the destruction of churches. Along with a number of other bishops, Kivengere risked his life to speak clearly and directly to Amin about his crimes. After he was exiled to Kenya, Kivengere was interviewed by journalists, and one of them asked, "Knowing how evil Idi Amin is, if you and he were in a room alone, and you had a gun and he did not, what would you do?" Kivengere answered, "I would give him the gun, for that is his weapon, not mine. Mine is the love of Jesus" (MacMaster 2006: 265).

It is easy to exaggerate the power of earthly political systems, and to imagine that physical force is the only form of power with which to counter them. In general, the spiritual world seems less real to us, and supplemental to the reality of the material world. But to look at power in this way is to make the gnostic mistake of divorcing the material from the spiritual in unbiblical ways. Both we and the world we live in are created wholes, and *all* power comes ultimately from God. The true distinction is between hidden and manifest forms of power (Newbigin 1989: 105). Throughout the

Bible, God repeatedly rejects apparent power in favor of apparent weakness, through which his real power operates more effectively. For instance, God used a boy, David, against a giant, Goliath; an outcast, Moses, against a mighty king, Pharaoh; and of course an unarmed teacher, healer, and preacher, Jesus, against not only the Jewish and Roman political authorities of the time, but against the whole human rebellion against God. Thus, when the Apostle Paul asked to have his "thorn in the flesh" removed, God replied, "My grace is sufficient for you, for power is made perfect in weakness." Afterwards Paul declared, "I will boast all the more gladly of my weaknesses, so that the power of Christ may dwell in me . . . whenever I am weak, then I am strong" (2 Cor 12:9–10).

Jesus both taught and demonstrated how apparent weakness can exert a tremendous force over the lives of people and the events of history. He praised the "poor in spirit," "the meek," and "the peacemakers" (Matt 5:3–9), and he instructed his disciples to love their enemies:

> You have heard that it was said, "An eye for an eye and a tooth for a tooth." But I say to you, do not resist an evildoer. But if anyone strikes you on the right cheek, turn the other also; and if anyone wants to sue you and take your coat, give your cloak as well; and if anyone forces you to go one mile, go also the second mile. Give to everyone who begs from you, and do not refuse anyone who wants to borrow from you.
>
> You have heard that it was said, "You shall love your neighbor and hate your enemy." But I say to you, Love your enemies and pray for those who persecute you, so that you may be children of your Father in heaven; for he makes his sun rise on the evil and on the good, and sends rain on the righteous and on the unrighteous. For if you love those who love you, what reward do you have? Do not even the tax collectors do the same? And if you greet only your brothers and sisters, what more are you doing than others? Be perfect, therefore, as your heavenly Father is perfect. (Matt 5:38–48)

What is notable about this passage is not only the reversal of the usual form of human morality, "love your neighbor and hate your enemies," but the real, concrete, and practical terms in which Jesus instructs us to love our enemies. We are not to resist them with their own forms of coercion, but to give to them generously, and to pray for them when they persecute us. This is what it means to be perfect as our heavenly Father is perfect.

Jesus' own death and resurrection make the point about strength in weakness the most clearly. During his lifetime, some of his followers were hoping that Jesus would take up arms against the Roman government along with other Jewish revolutionaries of the time. The Zealots, for instance, were using terrorist tactics to fight for Jewish freedom and to defend the true God against paganism. Some years before, the Maccabees had been successful for a short time in evicting the Romans from Palestine. It was the hope that he would lead another such revolt that caused people to cheer Jesus' final entrance into Jerusalem—and to quickly turn against him in disappointment when he was arrested and denounced by the Jewish authorities. But Jesus did not join the revolutionary movements of the time, either to defend God or his nation. Instead, on the night he was arrested, Jesus prevented his disciples from protecting him, and the next day allowed himself to be executed. Marshall points out:

> Aware that the established order would use lethal force to oppose his work, Jesus had three existing options. He could take the *revolutionary option* of the Zealots and strive to bring in the kingdom by military force. He could take the *withdrawal option* of the Essenes and advocate a retreat into the desert, away from the corruption of surrounding society. Or he could take the *establishment option* of the Temple rulers and seek to make the best of a poor situation by collaborating and compromising with the existing unjust order. Jesus rejected all three. Instead, he chose the way of nonviolent, sacrificial, peacemaking love and required the same of his followers. (1989: 60) [Emphases in the original.]

It is this rejection of the use of violence, both preached and modeled by Jesus himself, that has created the tension in the Christian church over military service. It is indeed difficult to imagine "what would Jesus do?" in military uniform.

The Christian story, however, is *not* one of defeat! On the contrary, our defeats in this life are only temporary, and we endure them in anticipation of the ultimate victory of God over all of the powers of this world. Jesus' resurrection was the sign that God's kingdom is at hand, that the victory over evil is already accomplished, and that we too will experience that victory through resurrection. Paul declares that Jesus "was crucified in weakness, but lives by the power of God" (2 Cor 13:4), and that he has "disarmed the rulers and authorities and made a public example of them, triumphing over them in it" (Col 2:10–15). This is because:

> He is the image of the invisible God, the first-born of all creation; for in him all things in heaven and on earth were created, things visible and invisible, whether thrones or dominions or rulers or powers—all things have been created through him and

> for him . . . and through him God was pleased to reconcile to
> himself all things, whether on earth or in heaven, by making
> peace through the blood of his cross. (Col 1:15–20)

The philosopher Friedrich Nietzsche despised Christianity for teaching a
"slave morality" of love and humility, rather than a "master morality" of
pride and strength. Because he was an atheist, Nietzsche failed to see the
real victory of God over all of creation through Christ's death and resurrection. Those of us living as citizens of the new kingdom have the opportunity
to view power differently, to see it as it truly is—made perfect by God in
apparent weakness, and victorious in the end through resurrection.

THE CHURCH AND POLITICS

So then, is it possible to be a Christian and still love your country? Certainly. In fact, Christians have always done so. Lamin Sanneh points out
that the love of their own countries that birthed the nationalist movements
in Africa, Asia, and Latin America was partially the result of Christianity
transforming the lives of converts and giving them a newfound pride in
their own languages and cultures (1993: 17).[17] But, to love a country really
means to love the *people* of the country. And for Christians, such love goes
beyond nationalist rhetoric, or patriotism, to God's transforming purposes
for them as set in the larger objectives of the kingdom of God. In the second
century, a letter was written describing "the manners of the Christians" living in Rome:

> With regard to dress, food and manner of life in general, they
> follow the customs of whatever city they happen to be living
> in, whether it is Greek or foreign. And yet there is something
> extraordinary about their lives. They live in their own countries
> as though they were only passing through. They play their full
> role as citizens, but labor under all the disabilities of aliens. Any
> country can be their homeland, but for them their homeland,
> wherever it may be, is a foreign country. (Martyr 1877: 86)

This surely describes how we Christians should live in our respective countries now. We should plunge ourselves deeply into the social, cultural, and

---

17. Sanneh suggests that when missionaries did the painstaking work of translating the Bible into vernacular languages, they had to learn the linguistic terms, and
therefore the worldviews, of local people. This gave those same people a pride in their
own cultures and histories that became the needed impetus to resist and reject colonial
oppression.

political life of the people we are with, but all the while maintain a larger view that refuses to be captured by the ideology of any political system.[18]

There are a number of principles we should follow in our relations to our countries. First, Lesslie Newbigin identifies the Christian political stance as one of "patient revolutionaries":

> We are not conservatives who regard the structures as part of the unalterable order of creation . . . and who therefore suppose that the gospel is only relevant to the issues of personal and private life. Nor are we anarchists who seek to destroy the structures. We are rather patient revolutionaries who know that the whole of creation, with all its given structures, is groaning in the travail of a new birth, and that we share this groaning and travail, this struggling and wrestling, but do so in hope because we have already received, in the Spirit, the first fruit of the new world (Rom 8:19–25). (1989: 209)

According to Newbigin, we are revolutionaries in the sense that we refuse to legitimize the evils of political systems as they are, but we are patient in waiting for the needed change because we know that God is in the process of redeeming all of creation, ourselves included. If we become impatient, we will inadvertently participate in, and even propagate, the evil that surrounds us. But if we remain patient revolutionaries, or "ordinary radicals," to use Shane Claiborne's term (2006), we can effectively serve our countries' true needs as citizens of the kingdom.

Second, our political involvement should always be in connection with the church. Martin Luther King, Jr. wrote:

> The church must be reminded that it is not the master or the servant of the state but rather the *conscience* of the state. It must be the guide and the critic of the state and never its tool. If the church does not recapture its prophetic zeal, it will become an irrelevant social club without moral or spiritual authority. If the church does not participate actively in the struggle for peace and for economic and racial justice, it will forfeit the loyalty of millions and cause men everywhere to say that it has atrophied. But if the church will free itself from the shackles of a deadening status quo and, recovering its great historic mission, will speak and act fearlessly and insistently in terms of justice and peace, it

---

18. This includes the ideology of democracy. Of course, there are many benefits to democracies, such as the relative empowerment of the populace and transparency of government. But there are detriments too, such as the marginalization of minorities and the power of the majority to do wrong. As Christians, we should remember that the kingdom of God is not, and never will be, a democracy.

will enkindle the imagination of mankind and fire the souls of men, imbuing them with a glowing and ardent love for truth, justice, and peace. (2010: 59–60) [Emphasis added.]

The church can play a strong and important role in critiquing the state for its abuse of power, its partiality to vested interests, and its desire for its own glory through war. As Christians, we should never fall into the trap of imagining the church to be simply a voluntary association under the authority of the state. The church is the body of Christ, who is Lord of all, and we are its members first and foremost.

Finally, William Temple, former archbishop of Canterbury, has suggested that the church as an institution should always remain independent of specific parties or policies in political debates. But it must announce Christian *principles* clearly, and insist on them without compromise:

> The method of the Church's impact upon society at large should be twofold. The Church must announce Christian principles and point out where the existing social order at any time is in conflict with them. It must then pass on to Christian citizens, acting in their civic capacity, the task of re-shaping the existing order in closer conformity to the principles . . . The Church is likely to be attacked from both sides if it does its duty. It will be told that it has become "political" when in fact it has been careful only to state principles and point to breaches of them; and it will be told by advocates of particular policies that it is futile because it does not support these. If it is faithful to its commission it will ignore both sets of complaints, and continue so far as it can to influence all citizens and permeate all parties. (1977: 58–59)

Temple illustrates his point by giving the example of the problem of unemployment. The church cannot, he suggests, determine the best economic policy for the government to enact, but it can declare that "a society of which unemployment . . . is a chronic feature is a diseased society, and that if you are not doing all you can to find and administer the remedy, you are guilty before God" (59). By stating the principle, the church reminds the government that it must act to fulfill its divinely ordained purposes, lest it be judged and condemned by a higher authority.

Yes, "we" Christians can, and should, love our countries. As human beings, we are members of families, ethnic groups, and nations. It is normal for us to care for our own people, as Jesus did the Jewish people. Yet, our *allegiance* to our own people must always be tempered by the higher allegiance we give to Christ and his kingdom, and the love we have for them must include a concern for their failings and a desire for their redemption. Redemption is a deeply political matter. It involves challenging the powers of darkness at work in the institutions of this world. And, as Newbigin has pointed out, they fight back. Still, we must take the risk and endure the suffering, as Jesus did, to free not only our own people, but *all* people, from the bondage of power misused by the principalities of this world. Though we do not always see immediate results, we are assured of the outcome because we know that God is working in hidden ways through our efforts, and because we know that his final victory is certain.

(CHAPTER 7) DISCUSSION QUESTIONS

1. Describe a Christian theology of political systems. What role do humans play, and what role does God play in the construction of political order? Is it possible for different types of systems to meet God's criteria for how political systems should function?

2. How should Christians practice their citizenship in earthly nations? Is this different than the way members of other religions, or secular people, practice their citizenship? If so, how?

3. While Christians legitimately disagree about whether they should engage in military service, they need not disagree on the importance of working toward alternatives to war. What are some alternatives to war that might bring about reconciliation with justice? How does the anthropology of political order (norms, legitimacy, etc.) assist us to think creatively about the possibilities?

4. How should the church speak to the state on matters of Christian conscience? How can we as ordinary Christians encourage the church to be the conscience of the state more effectively?

RECOMMENDED READINGS

Gutiérrez, Gustavo. 2007. *A Theology of Liberation.* Maryknoll, NY: Orbis.
Haugen, Gary A. 1999. *Good News about Injustice: A Witness of Courage in a Hurting World.* Downer's Grove, IL: InterVarsity.
King, Martin Luther, Jr. 2010. *Strength to Love.* Minneapolis: Fortress.
Temple, William. 1977. *Christianity and Social Order.* New York: Seabury.
Yoder, John Howard. 1994. *The Politics of Jesus.* Grand Rapids: Eerdmans.

Chapter 8

Can Art be Evil?

The Role and Purpose of Aesthetics in Culture

The American teenager in India wanted to learn classical Indian vocal music. Karnatic music is a 600-year-old tradition as intricate and as challenging as ballet. Performers train for a lifetime and sing for audiences of educated connoisseurs. The teenager's first problem was that the entire body of music was religious in nature. As a Christian, she would have to mimic the worship of Hindu gods and goddesses. Then, when she decided to go ahead, she was confronted by a Western friend who didn't like the sound and said passionately, "You're not going to learn that gosh-awful music are you?"

What is art? We know it includes music, painting, sculpture, dance, and other such "fine arts."[1] But it also includes more informal kinds of creating beauty. In fact, the first form of art is found on the human body, including tattoos, piercings, and make-up. Storytelling and drama, along with their modern forms, literature and film, are also included. What do all of these things have in common? The philosophical debate over the definition of art will probably never end, but for our purposes here, we will simply define art as an attempt to communicate with the use of beauty and skill (skill is the root meaning of "art"). A world without art would be a strictly utilitarian one. All communication and activities would be based purely on necessity and usefulness. So, art is an expenditure of time and energy that is

1. This chapter was read by Andrew Meneses, whose expertise in critical analysis of the arts made his affirmation of the chapter's content especially welcome.

beyond what is needed for utilitarian purposes, an elaboration on ordinary activities that requires skill, imbues beauty, and communicates the result to others.

With that definition, we now have to ask what beauty is. Human beings everywhere have an aesthetic sense that causes them to appreciate scenes in nature, the sound of singing, and healthy-looking faces and bodies. Likewise we are repulsed by ugliness in the form of violence and destruction in nature, or misshapen figures. Studies show that cross-culturally people will select the same faces as being the most beautiful, based on symmetry and other signs of health, regardless of the ethnicity of the observer or of the observed faces (Vera Cruz 2014). So, there appears to be an ability to appreciate beauty that is common to all human beings. As Christians, we might speculate that God has imbued humans with this ability to enable us to appreciate creation as it was meant to be. Both our senses and our understanding are involved. When we see, hear, touch, feel, or taste something beautiful, we enjoy both the sensation and what it means to us. That meaning has something to do with order and perfection, things which we only see in partial form in this life, but can imagine in their perfect form as God intended them in the beginning, and as he will restore them in the new heaven and new earth at the end of time.

Art, then, involves adding both beauty and meaning to things beyond what is strictly necessary to use them. This does not mean, however, that their usefulness is eliminated. In fact, most art is in the form of ornamentation. People paint pots intended to store water with intricate figures and designs. They sing chanting songs of crossing over into heaven to endure hard work in the fields. They carve elaborate stones to commemorate tombs, and weave beautiful fabrics to cover and protect their bodies. In fact, people work to beautify ordinary objects and activities nearly continually, and the "artists" include all of us. We select hair and dress styles daily, decorate our rooms and houses, and even doodle on paper in boring classes to add the significance that only the creation of beauty can bring to our lives.

In traditional societies, while there is some room for the artist's self-expression, the overall purpose of art is to express the identity, beliefs, and values of the community. Since art is typically produced on a part-time basis, along with other activities, everyone is an artist. The art itself is produced within an art tradition that largely determines its subject and style. It is evaluated by culture members for its beauty, evidence of skill, and the message it communicates within the tradition. As a result, artists are accountable to the communities in which they live, and their art is readily appreciated and supported by its audience. But in large and complex societies, there are full-time professional artists who create stand-alone art, not just ornamentation. Those who wish to enjoy it must go to special venues such as museums and concert halls (or in previous times, royal courts). Professional artists can develop more elaborate and highly skilled forms of art, but as a result, art becomes separated from ordinary life. In fact, the entire art world may become alienated from the rest of the culture.

In the West, due to historical developments in the concept of the individual, there is a belief that artists must be free to create art as a form of personal self-expression. This leaves the burden of communication to the art appreciators, who are expected to value what the artist has created whether or not they understand it, and whether or not they agree with it. This point was driven home in the 1980s when the artist Andres Serrano displayed a photograph of a crucifix submerged in a jar of his own urine. The artist was partially funded by the National Endowment for the Arts, and one of the prints of the photograph eventually sold for almost $300,000. Not a few viewers took offense, and the result was an international debate on the limits of individual self-expression in art.

The argument could be made that when the art community becomes separated from the larger public that it serves, the art itself becomes distorted. That is, having left behind the community's input, it begins to merely represent individual pathologies. No doubt art has a prophetic function, critiquing society and cultural values as from the outside. But sometimes this prophetic function can descend into pure hostility and nihilism. Meanwhile, members of the art world may develop a sense of identity as an elite community into which art appreciators must be initiated. The art that ordinary people like may be viewed derogatively as "common" or "popular," suggesting that "real" art can only be understood by the elect few.

It is true that appreciating any art form requires some education. The music that the American teenager wanted to learn in India sounded harsh to her friend. The teenager herself had spent hours in concert halls listening to the music and learning to hear and understand its subtleties. Even Indian appreciators of it tended to be from educated classes, as is the case with Western classical music. So any developed art form requires not only that artists be trained, but also that culture members learn how to appreciate it. In traditional societies, however, this education happens naturally as part of growing up in the culture, learning its art forms along with its worldview. In the West, the aesthetic education needed, along with the adoption of social, political, and moral views found in the art world, happens only to those who intentionally enter the segregated arena in which art is taking place, and the breakdown in communication with the general public can be significant.

THE MORALITY OF ART

As we have seen, according to the art community in the West, art is about the self-expression of the individual artist. According to anthropologists, art is a creative reflection of the culture in which it occurs. But in either case, individual or group, there is a question of the morality of art. Is art always an innocent moral good? Can art ever be evil? Consider the following two examples, the first a painting and the second a bodily alteration:

Figure 8.1: Can Art Be Evil?

Und Ihr habt doch gesiegt!

Source: Alamy Stock Photos

This picture is from a poster that is freely available on the internet. The inscription reads, ". . . and you were victorious after all," words that were printed on the back of the silver medal, "Blood Order," one of the highest awards of the Nazi party. This *is* a piece of art. It was no doubt painted to be used politically, but that does not make it less than art. Remember, most art is attached to a utilitarian purpose.

Is this painting evil? Why, or why not? The painting does not lack beauty. It is well composed, uses colors in an appealing manner (in the original), and reflects skill in drawing. Clearly, if there is evil in this piece of art, it is not in the picture itself, but in the message that it communicates to the viewers—a message about the superiority of the "master race" and the need to fight militantly to defend it. It communicates a constellation of ideas and practices that we know resulted in the torture and death of Jewish people and many others, and that continues to represent racism and hatred today. Does the argument hold that this piece of art is simply the self-expression of the artist and therefore cannot be judged for its morality?

The second example relates to women's beauty. In China, there was a thousand-year-old practice of breaking the bones of little girls' feet and binding them tightly to keep them small and "beautiful" for their husbands in later life. Women whose feet were broken and bound in this way were able to wear intricately designed shoes that reflected their high class status. But they also had to relearn how to walk and to endure continual pain and immobility throughout life. There are similar examples in the West. Nineteenth-century European corsets produced an exaggerated shapeliness in women by lacing them so tightly as to damage lungs and other internal organs. Even now American women subject themselves to extreme diets and unnecessary surgeries to achieve the ideal for feminine beauty. Are such practices simply culturally relative forms of beauty, not to be evaluated as more or less good or evil?

Perhaps we should ask, where do good and evil come from? As Christians we believe they both live, most immediately, in the human heart. Art, or the creation of beauty, is one of the finest products of the human heart. It reaches deep into our being below the level of consciousness to reveal things that cannot be fully articulated in any other way. Thus, if both good and evil reside in the human heart, we should expect to see them both reflected in art and in conceptions of beauty. At the level of the individual, artists' own struggles and temptations are reflected along with their virtues. At the level of the culture, the society's fundamental brokenness and its evil projects are represented along with its commitments to good and constructive things. In a sense, art reflects the very "soul" of the culture. So to suggest that it is morally neutral, or always good, is actually to trivialize it by detaching it from the culture's most important commitments. To recognize its capacity for *both* good and evil is actually to acknowledge its centrality to human life.

If there is morality in art, then as Christians we must know where to look for it. Clearly it is not in the materials used to create art, which are natural and human products, nor is it necessarily in the genres of art represented. The moral element of art must be in the message it communicates. That might seem obvious, but there is a vigorous debate in the West over a) how we can know what the message is, and b) whether or not it is important that the artist's intended message is correctly understood by the appreciators. In literature, scholars have declared "the death of the author," by which they mean that it is impossible to know what the author intended and that readers must make up their own minds on the meaning of a text. Defenders of this view point to the fact that language is a system unto itself which can only be understood by decoding words with reference to other words, not by reference to external objects.[2] The same is true of the elements of art forms, which also constitute a kind of "language" that is partially sealed off from real world meanings. In painting, for instance, abstract pictures juxtapose colors to one another, but do not refer to the real world at all. So, with abstract art, what is the "real" message?

Part of the solution to this problem is to remember the role of the culture. Normally, both the artist and the appreciators are members of the same culture, speak the same language, and therefore *can* communicate based on a common history and set of understandings with regard to symbols. Thus, in the case of Andres Serrano, one could suggest that, rather than a breakdown in communication, the difficulty was that the public understood all too well what he meant![3] Art, then, is a form of a culture-wide conversation. In this conversation, the artist's intention matters, but so does the evaluation of the appreciators. In general trust needs to be built up between the art community and the rest of the culture, and a conversation engaged around moral principles and social projects. In the end, art is not just a form of individual expression, nor is it inevitably good just because it is a cultural product. It is a collaborative project of the culture as a whole which must be evaluated not only in terms of its aesthetics, but also in terms of its intent.[4]

2. For instance, words like *up* and *down* are defined in contrast to one another, not by reference to a real direction. In the main, "up" is understood to be the opposite of "down" within a system of direction words. (Consider that the objective direction of "up" varies depending on where you are standing on the globe.) Much of language is like this, creating systems of understanding in our minds that are partially independent of reality.

3. Serrano declared that his art, which included many other provocative pieces, was intended not to criticize religion, but rather to criticize its misuse. Still, in his speaking tours, his antagonism to the Catholic Church (in which he had been raised) seemed evident, and the general public was skeptical of his statements.

4. Having said this, it is true that the message conveyed by a piece of art is often "inarticulate" in Michael Polanyi's sense (see chapter one). That is why people have gut level reactions, both positively and negatively, to it. I am suggesting that rather than dismissing these reactions, we should investigate them sensitively to understand the undercurrents of the message and/or the reasons for the responses of the culture members.

FORM AND MESSAGE

In traditional cultures there are many purposes for art. These purposes include: healing the sick (as with Navaho sand painters), calling upon supernatural spirits (as with Balinese dances), making political statements (as with Kwakiutl oratory), finding peace (as with Tibetan mandalas), remembering history (as with Hebrew poetry), prophesying to society (as with Native American ghost dances), and creating icons for worship (as with Hindu painting and sculpture). In particular, there is a strong association between art and religion, as objects of art are created for use in magic practices and animistic worship. Even in the West, almost all art had religious themes prior to the Enlightenment.

For Christians, a practical problem emerges: how to appreciate art as a reflection of culture while remaining faithful to Christian beliefs and practices. The American teenager had to sing songs of worship to Krishna and other Hindu gods in order to learn Indian classical music. Hopi Christians wanting to make the beautiful Kachina dolls of their culture must disassociate them from their traditional connection to potentially malevolent spirits. Maasai Christians must decide their level of participation in the elegant and powerful dancing of their culture, given its association with warfare. And, American Christians must choose whether to listen to secular music or watch television and movies with sexual and violent content, not to mention the atheistic and amoral assumptions that are embedded in the entertainment industry generally. Is there a limit to how far Christians can go in appreciating the art of their own or other peoples' cultures without compromising their commitment to Christ?

For over 2,000 years, Christians have responded to this problem by *adapting* local artistic and cultural forms to reflect Christian values and to convey the Christian message. This is in marked contrast to Islam, which denies the value of representational art and promotes Arabic culture as the pure form of the religion (Sanneh 1993). From the beginning, Christians have reshaped existing traditions to their own purposes, rather than reject them entirely. For instance, the Christmas tree was originally the center of pagan winter rituals. Some of the oldest hymns we sing are set to songs that were originally sung in taverns. These examples are from Europe, but Christians in all parts of the world have adapted their cultures' art forms to Christian purposes.

This process is not as simple as it sounds. We might imagine that it is just a matter of replacing the message while retaining the form. But the creation of the *connection* between form and meaning is at the heart of the construction of art. Can *any* form be adapted to the Christian message? Is there no message at all in the form itself? As an example, we might consider the heavy metal music scene in Western Europe and North America. Metal music is associated with particularly dark messages about death, apocalypse, and even the occult. Both performers and fans wear black clothing, jewelry that combines crosses with skulls, and dog collars and chains. At concerts, they make gestures such as the upraised fist with "devil's horns." The music itself is characterized by intentionally hard sounds made by highly distorted electric guitars and vocal screaming. The scene is clearly counter-cultural, so in truth, if there were no negative connotations to the form of the art, metal bands would not be able to make their point.

Yet, remarkably, there *is* a Christian metal scene! Below is an album jacket for a Christian band:

Figure 8.2: Letter to the Exiles: A Christian Metalcore Band

Source: Facedown Records

There are two questions to be answered in a situation like this, 1) why should we adopt the form?, and 2) how can we adapt it effectively, in such a way as to preserve the integrity and beauty of the art, while rejecting evil and promoting good? To answer the first question, Christians adopt cultural forms both because they wish to communicate the Christian message to others and because they appreciate the art itself. Thus, Christians in the metal scene both enjoy the music and want to reach others for Christ with it. This must be carefully done. Non-Christians are not drawn to the message when it is conveyed as a thinly veiled advertisement with a poor performance of the art. Christian artists must be just as skilled as non-Christian artists if they are to draw an appreciative audience. Moreover, there is an intrinsic value to the form of the art that must be respected. A "cheesy" adaptation of the form conveys inauthenticity, a characteristic that discredits the Christian message.

This leads to our second question, how can we effectively adapt the form? I have suggested that the form itself *does* have a message. So the first task is to determine what that message is, in cultural context, and why it is being conveyed. In the case of metal music, the message—conveyed in the color black, the distorted and screaming sounds, the apocalyptic lyrics, etc.—seems to be a prophetic announcement to the culture of its own impending doom. Is this message evil? Actually, there is a point of connection with the Christian message, which also predicts a final doom for this world as we know it. In fact, the lyrics in metal commonly incorporate biblical phrases and imagery for that reason. Furthermore, the appreciators of this art form tend to be at least somewhat alienated from the larger culture. That alienation is also something Christians should recognize. Through the centuries, and around the world, Christians have commonly found themselves at odds with their own cultures, as did Jesus himself.

These points of connection can be highlighted in the creation of a Christian form of the art. But the matter cannot be left at that. Christianity is centrally about the promise of purpose, hope, and a future, in the face of evil, death, and destruction. That hope must be woven into the art to convey the right message. Here is how Letter to the Exiles has done this in the lyrics to their song, "Make Amends," by Chris King:

> At what cost do I walk away,
> do I tear from me my own hate and let go?
> I have walked for so long, I have walked so far,
> from being a saint, and a long way
> from this holy ground my father made.
> Wandering feet remain without cause, without name.
> I carried this curse all the way,
> as I carried your hurt, as I carried your hate.
> Now I carry this broken body back to the beginning.
> I can rebuild these hands, rebuild this broken home.
> What will it take to forgive the fall of man, the fall in me? . . .
> With such subtle words the answer came
> like a call from that forgotten place.
> It will carry me. It calls to us.
> With all this darkness surrounding,
> Father would you even let us go home?
> If there is grace I pray it comes to us
> where my enemies walk as brothers beside me.[5]

5. "Make Amends," on the album of the same name, by Letter to the Exiles.

The lyrics here are reminiscent of the parable of the Prodigal Son, and as with Jesus' parable, they reach out to each of us to consider our own alienation from God. But they also provide the hope that God, as our Father, will welcome us home despite our sin and hatred. With the subtlety of indirect reference, they sketch out the possibility of redemption for those who have experienced the hard side of life and their own failings, thereby embedding the gospel of hope in an art form that was designed to convey a message of doom.

ART AND RELIGION

The message of Christianity can be planted in any cultural soil (after appropriate "soil analysis"). But what about the association between art and the other religions? Ironically, it is sometimes new converts who reject the use of their own cultural forms. For instance, in Africa, drums play a central role in witchcraft related practices. European and American missionaries, who have experienced drums in worship bands and who have enlightened beliefs about the value of retaining indigenous art forms, may be surprised to find that new converts do not want drums in churches. The reason is a combination of past association and continued belief that the drums really do call upon evil spirits. It is easy for cultural outsiders to dismiss such beliefs and the feelings elicited by them. Outsiders have never been under the power of the other religion. In the story at the beginning of this chapter, the American teenager could more easily learn Indian classical music than could her Indian Christian friends, since gods like Krishna had never been real to her.

Furthermore, it is secularist thinking, not Christian thinking, that would completely exclude the possibility of a real association between art forms and evil influence. Ex-alcoholics must carefully avoid all alcohol, partly because of their weakness for it, but also partly because of their knowledge of what it can do. Likewise, those who have been deeply into the evil side of a culture cannot simply adapt the art form without retaining some of its former impact. Keeping with our example above, members of the Christian metal scene tend *not* to have been previously immersed in the occult aspects of the secular metal scene. Christians who have been in that scene prior to their conversions are more likely to reject metal entirely as part of their own dark past.

Produced by Facedown Records in 2012. Chris King, vocals; Mark Randazzo, guitar; James Appleton, bass; Andy Amato, drums.

For these converts, the art form itself has a spiritual dimension. In fact, in traditional cultures most art is created for use in rituals that directly involve the spiritual world. These rituals include rites of passage, in which people are initiated into the various stages of life, rites of intensification, in which elements of nature are manipulated to benefit the group, and healing rites. In all of these cases, ritual specialists call down the spirits and persuade, manipulate, or coerce them to do what is needed. People make elaborate masks and special clothing, construct ornate paraphernalia, and perform dances and oratory for rituals such as these. The art they create is beautiful and meaningful in its context, but its intent is to control the world through magic. People believe the art forms literally contain the spirits that will assist them. In Bali, when elaborately carved and painted masks are worn, the spirit of the mask possesses the wearer. In India, when Hindu sculptors finish the construction of an idol, they perform a ritual to invest it with the god. Thus, the art of other religions is inextricably combined with those religions' conceptions of, and interaction with, ghosts, spirits, and gods.

This literalism, connecting the forms of art with the presence of spirits, should not surprise us. The relationship between the spiritual and material world is at the heart of religious practice, and art is often the vehicle for expressing that relationship. In the Eastern Christian church, icons are used to draw worshippers to God. The debate over this practice is as old as the faith itself, with some calling it "idolatry." But Eastern Christians are clear that they are not worshipping the icons. They point to Jesus' incarnation as evidence that God permits and even affirms our need to see him in material form. The icons provide a focal point for prayer, and thereby a window to the spiritual world, for ordinary human beings whose spirits are contained within material bodies, and therefore have material needs.

Figure 8.3: Jesus the Good Shepherd

Source: Skete.com. Image in the public domain

The Eastern Church acknowledges the danger and has taken steps to avoid idolatry, such as by prohibiting statues in the round. But it defends the use of icons in the church as a vehicle for incorporating art effectively into worship.[6]

Art is also used in the Western church to express spiritual realities, including God's presence. In the Catholic Church, a bell is rung to indicate the exact moment in which the elements of the sacrament become the body and blood of Christ. In Protestant churches, the cross is commonly portrayed at the front of the sanctuary and there may be pictures of Jesus on the walls. Again, this is in marked contrast to Islam, and even to Judaism, both of which have much stronger prohibitions on art to prevent idolatry. Strict Muslims allow only abstract designs, lest they be tempted to venerate the depictions they have made of God, humans, or nature. Jewish synagogues

---

6. In the early church, some argued that the rejection of icons was in response to criticism by Greek philosophers who viewed the worship of idols as a low form of religion. Thus the real issue was not idolatry, but an attempt to gain prestige for Christians in a world that supremely valued the mind over the body (Latourette 1999: 294).

are bare of all carved statues and images of divine beings. Both of these religions see Christian art, especially in sanctuaries, as coming close to idolatry.
Indeed the line between using an icon or image as a vehicle and worshipping it can be a thin one. Even Hindus say that they are not worshipping
stone statues, but rather the gods that they represent.

What, then, constitutes idolatry? The Old Testament says that we are
not to have any other gods before the one true God, nor are we to make any
images of created things and worship them (Exod 20:1–6). The New Testament says that idolaters have "exchanged the glory of the immortal God for
images,. . .they exchanged the truth about God for a lie and worshipped and
served the creature rather than the Creator" (Rom 1:23, 25). The catechism
of the Catholic Church (which allows for the lighting of candles and prayers
in front of statues) states that: "Idolatry consists in divinizing what is not
God. Man commits idolatry whenever he honors and reveres a creature in
place of God."[7] So, idolatry consists in redirecting our gaze from the one
true God to anything that he, or we, have made. When we redirect our gaze
in this way, we expect power, for good or for evil, from things that do not
have it. Christian ethicist Lewis Smedes remarks:

> It is simple to make an idol; slice one piece of created reality
> off the whole and expect miracles from it. The miracles may be
> positive or negative; they may heal or hurt. If the idol has power
> to heal, you keep it around you . . . If the idol threatens you, you
> place a taboo on it . . . Idols work both ways: we make an idol
> of something either by expecting too much good from it or by
> fearing evil from it. (1994: 36)

Smedes argument is in reference to the misuse of sexuality, which can
be closely linked to idolatry. In Hinduism, the largest and oldest religion of
worshipping icons, there is a long tradition of temple prostitution, along
with other forms of interweaving sex and worship (such as in Tantricism).
The Apostle Paul notes the connection in the passage from Romans cited
above: "therefore, God gave them up in the lusts of their hearts to impurity,
to the degrading of their bodies" (Rom 1:24). To worship creation seems to
lead naturally to the worship of fertility, to exaggerated and distorted views
of sex, and ultimately to the worship of our own bodies. The idolatry of
the West consists of expecting miracles from sex and from material wealth,
resulting in distorted relationships to these things which do not satisfy our
ultimate needs.

7. See "Catechism of the Catholic Church." http://www.vatican.va/archive/
ENG0015/__P7E.HTM. Accessed on 4/27/17.

Smedes suggests that the solution to the problem of idolatry is not to try to obliterate our connection to other created things, but to restore those things to their proper places, expecting only what they can really provide. Then, we must redirect our gaze back to God himself as the creator of all things. We are material beings. The use of artwork in the church can be an effective means of bringing body, mind, and soul into a focused gaze on the one true God. The temptation will always be there to redirect that gaze to the created world, and especially to ourselves. But the total rejection of representational art simply creates a negative idol out of fear. The Christian way is to appropriate art in the service of honoring God, serving others, and enjoying the life he has given us.

ART AND ETHNICITY

In the contemporary globalized world, art has become a vital element in the expression of ethnic identity. In chapter four, we saw that ethnic groups are socially constructed in contrast to other ethnic groups, and in response to the need to obtain and protect political and economic resources and interests. The result is a kind of marketplace or competition between ethnic identities in which symbols are used to mark out territory. Because ethnicity involves membership in cultural groups that have historical roots in certain places, the art of those places is especially valuable as a marker. So, for instance, Native American Indians are represented by their crafts, Europeans are associated with their history of fine arts, and Americans are known abroad through their film industry.

Yet ethnic groups no longer live exclusively in the places from which they have come. They have become transnational, living in different parts of the globe, but in constant communication with one another, and having a common identity. One might think that ethnicity would be on the decline as less and less people live out their lives in their homelands, but in fact the opposite is the case. Living abroad in multicultural environments causes people to value their original places and cultures all the more. Thus, some theorists have suggested that ethnicity is actually a *product* of globalization, rather than a survivor of it. In a world characterized by large numbers of massively uprooted people (immigrants, refugees, migrating laborers, and international travelers), ethnic identities are being actively created in order to provide people with a sense of belonging.

Two major theorists have described the role of symbols and imagery in this process, Benedict Anderson and Arjun Appadurai. Anderson has suggested that the rise of the mass media, beginning with the printing press, has made it possible for people to form "imagined communities" (1983). Unlike real communities, in which people have face-to-face contact, these communities are composed of people who do not know each other. Yet they are able to maintain a sense of membership in the group by virtue of speaking a common language that is standardized by the media and used to convey specific beliefs and values. Tacitly, the members of an imagined community construct a grand narrative of their history, identify heroes and hard times they have endured, and develop a sense of destiny. What holds them together is the belief that they are one kin with one homeland. Benedict was referring specifically to the rise of nationalism and the politics of democracy, but his concept of imagined communities has been broadened by others to include groups such as ethnic groups, and to investigate the ways in which people *invent* histories and traditions to create a sense of common identity.

Appadurai has studied the role of the imagination in what he calls the "deterritorialization" of culture (1996). He suggests that culture is traveling around the world through various "flows" of ethnicity, media, technology, finance, and politics. These various flows are not in sync with one another, and the disjunctures between them create unpredictable inconsistencies and clashes. So, for instance, in the "Arab Spring" of 2010 when multiple governments across North Africa and the Middle East were toppled by popular demonstrations, democracy, a political idea, was heavily promoted through the use of a then new form of media, Facebook. The end result, however, was not actually democracy in all cases. Once the governments were toppled, battles for control of the state broke out, and several governments were taken over by fundamentalist Muslims whose interest was in maintaining religious law. What began as a political movement, facilitated by a new technology, ended up promoting religious ends.

In dynamic and unpredictable processes such as these, symbolism plays a heightened role in the construction of people's images of themselves and others. In fact, people may intentionally stereotype themselves with the use of external images to create a stronger identity and to assert it on the global stage. Customs and traditions long forgotten, or ones newly invented, are picked up to play the role of identity markers. For example, the feathered headdress of Plains Native American Indians has been adopted as a symbol of Native American identity by members of the syncretistic religion, Umbanda, in Brazil where such headdresses were never previously used. Ironically, it was through the "cowboy" movies of Hollywood that these South Americans first encountered and then adopted the symbol of the headdress.[8]

---

8. See the film by anthropologist, Peter Fry, "Umbanda," the *Disappearing World*

Such inventions of tradition are part of what anthropologists call "the reproduction of culture." All culture is invented. But we do not reinvent every aspect of it in every generation. Much of it is passed down as tradition for reasons of economy—it would be very expensive in terms of time and energy (not to mention the negative consequences of trial and error), to continually reinvent everything. Still, cultures must change to adapt to new circumstances, and when they do they commonly represent these changes as rediscovered forms of "tradition" in order to give them legitimacy. People are more willing to adopt practices that they perceive to be representative of their own identity and background. The result is the dynamic reproduction of culture in the creation of "imagined communities" such as ethnic groups.

Art is deeply involved in the reproduction of culture and ethnicity. It provides a kind of memory for people, as well as an assertion of their identity to others. This is not done through specific works of art (though these may be influential sometimes), but rather through entire genres or art forms. An art genre is composed of symbolic elements and styles that are considered typical of a tradition and that are used to embody the message in a cultural context. That context includes the history and experience of a people. Thus, art genres are deeply representative of the ethnic groups from which they emerge, and in general should be preserved not only for their intrinsic beauty, but for the sense of history and identity which they provide.[9]

In the context of the global church, art genres can be a source of continually re-representing the Christian message in different forms of beauty emerging from various cultural backgrounds. Here, for instance, is a depiction of the Lord's Supper:

---

series, Chicago: Films Incorporated Video, 1991.

9. With globalization, "ethnic" art has become a commercial product, promoting ethnic groups and their cultures to consumers worldwide. The commodification of art has made it possible for us to experience the beauty of art from all around the world, but sometimes at the price of its authenticity. The difference is in the fact that art for sale must consider what buyers from other cultures will want, rather than what the home culture wishes to express.

Figure 8.4: The Lord's Supper

Source: The Lord's Supper © Vie de Jésus Mafa[10]

This artist has intentionally imitated a Western painting of an event in Christian history and transposed it into an African context. The positioning of the figures reminds the viewer of the painting of the Last Supper by Leonardo da Vinci. But the figures themselves—their dress, the objects, and the context—have been modified to reflect a normal setting in Africa. Thus, an African art genre has been used to portray a Christian theme borrowed from European history, and the message is clear: Jesus' sacramental supper is for African as well as Western Christians. This is one of the ways in which art genres can be used to link Christ to culture, embodying the Christian message so that it comes alive to people in their own contexts.

A CHRISTIAN THEOLOGY OF ART

Why do human beings create art? So far, we have noted that art is an elaboration of ordinary activities that creates beauty, that beauty has something to do with the order and perfection that God originally intended for creation, but that both goodness and evil can be conveyed through the art of our fallen world. We have investigated the nature of the relationship between art and the spiritual world, the possibility of art becoming idolatrous, the role of art in the construction of identities, and the process by which the Christian

10. https://www.librairie-emmanuel.fr/cartes-jesus-mafa-c-11295. Accessed 2/27/18.

message can be conveyed through different art forms. In all of this, we have not yet established the theological reason *why* people create art.

In short, Christians believe that people create art because they themselves are created in the image of the master Artist, and because they have been given dominion over the rest of creation. God, who is spirit, has expressed his own creativity by shaping the material world. Thus, creation reflects the glory of God in material form. Psalm 19:1 says, "The heavens declare the glory of God, the skies proclaim the work of his hands." As embodied creatures who are made in God's image, we human beings are both a work of God's art, and workers of art ourselves. Moreover, the theologian Eric Flett writes that, "the created order has been constructed in such a way that it requires the presence and agency of human persons as cultural beings to fulfill its *telos*" (2011: 236). This is a strong statement suggesting that our cultural activity is *necessary* for the world to achieve its ultimate purpose. That purpose is to sing praises to the Creator in loving response to him for having created everything. Note the musical analogy used to make this theological point. As the creatures uniquely made in God's image, our particular role as human beings is to bring the whole of creation into a relationship with God expressed through art.

It is precisely for this purpose that we have been awarded dominion over the earth. Psalm 8:3–6 says:

> When I consider your heavens, the work of your fingers,
> The moon and the stars, which you have set in place,
> What is mankind that you are mindful of them,
> Human beings that you care for them?
> You have made them a little lower than the angels
> And crowned them with glory and honor.
> You made them rulers over the works of your hands,
> You put everything under their feet.

As we saw in chapter two, the Old Testament understanding of "image" was as a vice-regent, a representative of the king. In the ancient world, images (statues) were placed in various parts of an empire to represent the king's reign. People encountering the statues were to honor the image in order to show their respect for the king (as in the story of Daniel). So, the image of God in human beings reflects God's power and his glory to the earth (Enns 2012: xv).

An artist has a kind of dominion over the material world that can be used to further its advancement toward its final *telos*, or purpose, which is to glorify God. That is why it is supremely important that art not be used for evil. Where evil is found in art, it is an expression of human rebellion against God and the sin-sickness at the very heart of our lives. Since sin is pervasive, we cannot expect that our art will be completely free of evil. But the Christian story is always one of redemption, and our art too can be redeemed. Thus, the best art is good because it puts the world back into a relationship with God based on a celebration of his "glory"—a word that also means beauty.

There are contemporary theologians who suggest that it is only through beauty that we are able to apprehend the truth of the Christian message. As we saw in chapter one, the truth itself cannot be finally determined by human beings. Our self-centeredness and willful blindness prevent us from accepting it, even when we can understand it. But it is possible for us to be *persuaded* of the truth through the appeal of its beauty. John Milbank says that the task of the church is not to make incontrovertible arguments for the faith, but to tell the Christian story, to proclaim Jesus as the Word, and to live that story out "in a manner that restores [its] freshness and originality" (1990: 381). David Bentley Hart writes that our theology must center on, "the beauty to whose persuasive power the Christian rhetoric of evangelism inevitably appeals" (2003: 1). According to these theologians, the best Christian theology tells a story of the peaceful world God intended in the creation and of his loving redemption of us after the fall, and contrasts it to the more violent stories that are offered by others to account for our present circumstances (such as that we are a competitive species, divided from one another by our "natural" pursuit of self-interest).

The Christian story, the story of God's first purposes for us, of our own rebellion and its devastating consequences, of God's tremendous love in sending his own Son to save us, of his Son's conquering of death and final victory over sin, and of the coming re-creation of the heavens and the earth, is appealing because it is beautiful. The beauty of the story reflects the heart of the Artist who made us, loves us, and who is redeeming us for himself. And, it is that story, in part or in whole, hidden or revealed, that is the central message of all truly Christian art.

(CHAPTER 8) DISCUSSION QUESTIONS

1. What is art, and what is its purpose?

2. What is the nature of the relationship between art and good or evil? How can Christians effectively interact with art to redeem it?

3. What is the role of art in the church? How might a carefully constructed theology of art enhance the use of art by Christians in worship services?

4. How can art be used to convey the Christian message to the world in a manner that is clear and penetrating, yet winsome?

RECOMMENDED READINGS

Wolterstorff, Nicholas. 1987. *Art in Action*. Grand Rapids: Eerdmans.

Trotter, Lilias. 2007. *A Blossom in the Desert*. Grand Rapids: Discovery House.

Appadurai, Arjun. 1996. *Modernity at Large: Cultural Dimensions of Globalization*. Minneapolis: University of Minnesota Press.

Hart, David Bentley. 2003. *The Beauty of the Infinite: The Aesthetics of Christian Truth*. Grand Rapids: Eerdmans.

Chapter 9

Why is It All about Jesus?

Christianity and the Other Religions

"Don't worry, just go ahead and be a good Muslim. Jesus will save you anyway!" The speaker was a Christian who believed that all people will be saved by Christ whether they accept him in this life or not. Her listener was a Muslim friend who was trying to convince her of the truth of Islam. To the speaker's surprise, her friend was not pleased with her reassurance. She had, in effect, told him that he was wrong no matter what, and that in the end he would be kidnapped into the Christian heaven!

Relating as Christians to members of other religions, or of no religion, is not easy.[1] When people disagree on their most fundamental beliefs, principles, and outlook on life, they can find it difficult to actually comprehend one another. They may be using the same words, such as *God* or *grace*, but with such different meanings that they talk in circles without really understanding the points of similarity or difference. Furthermore, the truths of religions cannot be proved beyond doubt. We can try to explain what we mean, and we can tell stories of our own and other people's experiences, but we cannot conclusively establish God's existence, or any other religious truth, by rational argument alone.[2] Even if we could, we would not be able

---

1. Barbara Hiebert Rowe and Andrew Bush read this chapter. I deeply appreciate their sensitive comments and their encouragement as I tackled a difficult subject.

2. This is in part because of the limitations and distortions of the human mind, and in part because God has chosen to remain partially hidden from us to allow us to choose freely to respond to him in love. It does not mean that rational arguments are

to convince others this way. Because of our human rebellion against God, none of us is an innocent seeker after truth. Our desire to know the truth is contaminated by our desire to defend ourselves and our own sense of security. That is why conversations about religion degenerate so easily into arguments. We all, including Christians, feel threatened when we encounter others who believe we are wrong, and we end up defending ourselves more than God.

Moreover, even when we are trusting that God can defend himself (and us), and are willing to engage in honest discussion across religious lines, we in the West can find it difficult to do so without being accused of being "arrogant" or "intolerant." As we saw in chapter five, Western culture is divided into two arenas: the public arena of the workplace, economy, and politics; and the private arena of family and religion. This arrangement is a compromise that benefits the state because it enables people from different backgrounds to live together as citizens of the same country. Those truths deemed necessary for a peaceful coexistence, such as the ones underlying the political and economic systems, are expressed openly in the public arena and with intent to find agreement. But those truths deemed (however wrongly!) as unnecessary for peaceful coexistence, such as the ones associated with personal morality and religion, are relegated to the private sphere where "tolerance," or agreeing to disagree, is strictly mandated by the culture. In sum, in the West you may use persuasion to convert people to your political or economic views, but you may not do so with your religious views. By preventing a legitimate public discussion of religion—that is, a discussion with intent to find *answers* to religious questions—the culture supports the state's efforts to preserve its own authority over civic life.

The problem with this solution is that it marginalizes, and even trivializes, religion. As we saw in chapter one, the philosophy of pluralism promotes the idea that religion is a private matter and suggests that since we cannot know religious truth with complete certainty we should simply accept the differences between us without attempting to resolve them. This idea has been so popular that many Christians at least tacitly espouse it, and as a result are hesitant to say what they think in religious discussions. But, if we unpack the various assumptions it contains, we will see that the philosophy of pluralism is not a tenable solution for anyone of any religion who actually *cares* about the truth.

---

useless. Such arguments can help confirm our faith by giving us a better understanding of it. But they play a supporting role, rather than the primary one, in establishing what we believe. The primary role is played by God's revelation of himself in Scripture, church tradition and personal experience, and by our faithful response to him.

To begin, we can ask ourselves whether there is truth in all religions. Surely the answer to this question is, "Yes!" Christian theologians acknowledge that, due to God's general revelation of himself through nature, thought, and experience, all people can have some knowledge of his existence (Rom 1:20). Thus Hindus, for instance, agree with Christians that the spiritual world exists and that it explains the events of this life. Muslims agree that God created us and will judge us at the end of time. Even atheists agree that human morality is important. There are many points at which we as Christians can affirm what others believe because we believe them too. The problem is that surface agreements such as these can hide deep disagreements, just as using the same words can hide different meanings. Hindus do not distinguish in absolute terms between gods and human souls, so in Hinduism people can become gods. Muslims do not accept Jesus' role as Savior, so in Islam people are judged solely based on their own merits. Atheists reject the idea that creation is imbued with God's purposes, so atheism bases its morality on human rational thought. These are all points of deep disagreement between Christianity and the other religions and philosophies of the world.

But perhaps there is an even deeper level at which all religions agree, a kind of generic religion that underlies them all. This is an appealing idea because it suggests that we need not worry about the differences because we agree on the most important things. Yet, the attempts to identify the specific elements of a generic religion have invariably resulted in the coopting of other religions into one religion. For instance, many people imagine that Hinduism is a particularly tolerant religion because Hindus believe that, "all paths lead to God." But what Hindus have traditionally meant by this was that a great unknowable reality exists behind what we can perceive, and that there are multiple paths *within Hinduism* to access that reality. These paths include the Hindu ways of knowledge, of meditation, of action, and of renunciation. They do not include the ways of salvation by Christ or of judgment by Allah. Nowadays, educated Hindus will say that the other world religions do lead to God too. But they mean the Hindu conception of God, and they assume that the central propositions of Hinduism, such as reincarnation and karma, are true for everyone. Thus, Hindus are actually incorporating other religions into their own cosmology, "all paths lead to the *Hindu* god (Brahman)." There are Christians who have done the same thing by proposing a universal religion behind all the varied religions of the world. When they do this, they assume a very particular character of God: that he is the creator, is wholly good, loves us all personally, and wants us to love him and one another. These are deeply Christian beliefs, not generic or neutral ones. So Christians who hope that all religions will agree on these points are in effect attempting to convert everyone to Christianity after all.

Lesslie Newbigin suggests that the different religions of the world "turn on different axes" (1995b: 171). He means by this that they are asking and answering different questions, and he suggests that when we attempt to merge the religions we distort others' answers to fit our own questions. For instance, Westerners have a fascination with the notion of reincarnation because they generally view life positively and would like to have more of it. But Hindus and Buddhists, who really believe in reincarnation, view life negatively and consider reincarnation a punishment for their sins. Their whole goal is to escape the cycle of rebirth. So adopting the Hindu doctrine of reincarnation to answer a Christian question about the limitations of our lives in the face of death distorts the original meaning of the doctrine. Once again, the deeper we look into what people actually mean by what they say, the more fundamental are the differences that we find.

This is most especially the case with the belief in God. Almost all religions acknowledge a spiritual world behind the phenomenal one, and many identify a single deity, often a creator, behind the multiplicity of spiritual beings (including polytheistic Hinduism). Thus, some have suggested that the different names for God mask a single underlying reality. This would be true if names were mere labels placed on the same underlying concept. But, as any linguist will attest, names are not merely labels. They are the surface forms of highly packaged conceptual understandings of the world. Thus, the different names for God can reflect radically different conceptions of God's identity and character. The Hindu Brahman is an impersonal force, the Muslim Allah is a righteous judge, and the Buddha is not a god at all, but a human being who ceased to exist after he became enlightened. There are also differences between the Jewish conception of Yahweh and the Christian understanding of the Trinity. And, there are variations in our personal conceptions of God depending on our individual thoughts and experiences. We Christians can become functioning polytheists when we refer to "my God" or "your God" in such a way as to imagine that we can define who God is according to our personal preferences. So, rather than suggest that everyone is right about God, it would probably make more sense to suggest that everyone is *wrong* about God, and that all of us must seek to know God's true character better than we currently do.

Newbigin suggests that the essence of a religion is its "final authority," the person, book, belief, or other source of commitment to which people turn to know the truth about God (1995b: 160). For Christians, that final authority is Jesus: a man who lived 2,000 years ago in Palestine, worked as a carpenter and helped to raise a family for thirty years, became an itinerant preacher announcing a new kingdom, was executed by the state on false charges after just three years of ministry, but was raised by God from the dead and has ascended to heaven leaving behind his Spirit to "teach [us] everything" (John 14:26). The idea that knowing Jesus is the only, or even the best, path to God is deeply offensive, a "stumbling block" or "scandal" (1 Cor 1:23), to most people, as Jesus himself predicted it would be (John 15:18–25). The reason for the offense is that it appears God has not been evenhanded. Why should a single person, living in a pinpoint of time and place, be the embodiment of God bearing his message to all the earth? Why should not God reveal his message freely at all times and places to everyone? We will probably never know in this life the full reason for God's choice to use incarnation and discipleship to deliver his message of redemption to humanity. But, says Newbigin, the significance of this circumstance is that we are humbled by having to receive the message from others, and being required as part of Christian living to pass it on (1995b: 174).

So how then do we work, play, converse, and live with the members of other religions? Newbigin points out that our own need for Jesus places us in the same position that they are in, at the foot of the cross (1995b: 181). Of course, the members of other religions do not recognize the cross. But as Christians, we believe all of humanity is in need of the same redemption, ourselves included. Later in this chapter, we will investigate the ways in which we can "speak," both literally and metaphorically, to others about Christ. But for now, it is important to note that there is no reason why we as Christians cannot cooperate with and participate in the abundant life-giving activities of non-Christians. From our common position at the foot of the cross, we can engage in peacemaking, assist the poor and marginalized, care for the environment, protect the abused, and in general work toward a better world. And, when we are working together with the members of other religions, or of no religion, conversations are possible that can be used by the Holy Spirit to accomplish his purposes.

THE ANTHROPOLOGY OF RELIGION

Anthropologists study religion along with the rest of human life and experience. But, because the vast majority of anthropologists are atheists, they tend to find religious beliefs and behavior mystifying. Typically they resolve this problem by reductionism, that is, by explaining religion in terms of one or another function of society. The early anthropologist Edward Tylor suggested that religion was the result of people's speculation about things they did not understand. He, and many others at the time, assumed that access to scientific knowledge would eliminate the need for religion. The sociologist Emil Durkheim suggested that religion was an expression of group solidarity, that is, of the human sentiment that binds society together. Karl Marx thought that religion was an illusion giving oppressed people false hope and preventing them from trying to change their circumstances. And Sigmund Freud thought that religion was an expression of the psychological need for an authority figure that would no longer be necessary when rational thought replaced our violent impulses. Most anthropologists have bought into one or another of these reductionist functional explanations for religion.

As believers, we *can* acknowledge the existence of the various "functions" of religion. It is true that our Christian faith answers many of our questions (Tylor), brings us together in community (Durkheim), reassures us with the hope of a better future (Marx), and satisfies our psychological needs, including the need for an authority in life (Freud). But that is not to say that any, or all, of these functions are the quintessential reason for religion. As total explanations, reductionist theories fall short of the mark, both because they fail to fully account for the significance and depth of religious experience, and because they cannot explain the remarkable complexity and variety of the world's religions. In fact, all such theories can easily be refuted. Against Tylor's theory we can point out that the religions do not provide simple or straightforward answers to intellectual questions, in fact they commonly raise new and more difficult questions; against Durkheim, we can demonstrate that the prophetic element in religions sometimes disrupts the social order and creates conflict rather than solidarity; against Marx we can object that, historically, many liberation movements for oppressed peoples have been religiously motivated; and against Freud we can point out that the progress of rational thought in science and philosophy, far from eliminating religion, has produced even deeper, more carefully considered theologies.

Anthropologists' attempts to explain religion by reductionism, then, are inadequate to the task of really understanding it. One anthropologist, Glenn Hinson, has suggested that ethnographers need to begin by taking at face value what religious people say about their own experiences. By ignoring their informants' explanations, and looking for alternative ones, anthropologists (along with other social scientists) are effectively saying, "since we *know* that the supernatural world does not exist, we must try to discover the *real* reason for religion." The result, says Hinson, is that:

> Supernatural experience is thus consigned to a reality apart,
> a realm where the "real" is defined only within the narrow

> parameters of belief. "That's what they believe," most ethnog-
> raphers seem to say, "and thus it's real *for them.*" What remains
> unsaid—but certainly not misunderstood—is the concluding
> codicil "but not for us, for we can see *beyond* the boundaries of
> their belief." Thus slips away any guise of ethnographic objectiv-
> ity, only to be replaced by implicit claims to a fuller knowledge
> and a more real reality. (2000: 330)

Were they to acknowledge the possible validity of religious beliefs and experiences, anthropologists would have to give up their sense of confidence
in their own naturalistic worldview . . . but they would understand religion
better as a result.

Hinson identifies three ways in which anthropologists dismiss religious
experiences: by ignoring what people say about them, by explaining them
away in terms of functions, or by assuming the people who have them are
delusional. Sometimes, says Hinson, anthropologists themselves experience
things that they cannot explain. When that happens, they usually attempt
to blame the stresses of fieldwork or absorption in the culture for producing a psychological effect. "In essence, most experiencing ethnographers,
like Ebenezer Scrooge in his encounter with the ghost of Marley, attribute
supernatural experience to that 'undigested bit of beef,' never considering
that on this one occasion their minds might *not* be playing tricks on them"
(2000: 333).

Hinson's own work on African American Christian worship services is
rich with ethnographic understanding, along with respectful acknowledgement of the possibility that his "consultants" may be right.[3] He points out
that most believers themselves acknowledge the possibility of false experiences, and have means of assessing whether experiences are authentic or
not. So the goal is a kind of team-work between ethnographers and consultants to discover the truth:

> To weight [strategies of ethnographic inquiry] with disbelief is
> to destroy their effectiveness and to abandon all claims to ob-
> jectivity. But to buoy them with openness is to invite dialogue,
> drawing our consultants fully into the search for understanding.
> With consultants as colleagues, and with our demand for total
> "explanation" dismissed as an exercise in imposed authority, we
> can jointly chart new paths of inquiry, drawing on collective

3. The difference between "informants" and "consultants" lies in the fact that the
former are used as sources of information which the anthropologist will write up and
interpret, while the latter are invited to assist in editing the final product, the ethnography. Consultants are co-writers together with the anthropologist, and so have greater
voice in what is said about them.

strengths to explore the experienced realities of belief. (2000:
334)

Notice that Hinson's approach to ethnographic understanding of religious
experience parallels Newbigin's approach to interacting with the members
of other religions. We begin with openness, trust, and humility, and proceed
by assisting one another to understand things that are beyond our compre-
hension in their totality.

Still, religious experience is not the only source of religious truth, and
it can be mistaken. Thus, all religions have teachings about what to believe,
how to interact with the divine, and how to live a moral life. These are
objective elements of the religion that form and shape experience, as well
as interpret it (cf. Lindbeck 1984). As Christians, we view peoples' experiences, beliefs, and practices as a combination of their own attempts to find
God, God's revelation of himself, and the devil's attempt to deceive them.
This means that what we might call "natural religion" is a human attempt
to understand the bigger questions of life in an arena that is a battleground
between God and the rebellious forces of evil arrayed against him in creation. With that larger view, it is possible to find value in the theorizing that
anthropologists do about the role of religion in society. Anthropological
theories can reveal the inner logic of people's thinking with respect to the
divine, the world, themselves, and good and evil.

Perhaps the most penetrating of these theories comes from the work
of Clifford Geertz, who has suggested that religion is a system of meaning
embodied in the symbols used in ritual (1973: 87–125). These symbols link
cosmology to morality in such a way as to cause each to reinforce the other.
For instance, the Buddhist term, *dharma,* means cosmic order, natural law
(or harmony), and human morality all at once. Its symbol is the wheel, with
each of the eight spokes of the wheel representing a specific teaching on
how to live. The wheel itself stands for the cycles of rebirth through which
a soul must go in order to be liberated from suffering. To achieve final liberation, or *nirvana,* Buddhists must follow their *dharma* by living rightly,
in accordance with natural law. Those who live wrongly, by *adharma,* are
being immoral and unnatural at the same time. The concept of *dharma,*
and its symbol, the wheel, link cosmology and morality to one another in a
mutually reinforcing manner.

Geertz believed that religion is ultimately a way of constructing meaning in life. He suggested that there are three "experiential challenges" that
can shake our sense of meaning: bafflement, suffering, and evil (1973: 100–
108). When we are baffled by things that don't make sense, from strange
lights in the night to peoples' odd behavior, we naturally attempt to close

the gap in our minds with an explanation. Religion provides us with "the proposition that life is comprehensible and that we can, by taking thought, orient ourselves effectively within it" (100). When we suffer, we not only wonder why we are suffering, but how to endure. Religion "rests ultimately on its ability to give the stricken person a vocabulary in terms of which to grasp the nature of his distress and relate it to the wider world" (105). And when we encounter evil or injustice in life, religion has the job of "affirming, or at least recognizing, the inescapability of ignorance, pain, and injustice on the human plane while simultaneously denying that these irrationalities are characteristic of the world as a whole" (108). With all three of these problems—intellectual, emotional, and moral—religion provides meaning in the face of "the dim, back-of-the-mind suspicions that one may be adrift in an absurd world" (102).

The answers that the religions give to life's questions are not simple ones. Geertz contrasts the religious perspective with the common-sense, the scientific, and the aesthetic perspectives (1973: 111). The common-sense perspective is characterized by a straightforward acceptance of experienced reality, the scientific perspective is characterized by doubt and systematic analysis, and the aesthetic perspective is characterized by attention to ap-pearances. What makes the religious perspective unique is the fact that it draws meaning and purpose from the widest possible "ultimate" reality (112). This wider reality is portrayed in ritual, where there is "a prior ac-ceptance of authority that transforms . . . experience" (109). Belief, then, comes from participating in rituals and accepting the religion's authority to provide the answers that we need to life's ultimate questions.

Geertz's work is valuable because it allows religion its own reason for being. But, even he is mainly addressing the problem that is most pressing for skeptical academics, namely, "Why does religion exist at all?" In the end, he too explains religion by subsuming it under culture as a natural phenom-enon (1973: 122). Some of the most recent studies of religion are even more reductionist than the earlier ones. There are cognitive psychologists who are suggesting that religion is an evolutionary by-product of human brain functioning (Boyer 2003), and economic sociologists who are suggesting that religion is a matter of markets, supply and demand, risk and rational choice (Sherkat and Ellison 1999). For those who do not have a religious commitment, the existence of religion continues to be an enigma.

For believers, however, the question is not, "Why does religion exist?," but "Which religion is right?" After all, the larger questions of life *do* need to be answered. In this sense, even atheists have a sort of religion, and the question is valid: How do we know the truth about life's ultimate meaning and purpose?

THE CHRISTIAN GOSPEL

In chapter one, we investigated the nature of scientific understanding and discovered that it does not actually provide complete objectivity or certainty, that it is a limited perspective, and that it too rests on faith. In fact, all knowing is a process of indwelling the truth, that is, mentally entering into it, in order to experience it as real. That experience of indwelling the truth provides us with a partially inarticulate or *tacit knowledge*, to use Michael Polanyi's term (1974: 55ff; 2009), upon which we act in the world. It is important for us to select carefully the beliefs that we choose to indwell. We are taking a significant risk of being wrong when we place our faith in one view of the world rather than another. So, a trusted authority in the context of a tradition is important to guide us in the process. Once we have taken the risk and committed ourselves to a chosen viewpoint, we must be willing to share it with others by inviting them to enter into it with us. Otherwise, we do not actually believe what we say we believe. All knowing is relational, says Parker Palmer (1993: 1ff), and requires not just a detached understanding, but a passion for the truth and compassion for others who need to know it. Though we do not possess the truth ourselves, we are *witnesses* to it, demonstrating a "proper confidence," to use Lesslie Newbigin's term (1995a: 105), that invites others to believe in what we say.

As Christians, we believe that God has revealed truth to us in two ways. First, he makes himself known to all the world through the evidence of nature and through the witness of the Holy Spirit in human hearts. Second, he communicates directly to particular people in chosen times and places through miracles, prophecies, Scripture, and especially through Jesus, who is the incarnation of himself. The former way, "general revelation," can be comprehended by everyone through human reason and conscience. The latter way, "specific revelation," is not knowledge that we can attain by our own efforts; it must be given to us. For instance, there is no empirical evidence that will provide certainty of our life after death. Nor is there any rational line of thought that will naturally lead to the idea that the death and resurrection of a single person, Jesus, should atone for the sins of humanity. It is only *after* we have received these truths and accepted them by faith that we can reason about them in order to understand further. We need special revelation in order to know the deepest and most important truths about God, the world, and ourselves.

Christians are sometimes confused as to what the primary source of God's special revelation is in Christianity. It is not the Bible per se, but rather the person of Jesus Christ who is revealed in the Bible who is our source. Put simply, Christians are the disciples of Jesus of Nazareth, whom we believe to have been God incarnate, and whom we take to be the Lord of our lives. The Bible is certainly the "word of God" in the sense that it is the account of God's whole revelation of himself, first to Israel and then to all the world, through history. Furthermore, it is a sacred and inspired text, not like any other book ever written, and the first guide to our faith and practice. But the Bible is most important to us because it reveals God's plan of salvation through Jesus, who is himself the *logos*, or the Word of God. It is by studying his life in the biblical text, praying to him as our friend and guide, following his instructions through the Holy Spirit as best we can, and most importantly, inviting him to live in our hearts to save us from sin and destruction and to transform us into his own image, that we become Christians.

This is an important point (and a theologically orthodox one) because it means that we are actually following a living person, not just a book of instructions. Furthermore, it means that the book itself can be translated into any language or culture, and convey the same salvific message needed to bring about a transformative encounter with Christ. Most Christians take the translatability of the Bible for granted. But, to show the difference, Muslims take the Qur'an (Koran) as their final authority rather than Muhammad, who was only a prophet. Thus they do not believe that the Qur'an can be translated without fatally distorting the message. The text itself, which is written in seventh-century Arabic, is considered to be directly from God without any human intervention.[4] Even the pronunciation of the text must be correct, since it is God's own words that are being spoken. Thus, those who convert to Islam must learn classical Arabic to read the true Qur'an, and must adopt Arabic customs and practices to be good Muslims (Sanneh 1993). This hermeneutic parallels the Muslim view of God as transcendent (above us) but not immanent (with us). Allah is perfect, and must not be contaminated by any human or earthly imperfection. Though he is "merciful," he does not accommodate himself to imperfect human history, language, or culture. So, in order to establish a relationship with God, human beings must take the critical first step of submitting themselves to Allah's will and of accommodating themselves to his commands.

Christians believe God to be both transcendent and immanent. His immanence is most clear in the incarnation, when *God* took the critical first step of becoming human in Jesus. The Bible too is an incarnational text. That is, it was written by human beings who, though under the influence of the Holy Spirit, were still psychologically present themselves in the writing.

---

4. Muslims believe that the messages from God contained in the Qur'an were delivered by the angel Gabriel to the prophet Muhammad. Muhammad, who was illiterate, simply memorized the messages he received. His illiteracy is taken as a sign that no human element entered into the Qur'anic text in any way.

As one theologian has put it, God inspired the human writers of the Bible, "not as dead passive things, but as free, integral, independent personalities, not as a mechanic uses his tools, not as a magician handles his puppets, but as a Living Spirit, breathing in and through living souls" (Evans 1891: 15).[5] Christians believe that God chooses to do his work, not just despite human weaknesses, but in and through them. The Apostle Paul says, "We have this treasure in clay jars, so that it may be made clear that this extraordinary power belongs to God and does not come from us" (2 Cor 4:7). Later he says that God's power is made perfect in our weakness (2 Cor 12:9). In Christianity, then, God accommodates himself to us so that we can be reconciled to him and begin to participate in the work that he is doing in the world.

What work is that? The treasure that Paul is referring to in the above passage is "the light of the knowledge of the glory of God in the face of Jesus Christ" (2 Cor 4:6), which shines through us to the world. So, it is Jesus himself who is our authority and the treasure, the gospel, that we offer to the world. After his conversion, Paul spent the rest of his life as a missionary, bringing the gospel, or "good news," of Jesus Christ to others. He declared that the man Jesus, who died and was resurrected for our sake, *is* God incarnate, the Lord of all (2 Cor 4:5). By believing in him, we can be reconciled to God and to one another and have everlasting life (John 3:16). This is the truth that we Christians believe is the most important one, and the one that must be shared with everyone.

The gospel that Paul and the other apostles witnessed to in the first century has been passed on ever since by missionaries. Through the Bible, it has been translated into countless languages and cultures. Missiologists call the effective translation of the gospel into a new culture, "contextualization" (Hiebert 2009). In order to be understood, the "good news" must be stated in local words, symbols, and figures of speech, and make sense in terms of local worldviews (Hiebert 2008). Then, once planted, the gospel takes root, grows, and eventually transforms not only the people, but the culture too,

---

5. Evans (1891: 41) suggests that the human element in the writing of the Bible is actually part of God's plan: "God is not limited as to his means and methods in communicating his will to men. Had a literal, stereotyped, incorruptible infallibility in every jot and tittle of the record been an indispensable requisite, God had a thousand resources at his command for securing such a record. That he chose men, yes, men, with all their ignorance and weakness and fallibility; that he entrusted his revelation to their stammering tongues and to their stumbling pens; that he deposited the interpretation of his eternal ways in earthen vessels, which could not escape the corruptions and mutilations of time; simply shows that a literal, particularistic infallibility is of less moment in the sight of God than some other things; of less worth, perhaps, than the thrill of a human touch, the glow of a red-hot word, the pulse of a throbbing heart, the lightening of a living eye, the flesh of a soul on fire; of less worth—who knows?—than the faltering of the pilgrim's foot; dearer to heaven than the lordly step of Gabriel."

under the influence of the Holy Spirit. This is not by any means a new process. Contextualization began with the New Testament, which was written
in Greek, not Hebrew, in order to be accessible to Gentiles.

Harriet Hill, a missionary with extensive experience in West Africa,
has demonstrated that the Bible is better understood when local terms are
used, rather than foreign ones, even when the local terms are only partially
accurate (2007). Hill compared conceptions of God, the devil, angels, and
demons among the Adioukrou of Ivory Coast. For the first two terms, *God*
and *the devil,* Bible translators used local equivalents despite the fact that
the Adioukrou thought God was married and had children, and that the
devil was just a psychic force in nature. For the second two terms, *angels*
and *demons,* new words and phrases were invented to avoid the association
with local gods. Eighty-five years after the translation, Hill found that the
Adioukrou had relegated the idea that God had a wife to an old folktale,
and they had altered their view of the devil to fit the biblical stories about
him. But they were still confused about who angels and demons were, and
considered them irrelevant to daily life. In their place, the Adioukrou had
retained the old gods, whom they appeased on the side to avoid becoming
possessed. The Adioukrou had successfully adjusted the meanings of local
terms to fit what they learned from the Bible, but had sidelined the foreign
terms and retained pre-Christian beliefs and practices in their place.

In fact, the gospel is like a prism in that it can be viewed from multiple
angles with beautiful effect. Missionaries commonly report that they have
understood the stories, symbols, and images of the Bible more deeply in
new cultural contexts. Sometimes they are deeply changed themselves by
the encounter, as was the case in the East Africa revival (discussed in chapter
four). Multilingual and cross-cultural Bible studies can be an especially effective means of gaining a fuller understanding of God's word. For example,
the Piro Indians of Peru use the same verb for "to believe" as they do for "to
obey," making it impossible to imagine believing without obeying. In the
Piro language, when Jesus says in John 14:1, "Believe in God, believe also
in me" he is simultaneously saying, "Obey God, obey also me." In Aztec, to
have faith is to "follow closely after" someone, making faith something that
we must do, rather than just think about in the abstract.[6] Examples such as
these show the value of Bible translation and of the contextualization of the
gospel to worldwide Christian faith and practice.

Translation and contextualization are possible because the gospel
message is not culture-bound. Since it is from God, it can be expressed in

6. These examples are from Sanneh (1993: 196), based on the work of Eugene Nida
(1952: 120–21).

any language or culture. Thus it is important that the gospel not be over-identified with a particular culture or its customs. The Apostle Paul stated clearly and on multiple occasions that Gentile Christians need not follow the religious customs and practices of the Jewish culture from which the gospel had originally come (Rom 9–10; 1 Cor 8; Gal 3–5). And, the early church took a stand that conversion to Christ was not a matter of adopting someone else's culture, but of allowing the gospel to penetrate and transform one's own culture. Not even Jewish culture could be the standard for correct interpretation of the gospel message to converts from other backgrounds (Walls 2002b: 68).

Most seriously, when the gospel message is over-identified with a certain language or culture, it loses its ability to challenge that culture, and may be used to affirm things in the culture that are not of God—a situation that missiologists call "syncretism." There are many cases of syncretism in the history of the church, including accommodations to Greek Gnosticism, to the European slave trade, to Indian caste, to African witchcraft, and to American racism, materialism, and militarism. Lesslie Newbigin comments:

> [The Church] can fail by failing to understand and take seriously the world in which it is set, so that the gospel is not heard but remains incomprehensible because the Church has sought security in its own past instead of risking its life in a deep involvement with the world. It can fail, on the other hand, by allowing the world to dictate the issues and the terms of the meeting. The result then is that the world is not challenged at its depth but rather absorbs and domesticates the gospel and uses it to sacralize its own purposes. (1989: 152)

Elsewhere, Newbigin calls this latter failing the "domestication" of the gospel (3). Just as wild animals are domesticated to be used for human purposes, so the gospel may be tamed to be used for the culture's purposes. First the message is distorted to fit the culture's previously held beliefs and values, and then the language, symbols and structures of the church are exploited to legitimize the culture's own power. The gospel's natural "wildness," the power of God, is prevented from transforming the culture in needed ways.[7]

In America, as we have seen, Christianity has been domesticated by a syncretism with pluralism. Due to its strong value on individualism, and its support of the state as the premier institution in society, American culture

---

7. Syncretism is in part an active rejection of the true gospel, and of Jesus himself, by the culture. Remember that Jesus, who *was* the gospel, was repeatedly rejected by the culture in which he lived, from the attempt to kill him after his first sermon in Nazareth (Luke 4:29), to the efforts to stone him in Jerusalem (John 10:31), to his final death on the cross. He was "the stone that the builders rejected" (Ps 118:22; Acts 4:11).

promotes a kind of functioning polytheism, in which each person may have their own invented conception of God. The sociologist Robert Bellah cites the example of an American woman who concocted a personal religion and called it "Sheilaism," after her own first name (2007: 221). By personalizing and relativizing religion, American culture prevents any challenge to its own authority in people's lives and reinforces the primacy of American citizenship. By co-opting the language, symbols, and institutions of the church, it convinces Christians that they need not make any difficult choices about whom to serve, God or country. The result is a dangerous subordination of the power of the gospel to loyalty to the world's dominant country (Meneses 2006).

There is always a danger that the gospel will be domesticated by the culture and that the church will agree to the terms of the deal in order to preserve its own safety and legitimacy. Still, contextualization is absolutely essential to the spread of the gospel, even in America. The British missiologist Andrew Walls reminds us that:

> No one ever meets universal Christianity in itself; we only ever meet Christianity in a local form, and that means a historically, culturally conditioned form. We need not fear this; when God became human, he became historically, culturally conditioned man, in a particular time and place. What he became, we need not fear to be. There is nothing wrong with having local forms of Christianity—provided that we remember that they *are* local. (2002b: 235)

In context, Walls is making the point that Americans too can celebrate their particular cultural expression of Christianity, so long as they remember that it is just one expression among many.[8] Moreover, everyone can offer their own expressions of the faith to the global church as unique contributions that complement the contributions of others. All this can be a true celebration of diversity, so long as we remember that Jesus is the true head of the church and are open to being corrected by others and by the Holy Spirit (1 Cor 12:12–26).

---

8. Walls (2002b: 234–45) has a perspective on American Christianity that is useful for identifying its strengths and weaknesses. He says that it is characterized by "vigorous expansionism; readiness of invention; a willingness to make the fullest use of contemporary technology; finance, organization, and business methods; a mental separation of the spiritual and the political realms combined with a conviction of the superlative excellence, if not the universal relevance, of the historical constitution and values of the nation; and an approach to theology, evangelism, and church life in terms of addressing problems and finding solutions."

In this last point, we are reminded that, while the gospel message is fully translatable, there is one term that is never translated, and that is Jesus' own name (though it is pronounced differently). The reason for this is that Jesus is a living person, not a theological concept. The very essence of the gospel is the historical account of his life, death, resurrection, and ascension into heaven, and the claim that this particular person is both Savior and Lord. Thus, the gospel is not just a new belief system. It is a grand story, or narrative, of the history of the world, its significance, and our place in it. Becoming a Christian is ultimately a matter of adopting that narrative and choosing to become a follower of Jesus. When we make this choice we come to indwell the story ourselves, and through our lives and our testimonies become the storytellers to others who are also invited to become Jesus' disciples (Newbigin 1989: 89).

The History of Christian Mission

How has the gospel been spread around the world? When Jesus had finished his time on earth and was ready to return to his Father, he left these instructions for his disciples:

> All authority in heaven and on earth has been given to me. Go therefore and make disciples of all nations, baptizing them in the name of the Father and of the Son and of the Holy Spirit, and teaching them to obey everything that I have commanded you. And remember, I am with you always, to the end of the age. (Matt 28:18–20)

With these words, Jesus declared his own authority over everything, instructed his disciples to make other disciples, and promised to be with them always. He also told them he would equip them for the task, saying, "You will receive power when the Holy Spirit has come upon you; and you will be my witnesses in Jerusalem, in all Judea and Samaria, and to the ends of the earth" (Acts 1:8).

The book of Acts records the dramatic outpouring of the Holy Spirit shortly afterwards at Pentecost, and the remarkable transformation of Jesus' first disciples from bumbling fishermen and tax collectors into powerful evangelists, apostles, and leaders of the early church. Dana Robert comments, "The transformation of a cowed and defeated handful of Jewish followers into a death-defying, multi-cultural missionary community was an amazing beginning to what is now the largest religion in the world" (2009:

12). The disciples, ones who follow, had become missionaries and apostles, ones who are sent (2009: 11).

As Jesus had predicted, his disciples went out to spread the gospel to the ends of the then known world.[9] The Apostle Paul made three missionary trips through the eastern Roman Empire, establishing churches throughout Greece and Asia Minor. As best we know from various church traditions, the Apostle Peter went to Rome where he was martyred, the Apostle Thomas to India where he established the Syrian church of Kerala and then was martyred, the Apostle Mark to Egypt where he established what became the Coptic Church, and the Apostle Philip to Ethiopia where he established what is now the Ethiopian Orthodox Church. So, within the lifetime of Jesus' disciples, the church had spread from Rome to India, and from Greece to Ethiopia.

When Jerusalem was destroyed in 70 AD and the Jewish people were sent into diaspora, many Christians were among them. These Christians took the gospel even farther. Jesus had predicted this too in his earlier words to the Samaritan woman at the well. When the woman raised the question of whether it was necessary to worship God in Jerusalem, Jesus responded that the true worshipers of God would worship him not just in Jerusalem, but *everywhere* "in spirit and truth" (John 4:23). In the first century, most people thought Christianity was a reform movement within Judaism and that its center would remain in Jerusalem. But when the church, under the guidance of the Holy Spirit, moved to incorporate Gentiles as full members without requiring them to observe Jewish law, there was a sea change in the understanding of God's message that caused Christians to reach out to any and all who would hear them. Then, the political circumstances of the time propelled them out of Jerusalem in all directions.

Christians living under the Roman Empire underwent severe persecution for over 300 years, primarily for their refusal to acknowledge the divinity of the emperor. From the destruction of Palestine to quell Jewish rebellion in the first century to the conversion of the Emperor Constantine in the fourth century, they were harassed, tortured, and killed. Meanwhile, the gospel was also being carried into the Persian Empire. There too, Christianity was seen as a threat to political power and to the state-sponsored Zoroastrian religion. The Roman and Persian Empires were rivals to one another, so when the Roman Empire finally ceased persecuting Christians and legitimized Christianity, the Persian Empire increased its persecution as a means of resisting Rome. Christians, despite their largely peaceful

9. The following history of Christian mission is broadly based on Bosch (2005), Latourette (1999), Neill (1990), and Robert (2009).

responses at this time, suffered tremendously for their faith, but did not stop carrying the gospel on.

The legitimization of Christianity in Rome had a powerful effect on the history of the church in Europe. As we saw in chapter seven, it made life easier for Christians, but at the price of compromise with political power. It also opened a public space for the discussion of theological issues, some of which became quite heated as the church endeavored to identify and consolidate its most central beliefs. One of these battles resulted in the exodus of a significant community of Christians east along the Silk Road. Known as the Nestorians after their theological leader, Nestorius, they took the gospel all the way from Persia to India, and then to China. Later, when Rome was sacked by "barbarians" from the north, tribal groups that had already become Christians carried the gospel to the northern parts of Europe, slowly replacing pagan deities and practices.

In all these various places and circumstances, Christians developed a good reputation for their care for the poor, concern for the oppressed, and for simple integrity. The historian Latourette comments, "In its first few centuries, within the Church which it had called into being Christianity had not only largely drawn the sting of slavery, given dignity to labour, and abolished beggary. It had also elevated the status of women and given new worth to childhood" (Latourette 1999: 248). Many social issues that we consider to be contemporary ones were in fact taken up by the church from the beginning. Christians were considered dangerous for their noncooperation with governments, but admirable for their willingness to give up their lives for their faith and for their care and concern for the suffering of others.

Unfortunately, under the long period of medievalism in Europe, the continued alliance of Christianity with political power encouraged many Christian kings to baptize their military exploits with Christian justifications and to coerce conversions as part of their expansionary projects. Many ordinary Christian people fell into nominalism and to syncretism with their cultures. As a result, monastic movements developed to preserve the gospel from social, political, and cultural corruption, and to continue to spread it to others. Robert comments, "Monks were the grassroots missionaries in the conversion of Europe. From the early centuries of the church, wandering celibate holy men and women were honored witnesses to the peaceful lifestyle and suffering of Jesus" (2009: 25). In fact, throughout history it has often been marginalized Christians who have reminded mainstream Christians of the radical call of Jesus to live in the world, but not be of it (John 17:14–19). From the monastics of Christian empires to the persecuted churches of non-Christian ones, like Jesus, they have spoken "truth to power" with their lives.

Though the European states were divided after the fall of the western half of the Roman Empire, the church remained formally united for several more centuries. This relative unity was in part due to the rivalry that Christians felt with Islam, which had burst out of Saudi Arabia in the seventh century. North Africa had been largely Christian under the Roman Empire, but it was converted to Islam with remarkable speed when it was overrun by the first wave of Muslims conquerors. Forced conversions were part of the reason, but Christian nominalism was also to blame as Christians who had once been willing to be persecuted for Christ took the safe and easy route of joining the religion of political power.

Eventually, the Eastern (Orthodox) and Western (Roman Catholic) branches of the church split from one another over theological issues and matters of church leadership. But when Byzantium was attacked by Turkish Muslims, Christians from Europe responded to the call of Pope Urban II to take back the Holy Lands in the Crusades. The terrible idea of a holy war had gripped the European Christians, who felt marginalized by Islam and were afraid of their own internal divisions. Latourette comments that the Crusades were "an aspect of the partial capture of the Church by the warrior tradition and habits of the barbarian peoples who had mastered Western Europe and had given their professed allegiance to the Christian faith" (1999: 414). As under the Roman Empire, syncretism with political power produced actions of which the church is now properly ashamed.

Still, despite cultural compromises and political blunders, Christianity continued to spread through Europe, into Africa, across Asia, and eventually to the Americas. As the colonial empires formed, Christian missionaries traveled the trade routes to new places. Right from the start, Catholic priests accompanied the conquistadors to Central and South America, and Protestant chaplains accompanied both military and trading companies to Africa and Asia (Robert 2009: 41). Once the empires were established, missionaries were able to move relatively freely around the world. It was the beginning of "globalization," a dramatic increase in communication, travel, awareness, and interconnectedness, and it yielded the first truly global church.

The colonial empires are now rightfully viewed as having been both exploitative and oppressive to the various peoples that they subjected and ruled. Furthermore, missionaries from Europe all too easily accepted the convenience and protection of the colonial powers. But missionaries and colonialists did not have the same purposes and commonly came into conflict with one another. Colonialism was primarily an economic enterprise, enriching European powers at the expense of the colonies. When missionaries, whose purpose was conversion and church building, were responded to with religious and cultural backlashes by local people, colonial governments stepped in to restrict them and even ban them from the colonies entirely. The missionary William Carey for instance, arrived in India in 1793 under a complete ban on missionary activity by the British East India Company. He had to hide from the company soldiers to preach the gospel. It took a massive campaign by Christians in England, and an act of parliament, to force the East India Company to permit missionaries to enter India legally.

Colonial missionaries were, no doubt, ethnocentric, as we all are. Still, they were not as insensitive to the value of culture as we now imagine. As early as 1659, a mission society founded by Pope Gregory XV sent the following instructions to its missionaries:

> Do not regard it as your task, and do not bring any pressure to bear on the peoples, to change their manners, customs, and uses, unless they are evidently contrary to religion and sound morals. What could be more absurd than to transport France, Spain, Italy, or some other European country to China? Do not introduce all that to them but only the faith, which does not despise or destroy the manners and customs of any people, always supposing that they are not evil, but rather wishes to see them preserved unharmed.[10] (Neill 1990: 153)

The Jesuits, founded in the sixteenth century, were early practitioners of "modern missions." They emphasized adaptation to local cultures, the ordination of local priests, the use of vernacular languages in liturgies, and Bible translation. Other Catholic orders, such as the Dominicans and Franciscans, refused to cooperate with colonial governments in Latin America over the slave trade, and protected the lives of Native American Indians by building them fortified villages. Eventually both of these orders were evicted from the Americas by their own governments for their efforts to protect indigenous peoples.

Protestant missions, coming out of a reform movement that declared *sola Scriptura* as its watchword, heavily emphasized Bible translation during the colonial period. In 1800 there were translations of the Bible (in whole or in part) into just seventy languages; one hundred years later that number

---

10. The instructions continue, "It is the nature of men to love and treasure above everything else their own country and that which belongs to it; in consequence there is no stronger cause for alienation and hate than an attack on local customs, especially when these go back to a venerable antiquity. This is more especially the case, when an attempt is made to introduce the customs of another people in the place of those which have been abolished. Do not draw invidious contrasts between the customs of the peoples and those of Europe; *do your utmost to adapt yourselves to them.*" [Emphasis added.] (Neill 1990: 153)

was 520 languages (Neill 1990: 216). By 2000, the number was 1500 languages.[11] Missionaries typically stayed longer and learned local languages more fluently than did colonial administrators, and thereby tacitly demonstrated the value of local cultures. In fact, according to historians, the translation of the Bible into new languages in the nineteenth century played a significant role in fueling the nationalist movements of the twentieth century (Sanneh 1993; Walls 2002a).[12] Bible translation implicitly valued local languages and cultures by refusing the notion that any of them were too "backward" to be vessels for God's message. As a result, in places where Bible translation took place, local cultures were revitalized and people were empowered against their colonial rulers. This eventually led to the rejection of colonialism, the development of independence movements, and the establishment of democracies with higher than average levels of good health, literacy, and economic development (Woodberry 2012).[13]

The nineteenth century saw an enormous movement of European missionaries to other parts of the world. Still, it was not these missionaries who were primarily responsible for the explosive growth of the global church under colonialism. Generally, it is difficult for cross-cultural missionaries to convince people to become Christians, given the differences in worldview. Their contribution is vital, since they are the first bearers of the message to the new culture. But it is the first converts who become the real evangelists to their own people. As Bishop Azariah of India put it, "No country can be fully evangelized except by its own sons [and daughters]" (Harper 2000: 43). New Christians are filled with enthusiasm, understand the mind-set of their own people, and can bridge the gaps that hinder conversion. For instance, William Carey brought very few people to Christ himself. But his first convert, Krishna Pal, brought hundreds into the church. After the king of Tahiti was converted, Tahitian Christians traveled to every island within a 2,000-mile radius spreading the gospel (Robert 2009: 49). In West Africa, the Liberian prophet William Wadé Harris led a mass movement

11. See "Growth of Scripture Translation and Publication Since 1800" at the United Bible Society web page: http://www.ubs-translations.org/about_us/#as. Accessed on 1/16/17.

12. There were missionaries who openly supported the independence movements. For instance, in India, Rev. E. Stanley Jones, an internationally renowned missionary, writer, and speaker, met with Mahatma Gandhi and defended India's right to independence. My own grandfather, John Nicholas Christian Hiebert, was a missionary to India at the time and also supported Gandhi.

13. Woodberry has conducted very carefully done statistical research to establish the fact that countries that had Christian missionaries under colonialism are more likely to be developed democracies now. The evidence is strongest for independent Protestant missionaries, as against state-sponsored church missionaries or Catholics.

into Christianity that crossed several countries and included over 100,000 converts. And, around the world, thousands of nameless "Bible women" and other evangelists have traveled on foot from village to village bringing people to Christ.[14]

Figure 9.1: Evangelism in Africa

Source: M. N. Daneel, 2014[15]

14. Historian Norman Etherington remarks, "the greatest difficulty faced by those who have tried to argue that Christian missions were a form of cultural imperialism has been the overwhelming evidence that the agents of conversion were local people, not foreign missionaries. None of them were coerced into believing and very few were paid" (cited in Andrews 2010: 677).

15. http://sites.bu.edu/shonareligion/. Accessed 2/27/18.

Since the twentieth century, indigenous mission movements have taken the gospel to the remotest places on earth and have spawned whole new denominations of Christians who are passionate for their faith. Now in the twenty-first century, the greatest missionary movements are not "from the West to the rest," they are from Asia, Africa, and Latin America to the whole world, including the West. As the missiologist Samuel Escobar puts it, missions is now "from everywhere to everyone" (Escobar 2003). Again, marginalized people have often been the ones to bring the gospel to centers of political and cultural power. Robert reminds us that refugee movements have been a primary means of the spread of the gospel throughout church history (2009: 75). In Latin America, concern for the poor has produced a new form of theology focused on the biblical message of liberation for the oppressed (Gutiérrez 2007). Around the world, Pentecostalism, with its appeal to ordinary people to be transformed by the power of the Holy Spirit, is the fastest growing form of Christianity. Nowadays, anthropologists have taken a new interest in this latter development, and are studying Pentecostalism from Africa to New Guinea to the United States. The dynamic growth of the church worldwide has caught the attention of social scientists who want to understand its meaning and its power (cf. Cannell 2006, Robbins 2004).

Confident Witness

What role do you and I have to play in this growth of the church? We are the disciples of the disciples of Jesus' disciples. What responsibility do we have to continue the work? Jesus' disciples once asked him, "What must we do to perform the works of God?" He answered, "This is the work of God, that you believe in him whom he has sent" (John 6:29). Our most important work, then, is to believe in Jesus ourselves. This is not a one time, and then it is done, thing! Rather it is a lifelong commitment to increasingly deep faith in God and in the One whom he has sent. Such belief is a matter of choice, but it is not a simple accomplishment. In many ways, the Christian message is not an easily believable one: that a single man in history was God incarnate, that through his death and resurrection all of humanity can be saved from destruction, that our lives have meaning, purpose, and hope because of him. Believing in Jesus is actually a very significant and difficult work that we perform for God!

One evidence of the strength of our own belief is our desire to tell others about it. Certainly that desire can be hindered by the rejection we experience when we attempt to share our faith. But the desire itself is rooted in our personal commitment to Christ, and it will overcome barriers when it is nurtured to full strength. The Apostle Paul wrote, "Pray for us as well that God will open to us a door for the word, that we may declare the mystery of Christ, for which I am in prison, so that I may reveal it clearly, as I should" (Col 4:3–4). Though he was trapped in prison for having shared the gospel, Paul's first desire was not to be set free, but to find an open door to further share Christ with others.

Christians are sometimes accused of having a sense of superiority when they witness to salvation through Christ. But we have already seen that this accusation can be a spurious attempt to quell the conversation. Furthermore, there is a link between our own circumstance and others' that, when remembered, naturally prevents a sense of superiority from contaminating the conversation. Newbigin says:

> Salvation is a making whole and therefore it concerns the whole. This means, in terms of my own spiritual life: (1) I am never permitted to think of my own salvation apart from that of God's whole family and God's whole world; (2) at no point—not even at the point of death—am I permitted to turn my back upon my neighbors, upon that bit of the world's life in which I have shared, which I have tried to serve, and without which I would not be a human being at all; (3) the end to which I look, for which I long, and in which I will rejoice, is not that I am saved but that my Lord shall "see of the travail of his soul and be satisfied." (1995a: 80)

Newbigin's point is that we are not saved by being *removed* from our social contexts. Rather it is in and through our connections with others, and with our cultures, that the message of salvation comes to us and is passed on. Our own struggles with belief, along with our wonderful experiences of God's presence and of the Holy Spirit's transformation of our lives, level the playing field between ourselves and those to whom we witness, making the conversation one of mutual assistance on the journey of life. When our hearts are in the right place, the salvation we long to see is of the entire earth, and for the glory of God.

It is important to remember that we do not do this work, either the work of believing or the work of witnessing, alone. The sharing of the gospel is not an individual sport, with highest honors going to the one with the most points. First, we look to invite others to Christ from the context of local churches in which we actively participate, demonstrating the community life that God intends for his redeemed people. Second, the spread of the gospel is actually a movement of the Holy Spirit, working through the church, and ahead of it, to redeem the world for God. We are exceedingly privileged to be allowed a role in that movement, but we are not ultimately responsible for it. Remembering this can remove some of the false pressure Christians feel to buttonhole others for Christ (which usually does not work well anyway). Jesus said that his yoke was easy and his burden light (Matt 11:30). Our great privilege is to simply watch and see God's marvelous work as it unfolds, and to participate in it when prompted and nudged to do so by the Holy Spirit. The results are up to him.

Finally, as we saw in chapter one, when given the opportunity (which we can request!), we should certainly share our faith with boldness. In Romans, Paul identified the need that motivates our passion to participate in God's work of salvation:

> The scripture says, . . . "Everyone who calls on the name of the Lord shall be saved." But how are they to call on one in whom they have not believed? And how are they to believe in one of whom they have never heard? And how are they to hear without someone to proclaim him? And how are they to proclaim him unless they are sent? As it is written, "How beautiful are the feet of those who bring good news!" (Rom 10:11–15)

The gospel is not always immediately understood to be good news. This is because "it is a secret in that it is manifest only to the eyes of faith" (Newbigin 1995a: 188). Yet, the gospel should not be buried like a treasure in the church grounds. It is meant to be revealed to the world for the world's redemption. When you share your faith with boldness, especially by risking comforts, reputations, safety, and even lives, the Scriptures say that you are beautiful in God's eyes.

(CHAPTER 9) DISCUSSION QUESTIONS

1. What experiences have you had with talking about religion with other people? What difficulties did you encounter, and what opportunities did you see?

2. What can we learn from the anthropology of religion that is helpful in terms of understanding our own and others' religious beliefs, practices, and experiences? How can we accept others' insights without abandoning our own most central commitments?

3. What actually is the Christian gospel, or "good news"? How can it can be framed in clear simple terms, without jargon, so that those who do not come from a Christian background can understand what it means?

4. Describe some of your own struggles with belief. Looking back at your own spiritual history, how has God encouraged you to believe, and gone before you to enable you to share your faith with others?

RECOMMENDED READINGS

Hiebert, Paul G. 1985. *Anthropological Insights for Missionaries.* Grand Rapids: Baker.

———. 2008. *Transforming Worldviews: An Anthropological Understanding of How People Change.* Grand Rapids: Baker Academic.

Hinson, Glenn. 2000. *Fire in My Bones: Transcendence and the Holy Spirit in African American Gospel.* Philadelphia: University of Pennsylvania Press.

Robert, Dana L. 2009. *Christian Mission: How Christianity Became a World Religion.* Malden, MA: Wiley-Blackwell.

Walls, Andrew. 2002a. *The Cross-Cultural Process in Christian History.* Maryknoll, NY: Orbis.

———. 2002b. *The Missionary Movement in Christian History.* Maryknoll, NY: Orbis.

Chapter 10

Studying and Living the Image

Conclusions

> For I am not ashamed of the gospel; it is the power of God for
> salvation to everyone who has faith, to the Jew first and also to
> the Greek (Rom 1:16).

It is not easy to be a Christian anthropologist. First, our society is divided
into public and private arenas, with religious thoughts and sensibilities
forbidden in the public square and the value on "tolerance" inhibiting honest
discussion across the boundaries. The academy, which is largely composed
of public institutions (with government funding), restricts its discourse to
secular language. Then, anthropology in particular has an uneasy relationship with Christianity. Its disapproval of the work of missionaries and its
ambivalence over Christianity's role as the dominant religion of the West
has caused it to be especially uncomfortable with Christians. For its part, the
church has sometimes unnecessarily resisted anthropology's propositions
on certain subjects (such as evolution). No doubt the church needs to listen
longer and better before it reacts to scientific theories and findings. But, as a
discipline rooted in the worldview of the Enlightenment, anthropology rests
on assumptions and presumptions that exclude religious interpretations,
and so it presents its case in terms that are immediately problematic for
people of faith. With such a divergence, the idea of being both a Christian
and an anthropologist can seem difficult at best, impossible at worst.[16]

16. An anthropologist who is the chair of one of the top departments of anthropology in the country says that he regularly gets the question from students, "Does being

I grew up in India as a child of missionaries. My parents were dedicated Christians involved in the work of the kingdom of God for the global church. I accepted Christ at an early age and subsequently attended a variety of churches of different denominations (Mennonite, Presbyterian, Lutheran, and Assemblies of God) and in a number of countries. Thus, I came to know the richness of the Christian faith and to love the worldwide church. But, when I went to college, and then on to graduate school, I discovered the prejudice that most anthropologists had against Christianity. It was a time, the 1970s, when Christians, and especially missionaries, were the "bad guys" in the moral universe of anthropology. Sitting in classrooms, listening to hostile jokes, and knowing I would pay a price if I spoke up, I learned to keep silent. Yet all this struck me as most unfair. Anthropology was a discipline that tried to understand people by having sympathy for them. Why did it not apply this same principle, much less its famed relativism, to Christians and Christianity?

Still, I persisted in becoming an anthropologist because I also loved the study of people and cultures. I did my doctoral fieldwork among merchants in an open-air market in southern India, and completed my degree from the University of California, San Diego.[17] The next step was to publish my work. But when I tried to write for publication, I found myself unable to use the restricted language of the anthropological discourse. I simply could not accept the packaged assumptions of the discipline, not even provisionally, for the purpose of adding my voice to the conversation. It was only much later, after I was employed by Eastern University (a Christian liberal arts institution in the Philadelphia area), that I discovered another discourse, the deep and rich world of "faith and learning integration," which intentionally relates bodies of knowledge from the various academic disciplines to Christian thought and practice. That experience was like opening the door, as Dorothy did, from the black-and-white world of Kansas to the colorful world of Oz. There was just so much to explore!

The first step I took was to go back to India and enhance my understanding of my ethnographic subjects by studying the lives of Dalit ("untouchable") women selling vegetables on street corners and in the

---

an anthropologist mean you can't be a Christian?" He assures these students that you can, but notes the background assumption that there is a natural hostility between the two (personal communication).

17. I was mentored by Dr. F. G. Bailey, whose assistance with my dissertation and continued friendship over the next thirty-five years fills me with gratitude even now. Dr. Bailey is an agnostic. He and I have had a long and friendly debate over Christianity that has been very enriching, at least to me. There is one point about which we are in complete agreement—the importance of *good writing!*

marketplace. The ethnography I wrote about their lives explicitly incorporated a Christian perspective into the analysis, and made the argument that Hindu cosmology was imprisoning these women where Christianity would have set them free. I wrote that book fully expecting that it would never be published, since it fell into the gap between Christian and secular publishers' purposes and market audiences. Remarkably, the University Press of America, which publishes academic books in an unbiased fashion, was willing to publish it (Meneses 2007). From that point on, my trajectory was set: in order to speak or write authentically, I would have to integrate my Christian faith with my anthropology. Since then, I have worked hard through research projects and new programs at Eastern to create an arena in which this can be done, not only by me but by others as well (Meneses et al. 2014).[18]

THE ANTHROPOLOGY OF CHRISTIANITY

Happily, since my graduate school days, the situation for Christians in anthropology has improved significantly. In the 1990s, a movement to study Christians as Christians was begun. One of the stories from the beginning of that movement makes the point about anthropology's previous (and sometimes continuing) prejudice. A doctoral student by the name of Joel Robbins went to Papua New Guinea to study a small group called the Urapmin. He had been trained, as had all anthropologists up to that point, to ignore elements of the culture that were deemed "modern," and to try to reconstruct the traditional forms—a technique that caused anthropology to image traditional cultures as pristine, and all outside influence as damaging. When he got to his field site, Robbins discovered that the Urapmin were all Christians. Robbins thought (quite rightly!) that as an ethnographer he should simply study them as they were rather than reconstruct their pre-Christian past. In doing so, he found that the Urapmin were not just nominally Christian, nor had they been manipulated or coerced to become Christians by missionaries. The Urapmin had actively sought Christianity, which they had heard about in the neighboring valley, and they were intensely serious about reformulating their traditional beliefs and practices to become good Christians. Robbins says, "They did not adopt Christianity in bits and pieces seized upon as syncretic patches for a traditional cultural

18. See Eastern University's webpage at www.eastern.edu. We have an undergraduate degree entitled the BA in Global Studies and Service, and a graduate degree entitled the MA in Theological and Cultural Anthropology. There is also a research project entitled *On Knowing Humanity*, originally sponsored by the John Templeton Foundation, that has produced an edited volume (Meneses and Bronkema 2017) and a peer-reviewed online journal, the *On Knowing Humanity Journal* (www.okhjoural.org).

fabric worn thin in spots by their attempts to stretch it to fit new situations. Rather, they took it up as a meaningful system in its own right, one capable of guiding many areas of their lives" (2004: 3). Robbins went on to write about the Christianity he found in the highlands of Papua New Guinea and to describe it in sympathetic terms.

Since then, Robbins (who is not himself a Christian) has continued to confront what he calls "the anthropological aversion to Christianity" (2004: 29). In an article entitled, "Anthropology and Theology: An Awkward Relationship," he has suggested three ways in which anthropology might benefit from Christian theology: 1) by investigating the historical role of theology in the formation of anthropology as a discipline, 2) by reading theology to understand the ethnography of Christians, and most significantly, 3) to consider theological arguments and paradigms and how they might inform anthropology's purposes. Robbins describes this last way as a willingness "to assume that the encounter with theology might lead anthropologists to revise their core projects" (2006: 287). Throughout his work, Robbins has insisted on taking Christian beliefs and practices seriously, and he has addressed Christians as intellectual equals, rather than just as objects of study.

CHALLENGES TO SECULARISM

There are other anthropologists who have questioned the commitment to secularism that prevents scholars from speaking from positions of faith. Their approach is to identify the fact that secularism is not the epistemological or ontological neutral ground that it pretends to be. Talal Asad, who is a well-recognized Muslim anthropologist, studies secularism from a genealogical (historical) perspective, and critiques anthropology's adoption of its assumptions.[19] Asad views secularism as having emerged from the excessive confidence of the European scholars of the Enlightenment who decided that their own observations of reality were clear and unprejudiced while others were blinkered and bound by religion and tradition (Asad 2003: 13). Max Weber, for instance, described premodern times as "enchanted" by the magical beliefs of religion, while modernity was "disenchanted" by the light of human reason. Asad points out that secularism is not actually based on a disembedded universal rationality, but rather on a specific political philosophy rooted in "a distinctive conception of nature as deep reality" (2003: 57).

19. The "genealogical" method was developed by Michel Foucault (following Nietzsche) and is characterized by a close investigation of the interrelatedness of meanings in a particular time period while noting the exercise of power in promoting conceptions that come to be considered the "truth."

That is, the presumption of modern secularism is that only nature is truly real, and that the rational human mind can discover the truth best when unhampered by religious fantasies.[20]

Asad notes the significant role that secularism has played in the development of the modern nation-state. Secularists tend to blame religion for war and violence and to credit the state for keeping the peace. But, in actuality, the modern world has simply been "shifting the violence of religious wars into the violence of national and colonial wars" (2003: 7). It is true that the European wars of the sixteenth and seventeenth centuries, following the Reformation, were devastating wars of religious difference (and *between* Christians!). But, as we saw in chapter seven, no century in human history has been as bloody as the twentieth century. There were two world wars as colonialism broke up, and countless civil wars within the nation-states that were formed thereafter. These were not religious wars; they were wars conducted by secular states and with the principles of nationalism.

Still, despite its failure to resolve differences in the political sphere, most people are convinced that secularism is absolutely necessary in science. Specifically, the belief is that by eliminating background identities such as those provided by religion and culture, scientists will be able to transcend their private perspectives and come to rational agreement on publicly accepted truth. Most anthropologists, says Asad, view anthropology's epistemological subject position (themselves) as modern, transcendent, and culture-free, while imaging the objects of their study as "nonmodern, local, [and] traditional" (Asad 1993: 19). They therefore fail to recognize that science is in fact a Western project with specifically modern claims and assumptions.

What does this critique mean for anthropology as a science? It means the field needs to be broadened in at least two ways. First, in anthropological analysis, the ground should be made level between scholars of different background beliefs. There can be no privileging of scholars without religious commitments over those with them, or even a restriction on bringing religiously-based thought into the academic discourse, so long as the thought itself is well considered and appropriate to the topic at hand. It is entirely possible that religious thought may add value to the conversation even for those who do not accept the source. Second, in data collection, ethnographers should increase the respect and the *credence* that they give to the people they study. That is, rather than assuming they know better about what is real and what isn't, ethnographers must work harder to accept

20. See also, Dipesh Chakrabarti (2007), who makes a similar argument from the perspective of Hinduism. For a critique of secularism from a Christian perspective, see Charles Taylor (2007).

informants' statements in their own terms without too quickly or easily ana-lyzing them in external terms.

Accepting informants' statements in their own terms does not mean the elimination of critical thought. On the contrary, it means widening the arena of critical thought to include matters beyond those observable in na-ture. Most people believe in the existence of God and the spiritual world in one form or another, and many claim direct experience of that world. Ethnographers must study these claims to religious experience without re-ducing them to categories and explanations that fit the ethnographer's own notions of reality. Glenn Hinson points out that, "Working from a posi-tion of unarticulated disbelief, most ethnographers simply refuse to accept believers' words at face value. To do so, they argue, would be to sacrifice their objectivity, to risk losing their scholarly perspective" (2000: 324). But, says Hinson, "When the urge to explain overrules the desire to learn . . . the victim is understanding. Thus the conversation ends, the two sides still separated by a chasm of belief" (323).

How, then, can anthropologists analyze the data on religious experi-ence that they have collected? Typically, in Western science, analysis is done by positing the existence of laws underlying the data that explain things. In the social sciences, this has often been done through a process of "unmask-ing," or claiming to know the "real" reasons for people's beliefs and behaviors apart from their own explanations. Often, as in the work of Michel Foucault, the exercise of power is believed to be the bottom line on what people are actually doing, the "law of gravity," so to speak, of human behavior. When that exercise of power has been described, people's own claims about their motivations are dismissed as ruses, and the situation needs no further ex-planation in the eyes of the anthropologist.

There is, however, another possibility for doing good analysis. Rather than unmasking people's beliefs and behaviors, it is possible to place them in larger contexts of understanding through a process of "framing." Theo-logians, such as John Milbank (1990), use this process to make sense of our world in terms of the Bible and traditions of church history. Different frames will produce different understandings of the same situation. But dia-logue can be had between scholars of different backgrounds, using different frames, that is productive of a richer understanding than is possible with the reductive and even cynical approach of the secular social sciences.

The matter is an important one because, as Clifford Geertz reminds us, scholarly work is not just an academic enterprise. It has *moral* purpose:

> When I try to sum up . . . John Dewey's work, what I come up
> with is the succinct and chilling doctrine that thought is conduct

and is to be morally judged as such . . . It is the argument that the
reason thinking is serious is that it is a social act, and that one is
therefore responsible for it as for any other social act. (2000: 21)

Under Enlightenment-based rationalism, the academy has become danger-
ously comfortable with the notion that science is just a matter of discovering
truth apart from its uses. For instance, according to the film documentary,
The Day After Trinity, when scientists first tested the atomic bomb in the
deserts of New Mexico, they speculated that it might vaporize the entire
earth's atmosphere—yet they went on with the test in the interest of scientific knowledge! (Palmer 1993: 1). Viewing all thought is a social act that can
be judged on moral grounds reminds us that science has a responsibility to
the public that can be usefully informed by religious perspectives. After all,
the religions have thought a lot about morality!

CHRISTIAN WITNESS TO THE ACADEMY

The Christian philosopher Nicholas Wolterstorff has suggested that, rather
than too resistant, most Christian scholars are entirely too conformist to the
latest trends in science (1999: 24). In an attempt to harmonize science with
their Christian beliefs, they either a) revise their own faith commitments
to fit the latest scientific theories, b) try to put scientific theories unaltered
into a larger Christian context, or c) insist that it is only in the application of
theories that we can incorporate our Christian thought, not in the theorizing itself (81). Instead, Wolterstorff writes,

> The Christian scholar ought to allow the belief-content of his
> [or her] authentic Christian commitment to function as control
> within his devising and weighing of theories. For he like every-
> one else ought to seek consistency, wholeness, and integrity in
> the body of his beliefs and commitments. (1999: 76)

According to Wolterstorff, all scholars are operating within traditions that
have "control beliefs," or "beliefs as to what constitutes an acceptable *sort*
of theory on the matter under consideration" [emphasis in the original]
(67). These control beliefs guide scientists' inquiries at every stage, from
determining the most important questions to ask, to selecting methods of
gathering information, to accessing the plausibility structures that permit or
deny certain interpretations of the data, and to presenting final conclusions
based on various levels of theorizing. In the secular academy, the control
beliefs include the notions that: 1) there is a real external world, 2) the
world can be explained in its own terms, without reference to God or other

"supernatural" beings, 3) existence is taken as a given, without any higher purpose, and 4) the future will be like the past in terms of the laws of nature.

Wolterstorff's point is that Christians must not accept control beliefs such as these, even provisionally, for the purpose of doing scientific theorizing. To the contrary, we must identify and acknowledge the control beliefs we have as Christians, and allow them to guide our scholarly work at every stage. Christian control beliefs include the notions that: 1) the real world includes not only the natural phenomena that we observe directly, but spiritual phenomena that we experience or observe indirectly, 2) natural phenomena must be explained by reference to the larger spiritual world, 3) existence has a purpose, and one that we can know through God's revelation in nature and in Scripture, and 4) time is limited and linear, and history, which has a beginning and an end, is the means by which God is working out his purposes for us and for creation.

Christian control beliefs such as these, says Wolterstorff, should guide our acceptance or rejection of scientific projects, cause us to develop research in new directions, and even assist us in developing a critique of science as a whole. In fact, given the arbitrary strictures of secular scholarship, some of the work of Christian scholars will necessarily be "in defiance of the academic establishment" (1999: 107).

Yet Wolterstorff reminds us that being a scholar is a part of God's mandate to humanity to "fill the earth and subdue it" (Gen 1:28), that is, to create culture:

> The Protestant tradition . . . understood the development of scholarship as an essential component in cultural formation— not just as an instrument of self-improvement, and not just as an instrument for beneficial alteration of one's circumstances, but as something good in its own right. God has declared it such, and enjoined its pursuit, so that it is part of [humanity's] obedient response to the cultural mandate. (1999: 140–1)

Wolterstorff is referring to the work of full-time scholars. But each of us is a scholar in the sense that we consider our circumstances and what we know about the world, theorize about it, and come to conclusions. Furthermore, we share our ideas with one another and develop common understandings of God, ourselves, and creation. In doing these things, we are fulfilling part of the cultural mandate we have been given as human beings by God.

Scholars who have authentic Christian commitment, says Wolterstorff, are members of a community of people who have been called out by God to be: 1) *witnesses*, in that they "proclaim that God is working in the world to bring about an order of things in accord with the goals he had when he created them," 2) *agents*, in that they "bring about such an order," and 3) *signs* (my term), in that they are a people "called to give indication in its own life of what such an order would be like" (1999: 73). As witnesses, agents, and signs of the kingdom of God, Christian scholars convey God's good news of redemption to the whole world.

CHRISTIANS IN ANTHROPOLOGY

So, how can Christian anthropologists speak to the secular discipline in such a way as to be heard, understood, and taken seriously? Moreover, how can our work become a source of valuable theorizing by others, including those who do not share the beliefs and assumptions of the Christian faith? What will be the value added of Christians researching, studying, and writing *as Christians* in this science?

The answer lies in the fact that our backgrounds are not just limitations on our understanding. They are also sources of knowledge from tradition and experience. For instance, who knows most about motherhood? Or about deep sea fishing? Or about living at high altitudes? Of course, it is the people who have lived in those circumstances. Anthropology has always recognized this, and has conducted careful ethnography to learn what other people know about their own situations. The goal, says Clifford Geertz, is to address humanity's ultimate questions by helping "to make available to us answers that others . . . have given, and thus to include them in the consultable record of what man has said" (1973: 30).

Yet anthropology has rightly insisted that an external evaluation of people's traditions and experiences is needed. We cannot simply buy into the beliefs that all illness is caused by witches, that hallucinogenic drugs are a legitimate means of contacting the spiritual world, or, for that matter, that God and the human soul do not exist unless proven to be there. Anthropology's mistake has not been its theorizing about people's beliefs and practices. Its mistake has been its assumption that there is a single, correct, external vantage point from which all evaluations must be made, and that that vantage point is the secular, naturalist one. So, what Christian scholars can add is *another vantage point* from which to express and to evaluate the human condition.

If this is to happen, that is, if multiple vantage points are to be allowed in anthropology, there are at least four barriers to be crossed: 1) the resistance in the academy to religious thought as such, 2) the resistance to giving up the the privileged position of secular naturalistic control beliefs, 3) the need for a living, growing language (or languages) with which to understand one another across the divide of different background beliefs, and 4) the need for everyone to speak openly and honestly about what their control and/or background beliefs actually are, and how they inform thought. Some of these are not actually new barriers to collaborative work. It has always been challenging for scholars from different theoretical perspectives to find ways to communicate and to work on common problems.

Currently, there are a number of well-respected philosophers who are working on the matter of how to communicate across background beliefs. Hans-Georg Gadamer has suggested that our "prejudices," that is, the limitations of the horizon of our understanding as seen from a particular vantage point, are actually a *precondition* (necessary) to understanding, and that a "fusion of horizons" is possible when we share what we know with one another (2013). Jürgen Habermas has suggested that people can come to common understanding by means of a "communicative rationality," a type of rationality based not on reasoning about the world but on our purposes in interpersonal communication (1985). As Christians, we know that no form of human reason will completely solve the problem of differences in understanding. We do not believe that the truth can be fully established by human effort, or even that human beings are entirely well intended in the process. Yet, Gadamer and Habermas remind us that we do have God-given abilities to think and to communicate in ways that can be effective in witnessing to truth, both as we discover it in the world and as God reveals it to us.

It is true that the current language of the discipline of anthropology will have to be expanded if faith-based thought is to be included. This is not a small matter because language is more than a set of labels on things. As any linguist will attest, a language is composed of highly constructed terms that force the speaker to view the world in a certain way. For instance, while anthropologists refer to human beings as a "species," theologians call them a "creature." Packaged into the term *species* is the notion that we are animals, with an evolutionary history, in competition with other animals for eco-niches, and with certain unique abilities, but no higher purpose beyond our own survival. On the other hand, packaged into the term *creature* is the notion that we have been created by God, placed in a world intended for harmony, not competition, and with a divinely appointed purpose, to care for the earth. We cannot resolve linguistic differences such as this one by simply agreeing on which term to use, *species* or *creature*. The debate is encoded in the terms themselves. Yet perhaps no discipline knows better the need for translation in the scientific enterprise than anthropology! Thus far, all Christian anthropologists have had to learn the language of secular, naturalist science, and to think, teach, and write in that language. Few secular anthropologists have attempted to learn the language of Christian theology, much less apply it to their studies as a critical tool. So, an expanded language of anthropology will need to include new terms borrowed from elsewhere as a means of exploring new ideas.

Finally, if the anthropological discourse is to be expanded to include religious perspectives, it will not be enough for the academy to broaden its parameters and provide the space. Christians and others must be willing to step up to the plate and begin to say openly all that they really think about the subjects of their study. They must declare publicly what their true intellectual position is and what it means for their scholarship. Then, as with any new movement in science, we can expect unpredictable, but exciting, developments in the field as it endeavors to understand human beings and their cultures more fully.

As we have seen, there is a new openness in anthropology to the scholarship from theology, and perhaps to religiously-based scholarly thought in general. This is not to say that secular anthropologists are ready to give up their privileged position with respect to control beliefs. Perhaps that is understandable, given the need for any discipline to have a structure based on its history of development. Yet any *living* discipline must be willing to grow and change, always allowing for the input from outside that will rejuvenate it and provide it with a path forward. In this sense, allowing anthropologists with religious commitments to speak freely, with the full set of their intellectual tools, may be the means of both reinvigorating the discipline and putting it into better communication with its own public audience (Meneses et al. 2014: 88ff).

THE BIGGER PICTURE

Lesslie Newbigin reminds us of the significance of the time in which we are living:

> The meaning of contemporary history is that it is the history of the time between Christ's ascension and his coming again, the time when his reign at the right hand of God is a hidden reality, the time in which signs are granted of that hidden reign but in which the full revelation of its power and glory is held back in order that all the nations—all the human communities—may have the opportunity to repent and believe in freedom. (1989: 128)

In the world of scholarship, as in the world in general, we Christians believe that Jesus is sovereign over all things. Yet, the reality of that bigger picture is intentionally hidden by God so that people can choose freely whether to reconcile with him and join the community of his followers, or not. Still, to guide the world in the right direction, God has provided signs of Christ's reign and has chosen us as Christians to be witnesses to these signs until the time when his reign is made evident to everyone.

One of the most important signs of the reality of Jesus' reign, according to Newbigin, is to be found in the distinguishing mark of the community of faith:

> One of the marks of the Biblical counterculture will be a confident hope that makes hopeful action possible even in situations which are, humanly speaking, hopeless. That hope is reliable, because the crucified Lord of history has risen from the dead and will come in glory. (1989: 101)

When we as Christians demonstrate "confident hope" for ourselves, others, and the world, and when we contribute positively to the efforts of others to improve the world, such as through well done faith-integrated scholarship, we become witnesses, agents, and signs of the partly invisible, yet fully present, kingdom of God. This is the bigger picture, the Christian frame, within which we work and to which we witness for the world's redemption.

(CHAPTER 10) DISCUSSION QUESTIONS

1. What experiences have you had of the difficulty of integrating Christian faith with academic knowledge?

2. How have you seen the commitment to secularism restrict scholarship and the scientific enterprise?

3. How might your field of study be different if it were put into direct engagement with Christian theology?

4. How can we be witnesses, agents, and signs of the kingdom of God in our scholarly work?

RECOMMENDED READINGS

Asad, Talal. 2003. *Formations of the Secular: Christianity, Islam, Modernity.* Stanford, CA: Stanford University Press.

Meneses, Eloise, Lindy Backues, David Bronkema, Eric Flett, and Benjamin Hartley. 2014. "Engaging the Religiously Committed Other: Anthropologists and Theologians in Dialogue." *Current Anthropology* 55(1) 82–104.

Milbank, John. 1990. *Theology and Social Theory: Beyond Secular Reason.* Malden, MA: Blackwell.

Taylor, Charles. 2007. *A Secular Age.* Cambridge, MA: Harvard University Press.

Wolterstorff, Nicholas. 1999. *Reason within the Bounds of Religion.* Grand Rapids: Eerdmans.

References

Anderson, Benedict. *Imagined Communities: Reflections on the Origin and Spread of Nationalism*. New York: Verso, 1983.

Andrews, Edward E. "Christian Missions and Colonial Empires Reconsidered: A Black Evangelist in West Africa, 1766–1816." *Journal of Church and State* 51(4) (2010) 663–91.

Appadurai, Arjun. *Modernity at Large: Cultural Dimensions of Globalization*. Minneapolis: University of Minnesota Press, 1996.

Archer, Dane, and Rosemary Gartner. *Violence and Crime in Cross-National Perspective*. New Haven, CT: Yale University Press, 1987.

Asad, Talal. *Formations of the Secular: Christianity, Islam, Modernity*. Stanford, CA: Stanford University Press, 2003.

———. *Genealogies of Religion: Discipline and Reasons of Power in Christianity and Islam*. Baltimore: Johns Hopkins University Press, 1993.

Barth, Fredrik. "Introduction." In *Ethnic Groups and Boundaries: The Social Organization of Cultural Difference*, 9–38. Long Grove, IL: Waveland, 1998.

Bateson, Gregory. *Steps to an Ecology of Mind*. New York: Ballantine, 1978.

Behe, Michael. *Darwin's Black Box*. New York: The Free Press, 1996.

Bellah, Robert, et. al. *Habits of the Heart: Individualism and Commitment in American Life*. Los Angeles: University of California Press, 2007.

Benedict, Ruth. *Patterns of Culture*. Boston: Mariner, 2006.

Berger, Peter, and Thomas Luckmann. *The Social Construction of Reality: A Treatise in the Sociology of Knowledge*. New York: Anchor, 1967.

Boas, Franz. *Race, Language, and Culture*. Chicago: University of Chicago Press, 1995.

Bodley, John. *Anthropology and Contemporary Human Problems*. Lanham, MD: AltaMira, 2008a.

———. *Victims of Progress*. Lanham, MD: AltaMira, 2008b.

Bohannan, Paul. *Social Anthropology*. New York: Holt, Rinehart and Winston, 1963.

Bohannan, Paul, ed. *Law and Warfare: Studies in the Anthropology of Conflict*. Garden City, NY: The Natural History Press, 1967.

Bosch, David. *Transforming Mission: Paradigm Shifts in Theology of Mission*. Maryknoll, NY: Orbis, 2005.

Boyer, Pascal. "Religious Thought and Behaviour as By-Products of Brain Function." *Trends in Cognitive Sciences* 7(3) (2003) 119–24.

Boyd, Gregory. *Satan and the Problem of Evil*. Downer's Grove, IL: IVP Academic, 2001.

Brown, Michael F. "Cultural Relativism 2.0." *Current Anthropology* 49(3) (2008) 363–73.

Cannell, Fenella. *The Anthropology of Christianity.* Durham, NC: Duke University Press, 2006.

Carvalli-Sforza, L. Luca, Paolo Menozzi, and Alberto Piazza. *The History and Geography of Human Genes.* Princeton, NJ: Princeton University Press, 1994.

Chakrabarti, Dipesh. *Provincializing Europe: Postcolonial Thought and Historical Difference.* Princeton, NJ: Princeton University Press, 2007.

Chagnon, Napoleon. *Yanomamo: The Fierce People.* New York: Holt, Rinehart and Winston, 1977.

Chesterton, G. K. *St. Francis of Assisi.* Bournemouth, UK: Image, 1987.

Chowdhry, Prem. "Customs in a Peasant Economy: Women in Colonial Haryana." In *Recasting Women: Essays in Indian Colonial History,* edited by Kumkum Sangari and Sudesh Vaid, 302–36. New Brunswick, NJ: Rutgers University Press, 1997.

Claiborne, Shane. *The Irresistible Revolution: Living as an Ordinary Radical.* Grand Rapids: Zondervan, 2006.

Claussen, Jan. *Apples and Oranges: My Journey to Sexual Identity.* Orlando, FL: Houghton Mifflin, 1999.

Collins, Francis S. *The Language of God: A Scientist Presents Evidence for Belief.* New York: The Free Press, 2006.

Colson, Elizabeth. *Tradition and Contract: The Problem of Order.* Chicago: Aldine, 1974.

Cronk, Lee. "Reciprocity and the Power of Giving." In *Conformity and Conflict: Readings in Cultural Anthropology,* 14th ed., edited by James W. Spradley and David W. McCurdy, 119–24. New York: Pearson, 2012.

Darwin, Charles. *The Origin of Species.* New York: Penguin, 1968.

Dawkins, Richard. *The Blind Watchmaker.* New York: W. W. Norton, 1986.

Dembski, William A. *The Design Inference: Eliminating Chance through Small Probabilities.* Cambridge: Cambridge University Press, 2006.

Denton, Michael. *Evolution: A Theory in Crisis.* Bethesda, MD: Adler and Adler, 1986.

de Tocqueville, Alexis. *Democracy in America.* New York: Bantam, 2000.

DeYoung, Curtiss Paul, Michael O. Emerson, George Yancey, and Karen Chai Kim, eds. *United by Faith: The Multicultural Congregation as an Answer to the Problem of Race.* New York: Oxford University Press, 2003.

Dix, Gregory, ed. *The Treatise on the Apostolic Tradition of St. Hippolytus of Rome.* London: S.P.C.K., 1968.

Douglass, William A. "Sheep Ranchers and Sugar Growers: Property Transmission in the Basque Immigrant Family of the American West and Australia." In *Households, Comparative and Historical Studies of the Domestic Group,* edited by Robert McC. Netting, Richard R. Wilk, and Eric J. Arnould, 109–29. Los Angeles: University of California Press, 1984.

Ember, Carol, and Melvin Ember. "War, Socialization, and Interpersonal Violence." *Journal of Conflict Resolution* 38 (4) (1994) 620–46.

Enns, Peter. *The Evolution of Adam: What the Bible Does and Doesn't Say about Human Origins.* Grand Rapids: Brazos, 2012.

Escobar, Samuel. *The New Global Mission: The Gospel from Everywhere to Everyone.* Downers Grove, IL: IVP Academic, 2003.

Evans, Llewelyn J. "Biblical Scholarship and Inspiration." In *Inspiration and Inerrancy: A History and a Defense,* edited by Henry Preserved Smith, 25–87. Cincinnati: Robert Clark and Co., 1893.

Evans-Pritchard, E. E. *Witchcraft, Oracles, and Magic among the Azande.* Abridged ed. New York: Oxford University Press, 1976.

Fabbro, David. "Peaceful Societies: An Introduction." *Journal of Peace Research* XV(1) (1978) 67–83.

Ferguson, Niall. *The War of the World: Twentieth-Century Conflict and the Descent of the West.* New York: Penguin, 2006.

Ferguson, R. Brian. "Ten Points on War." In *The Anthropology of War: Views from the Frontline,* edited by Alisse Waterston, 32–49. New York: Berghahn, 2009.

Firth, Raymond. *We, the Tikopia: A Sociological Study of Kinship in Primitive Polynesia.* Abingdon, UK: Routledge, 2004.

Flett, Eric. *Persons, Powers, and Pluralities: Toward a Trinitarian Theology of Culture.* Eugene, OR: Pickwick, 2011.

Foster, Brian. "Ethnicity and Commerce." *American Ethnologist* 1(3) (1974) 437–48.

Freeland, Stephen J., and Laurence D. Hurst. "The Genetic Code is One in a Million." *Journal of Molecular Evolution* 47 (1998) 238–48.

Friedan, Betty. *The Feminine Mystique.* New York: Bantam Doubleday Dell, 1983.

Gadamer, Hans-Georg. *Truth and Method.* London: Bloomsbury, 2013.

Geertz, Clifford. *Available Light: Anthropological Reflections on Philosophical Topics.* Princeton, NJ: Princeton University Press, 2000.

———. *The Interpretation of Cultures.* New York: Basic, 1973.

George, Susan. *A Fate Worse than Debt.* London: Penguin, 1988.

Goldschmidt, Walter. "Inducement to Military Participation in Tribal Societies." In *The Anthropology of War and Peace: Perspectives on the Nuclear Age,* edited by Paul R. Turner and David Pitt, 15–31. Granby, MA: Bergin and Garvey, 1989.

Goodale, Mark. "Introduction to 'Anthropology and Human Rights in a New Key.'" *American Anthropologist* 108 (1) (2006) 1–8.

Gordon, Cyrus H., and Gary A. Rendsburg. *The Bible and the Ancient Near East.* New York: W. W. Norton and Co., 1998.

Gould, Stephen Jay. *The Mismeasure of Man.* New York: W. W. Norton, 1996.

———. *The Panda's Thumb: More Reflections on Natural History.* New York: W. W. Norton, 1992.

———. *The Richness of Life: The Essential Stephen Jay Gould.* Edited by Steven Rose. New York: W. W. Norton & Co., 2007.

———. *The Structure of Evolutionary Theory.* Cambridge, MA: The Belknap Press of Harvard University Press, 2002.

Gutiérrez, Gustavo. *A Theology of Liberation.* Maryknoll, NY: Orbis, 2007.

Habermas, Jürgen. *The Theory of Communicative Action, Vol. 1.* Boston: Beacon, 1985.

Harper, Susan. *In the Shadow of the Mahatma: Bishop V. S. Azariah and the Travails of Christianity in British India.* Grand Rapids: Eerdmans, 2000.

Harrison, Lawrence E., and Samuel P. Huntington, eds. *Culture Matters: How Values Shape Human Progress.* New York: Basic, 2000.

Hart, David Bentley. *The Beauty of the Infinite: The Aesthetics of Christian Truth.* Grand Rapids: Eerdmans, 2003.

Hasluck, Margaret. "The Albanian Blood Feud." In *Law and Warfare: Studies in the Anthropology of Conflict,* edited by Paul Bohannan, 381–408. Garden City, NY: The Natural History Press, 1967.

Hatch, Elvin. *Culture and Morality: The Relativity of Values in Anthropology.* New York: Columbia University Press, 1983.

Haugen, Gary A. *Good News about Injustice: A Witness of Courage in a Hurting World.* Downer's Grove, IL: InterVarsity, 1999.

Hiebert, Paul G. *Anthropological Insights for Missionaries.* Grand Rapids: Baker, 1985.

———. *The Gospel in Human Contexts: Anthropological Explorations for Contemporary Missions.* Grand Rapids: Baker Academic, 2009.

———. *Transforming Worldviews: An Anthropological Understanding of How People Change.* Grand Rapids: Baker Academic, 2008.

Hill, Harriet. "The Effects of Using Local and Non-Local Terms in Mother-Tongue Scripture." *Missiology* XXXV(4) (2007) 383–95.

Hinson, Glenn. *Fire in My Bones: Transcendence and the Holy Spirit in African American Gospel.* Philadelphia: University of Pennsylvania Press, 2000.

Hoebel, E. Adamson. *The Cheyennes: Indians of the Great Plains.* Florence, KY: Wadsworth, 1978.

Hume, David. *An Enquiry Concerning Human Understanding.* Indianapolis: Hackett, 1993.

John of the Cross. *Ascent of Mt. Carmel.* Edited and translated by E. Allison Peers. New York: Image, 1958.

Kaessmann, Henrik, et al. "Extensive Nuclear DNA Sequence Diversity Among Chimpanzees." *Science* 286 (1999) 1159–62.

Keller, Timothy. *Generous Justice: How God's Grace Makes us Just.* New York: Dutton Adult, 2010.

Kelly, Raymond C. *Warless Societies and the Origin of War.* Ann Arbor, MI: University of Michigan Press, 2000.

Kelsey, David H. *Eccentric Existence: A Theological Anthropology.* Louisville, KY: Westminster John Knox, 2009.

King, Martin Luther, Jr. *Strength to Love.* Minneapolis: Fortress, 2010.

———. *A Testament of Hope: The Essential Writings and Speeches of Martin Luther King, Jr.* New York: HarperOne, 1990.

Kisare, Z. Marwa. *Kisare: A Mennonite of Kiseru. An Autobiography as told to Joseph C. Shenk.* Salunga, PA: Eastern Mennonite Board of Missions and Charities, 1984.

Korten, David C. *When Corporations Rule the World.* West Hartford, CT: Kumarian, 1996.

Kuhn, Thomas. *The Structure of Scientific Revolution.* Chicago: University of Chicago Press, 1996.

Lamoureux, Denis O. *Evolutionary Creation: A Christian Approach to Evolution.* Eugene, OR: Wipf & Stock, 2008.

———. "Robert A. Larmer on Intelligent Design: An Evolutionary Creationist Critique." *Christian Scholar's Review* XXXVII (1) (2007) 77–90.

Lang, Sabine. *Men as Women, Women as Men: Changing Gender in Native American Cultures.* Austin, TX: University of Texas Press, 1998.

Latourette, Kenneth Scott. *A History of Christianity, Vols. I and II.* Peabody, MA: Prince, 1999.

Leach, Edmund. *Political Systems of Highland Burma.* Boston: Beacon, 1965.

Lebacqz, Karen. *Six Theories of Justice: Perspectives from Philosophical and Theological Ethics.* Minneapolis: Augsburg, 1986.

Lee, Benjamin. "The Subjects of Circulation." In *The Postnational Self: Belonging and Identity,* edited by Ulf Hedetoft and Mete Hjort, 233–49. Minneapolis, MN: University of Minnesota Press, 2002.

Lee, N. Y. Louis, and P. N. Johnson-Laird. "Are There Differences in Cross-Cultural Reasoning?" Proceedings of the 28th Annual Meeting of the Cognitive Science Society. 459–64, 2006.

Lindbeck, George A. *The Nature of Doctrine: Religion and Theology in a Postliberal Age.* Louisville, KY: Westminster John Knox, 1984.

Lugo, Luis. "Caesar's coin and the Politics of the Kingdom: A Pluralist Perspective." In *Caesar's Coin Revisited: Christians and the Limits of Government,* edited by Michael Cromartie, 1–29. Grand Rapids: Eerdmans, 1996.

Luria, A. R. *Cognitive Development: Its Cultural and Social Foundations.* Cambridge, MA: Harvard University Press, 1976.

MacMaster, Richard K., with Donald R. Jacobs. *A Gentle Wind of God: The Influence of the East Africa Revival.* Scottdale, PA: Herald, 2006.

Marshall, Chris. *The Little Book of Biblical Justice.* Intercourse, PA: Good, 1989.

Martyr, Justin. *The Apologies of Justin Martyr: To Which is Appended the Epistle to Diognetus.* New York: Harper & Brothers, 1877.

Marx, Karl. *Capital: A Critique of Political Economy, Vol. I.* New York: Penguin Classics, 1990.

———. *Capital: A Critique of Political Economy, Vol. II.* New York: Penguin Classics, 1978.

———. *Capital: A Critique of Political Economy, Vol. III.* New York: Penguin Classics, 1981.

Mauss, Marcel. *The Gift: The Form and Reason for Exchange in Archaic Societies.* New York: Norton, 2000.

McClusky, Laura J. *"Here, Our Culture is Hard": Stories of Domestic Violence from a Mayan Community in Belize.* Austin, TX: University of Texas Press, 2001.

McGee, R. Jon, and Richard L. Warms, eds. *Anthropological Theory: An Introductory History.* New York: McGraw-Hill, 2008.

McGrath, Allister E. *A Fine-Tuned Universe: The Quest for God in Science and Theology.* Louisville, KY: Westminster John Knox, 2009.

McMichael, Philip. *Development and Social Change: A Global Perspective (Third Edition).* Thousand Oaks, CA: Pine Forge, 2004.

Mead, Margaret. *Sex and Temperament in Three Primitive Societies.* New York: Dell, 1963.

Meeks, M. Douglas. *God the Economist: The Doctrine of God and Political Economy.* Minneapolis: Fortress, 2000.

Meneses, Eloise. "Bearing Witness in Rome with Theology from the Whole Church." In *Global Theologizing: Belief and Practice in an Era of World Christianity,* edited by Craig Ott and Harold A. Netland, 231–49. Grand Rapids: Baker Academic, 2006.

———. *Love and Revolutions: Market Women and Social Change in India.* Lanham, MD: University Press of America, 2007.

Meneses, Eloise, Lindy Backues, David Bronkema, Eric Flett, and Benjamin Hartley. "Engaging the Religiously Committed Other: Anthropologists and Theologians in Dialogue." *Current Anthropology* 55(1) (2014) 82–104.

Meneses, Eloise, and David Bronkema, eds. *On Knowing Humanity: Insights from Theology for Anthropology.* Abingdon, UK: Routledge, 2017.

Middleton, J. Richard. *The Liberating Image: The Imago Dei in Genesis 1.* Grand Rapids: Brazos, 2005.

Milanovic, Branko. "True World Income Distribution, 1988–1993: First Calculation Based on Household Surveys Alone." Washington, DC: World Bank, 1999.

Milbank, John. *Theology and Social Theory: Beyond Secular Reason.* Oxford, UK: Blackwell, 1990.

Morgan, Lewis Henry. *Ancient Society.* Tucson, AZ: University of Arizona Press, 1985.

Mtika, Mike Njalayawo. "Subsistent and Substantive Communities under Attack: The Case of Zowe in Northern Malawi." In *Christian Mission and Economic Systems: A Critical Survey of the Cultural and Religious Dimensions of Economies,* edited by John Cheong and Eloise Meneses, 179–210. Pasadena, CA: William Carey Library, 2015.

Myers, Bryant. *Walking with the Poor: Principles and Practices of Transformational Development.* Maryknoll, NY: Orbis, 2011.

Narayan, Deepa, et. al. *Voices of the Poor: Can Anyone Hear Us?* Oxford: Oxford University Press, 2002.

Neill, Stephen. *A History of Christian Missions.* New York: Penguin, 1990.

Newbigin, Lesslie. *The Gospel in a Pluralist Society.* Grand Rapids: Eerdmans, 1989.

———. *The Open Secret: An Introduction to the Theology of Mission.* Grand Rapids: Eerdmans, 1995a.

———. *Proper Confidence: Faith, Doubt, and Certainty in Christian Discipleship.* Grand Rapids: Eerdmans, 1995b.

Nida, Eugene. *God's Word in Man's Language.* New York: Harper and Brothers, 1952.

Okkenhaug, Inger Marie. "Women in Christian Mission: Protestant Encounters from the 19th and 20th Century." *Kvinneforskning, Journal of Gender Research in Norway.* Oslo: Kilden, 2004. http://eng.kilden.forskningsradet.no/artikkel/vis.html?tid=54092&within_tid=540802004.

Ong, Aihwa. *Flexible Citizenship: The Logic of Transnationality.* Durham, NC: Duke University Press, 1999.

Ortner, Sherry. "Is Male to Female as Nature is to Culture?" In *Women, Culture and Society,* edited by Michele Zimbalist Rosaldo and Louise Lamphere, 68–87. Stanford, CA: Stanford University Press, 1974.

Palmer, Parker. *To Know as We are Known.* New York: HarperOne, 1993.

Paris, Jenell. *The End of Sexual Identity: Why Sex is Too Important to Define Who We Are.* Downer's Grove, IL: InterVarsity, 2011.

Pennock, Robert T. *Intelligent Design Creationism and its Critics: Philosophical, Theological, and Scientific Perspectives.* Cambridge, MA: The MIT Press, 2001.

Peoples, James, and Garrick Bailey. *Humanity: an Introduction to Cultural Anthropology.* Belmont, CA: Thomson Wadsworth, 2006.

Piaget, Jean. *The Psychology of the Child.* New York: Basic, 1969.

Pierson, Paul. "Arthur F. Glasser: Citizen of the Kingdom." In *The Good News of the Kingdom,* edited by Charles Van Engen, et al., 3–9. Maryknoll, NY: Orbis, 1993.

Polanyi, Michael. *Personal Knowledge: Towards a Post-Critical Philosophy.* Chicago: University of Chicago Press, 1974.

———. *The Tacit Dimension.* Chicago: University of Chicago Press, 2009.

Porter, Benita. *Colorstruck.* New York: BQ, 1991.

Priest, Robert J. and Alvaro Nieves, editors. *This Side of Heaven: Race, Ethnicity and Christian Faith.* Oxford: Oxford University Press, 2007.

Rempel, John. "Remember the Sabbath." *The Mennonite,* February 1, 2000, 6–7.

Ritchie, Mark. *Spirit of the Rainforest: A Yanomamo Shaman's Story.* Wauconda, IL: Island Lake, 2000.

Robbins, Joel. "Anthropology and Theology: An Awkward Relationship." *Anthropological Quarterly* 79 (2) (2006) 285–94.

———. *Becoming Sinners: Christianity and Moral Torment in a Papua New Guinea Society.* Los Angeles: University of California Press, 2004.

Robert, Dana L. *Christian Mission: How Christianity Became a World Religion.* Malden, MA: Wiley-Blackwell, 2009.

———. "World Christianity as a Women's Movement." *International Bulletin of Missionary Research* 30 (4) (2006) 180–88.

Rosenberg, Noah, et. al. "Genetic Structure of Human Populations." *Science* 298 (2002) 2381–85.

Ross, Marc Howard. "Internal and External Conflict and Violence: Cross-Cultural Evidence and a New Analysis." *Journal of Conflict Resolution* 29 (4) (1985) 547–79.

Sachs, Jeffrey D. *The End of Poverty: Economic Possibilities for our Time.* New York: Penguin, 2005.

Said, Edward. *Orientalism.* New York: Vintage, 1979.

Sanneh, Lamin. *Religion and the Variety of Culture: A Study in Origin and Practice.* Valley Forge, PA: Trinity, 1996.

———. *Translating the Message: The Missionary Impact on Culture.* Maryknoll, NY: Orbis, 1993.

Sen, Amartya. *Development as Freedom.* New York: Anchor, 1999.

Sharp, Douglas R. *No Partiality: The Idolatry of Race and the New Humanity.* Downers Grove, IL: InterVarsity, 2002.

Sherkat, Darren, and Christopher Ellison. "Recent Developments and Current Controversies in the Sociology of Religion." *Annual Review of Sociology* 25 (1999) 363–94.

Sider, Ronald. *The Scandal of the Evangelical Conscience: Why are Christians Living Just Like the Rest of the World?* Grand Rapids: Baker, 2005.

Smedes, Lewis. *Sex for Christians: The Limits and Liberties of Sexual Living.* Grand Rapids: Eerdmans, 1994.

Smith, Steven D. *The Disenchantment of Secular Discourse.* Boston: Harvard University Press, 2010.

Songer, Harold S. "Church." In *Holman Bible Dictionary,* edited by Trent C. Butler, 259–61. Nashville, TN: B&H, 1991.

Swartley, Willard M. *Slavery, Sabbath, War, and Women: Case Studies in Biblical Interpretation.* Scottdale, PA: Herald, 1983.

Sweet, Frank W. *Legal History of the Color Line: The Rise and Triumph of the One Drop Rule.* Palm Coast, FL: Backintyme, 2005.

Taylor, Charles. *A Secular Age.* Cambridge, MA: The Belknap Press of Harvard University Press, 2007.

Tefft, Stanton. "Cognitive Perspectives on War Traps: An Alternative to Functional Theories of Warfare." In *The Anthropology of Peace: Essays in Honor of E. Adamson Hoebel,* 29–53. Studies in Third World Societies, #47. Williamsburg, VA: College of William and Mary, 1992.

Temple, William. *Christianity and the Social Order.* New York: Seabury, 1977.

Troeltsch, Ernst. *The Social Teachings of the Christian Churches.* Louisville, KY: John Knox, 1992.

Trotter, Lilias. *A Blossom in the Desert*. Grand Rapids: Discovery House, 2007.

Turnbull, Colin. *The Forest People*. New York: Touchstone, 1987 (1961).

Tylor, Edward B. *Primitive Culture*. Mineola, NY: Dover, 2016 (1871).

Uchendu, Victor. "The Dilemma of Ethnicity and Polity Primacy in Black Africa." In *Ethnic Identity: Cultural Continuities and Change*, edited by George De Vos and Lola Romanucci-Ross, 265–75. New York: Mayfield, 1975.

Unander, Dave. *Shattering the Myth of Race*. Valley Forge, PA: Judson, 2000.

Valentine, David. "'I Went to Bed with My Own Kind Once': The Erasure of Desire in the Name of Identity." *Language & Communication* 23 (2002) 123–38.

Van Leeuwen, Mary. *Gender and Grace: Love, Work and Parenting in a Changing World*. Downers Grove, IL: InterVarsity, 1990.

Van Rheenen, Gailyn. "A Theology of Culture: Desecularizing Anthropology." *International Journal of Frontier Missions* 14 (1) (1997) 33–38.

Vera Cruz, Germano. "Cross-Cultural Study of Facial Beauty." *Journal of Psychology in Africa* 23 (2013) 87–90.

Vitz, Paul. *Psychology as Religion: The Cult of Self-Worship*. Grand Rapids: Eerdmans, 1994.

Volf, Miroslav. *Exclusion and Embrace: A Theological Exploration of Identity, Otherness, and Reconciliation*. Nashville, TN: Abingdon, 1996.

Walls, Andrew. "The American Dimension of the Missionary Movement." In *The Missionary Movement in Christian History*, 221–40. Maryknoll, NY: Orbis, 2002a.

———. "From Christendom to World Christianity" in *The Cross-Cultural Process in Christian History*, 49–71. Maryknoll, NY: Orbis, 2002b.

Weber, John C. B. *A History of the Dalit Christians in India*. San Francisco: Mellen University Research Press, 1992.

Weber, Max. *The Sociology of Religion*. Boston: Beacon, 1971.

Webster, John C. B. *A History of Dalit Christians in India*. San Francisco: Mellen Research University Press, 1992.

Weisbrot, Mark. "Ten Years After: The Lasting Impact of the Asian Financial Crisis." Center for Economic and Policy Research. Washington, DC, 2007.

Whiting, Beatrice. *Paiute Sorcery*. Viking Fund Publications in Anthropology, #15. New York: Wenner-Gren Foundation, 1950.

Wilcox, David L. *God and Evolution: A Faith-Based Understanding*. Valley Forge, PA: Judson, 2004.

Wolterstorff, Nicholas. *Art in Action*. Grand Rapids: Eerdmans, 1987.

———. *Reason within the Bounds of Religion*. Grand Rapids: Eerdmans, 1999.

Woodberry, Robert D. "The Missionary Roots of Liberal Democracy." *American Political Science Review* 106 (2) (2012) 244–74.

Wright, Christopher J. H. *Old Testament Ethics for the People of God*. Downer's Grove, IL: InterVarsity, 2004.

Wuthnow, Robert. *God and Mammon in America*. New York: The Free Press, 1994.

Zihlman, Adrienne L. *The Human Evolution Coloring Book*. New York: Harper Resource, 2000.

Index